ALL GREAT DISCOVERIES ARE MADE
BY   MEN   WHOSE   FEELINGS   RUN
AHEAD OF THEIR THINKING.

ELMER G. LETERMAN

ELMER LETERMAN'S BOOK OF USEFUL QUOTATIONS

OTHER BOOKS BY ELMER LETERMAN:

How Showmanship Sells
The Sale Begins When The Customer Says "No"
Commissions Don't Fall From Heaven
Personal Power Through Creative Selling
The New Art of Selling

Elmer Leterman's Book Of Useful Quotations

By ELMER LETERMAN

Published By
DROKE HOUSE/HALLUX
Atlanta, Ga.

INTRODUCTION

The most important product you have to sell is *yourself!*

And your ability to sell yourself has everything to do with how much you are worth — in friends and financially.

In the pages of this book, I want to share with you some of my own words and the words of many other men in all phases of business.

What these men have to say has proven valuable to me, as an individual and as a salesman.

Regardless of the subject, they are imparting wisdom based on their own observations and experiences. Most of them are at the top in their particular business or profession. And they got there by selling themselves and their products.

They are men who are worthy of being quoted simply because of their positions. The added value is that what they say is *valuable* and *useful* to every person involved in sales — and we are *all* involved in sales.

I find their words inspiring and practical.

I find myself quoting them to my clients for two reasons:
1. Their names are recognized.
2. Their words can help get a valuable point across at an important time.

Selling takes on many guises. It can be called advertising, merchandising, publicity, public relations, sales promotion, propaganda, diplomacy or leadership.

All of us are engaged in exchanging our labor, skills, talents and know-how for goods and services we need, by the use of money. Wherever we make these exchanges is the market place for our particular commodity. We trade something we have for something we need through the medium of money. To make the trade there must be some kind of sell: soft sell, hard sell, medium sell; subtle, blatant, or perhaps a hidden persuader. Dishonest it need never be, but *selling* it must be.

And I think the men quoted in this book would agree that, whatever topic they are discussing, they are still selling — themselves and their ideas, as well as the products associated with their names.

I started to title this book *The American Businessman Speaks*, because it is comprised of quotations by and about business that I have collected and used during my career.

But then I realized that what I have always maintained is true: All Business Is Selling — and All Businessmen Are Salesmen.

I hope that you find these quotations as inspiring and useful in your selling career as I have in mine.

Elmer Leterman

Elmer G. Leterman

Elmer G. Leterman, master insurance salesman, author, clothes designer and one of the world's greatest salesmen.

Born in Charlottesville, Va, the son of a department store owner who later sold insurance, he came from a modest home. Even as a boy he dreamed dreams and left home at an early age to work as a woolens salesman in New York City. By the age of 25 he was earning $25,000 a year — a fabulous amount in those days.

Later he decided to sell insurance and was launched on his new career at a dinner given by William Zeckendorf, New York real estate man. As a result Mr. Zeckendorf's guests purchased some $1,200,000 worth of insurance. Since then Elmer Leterman has never seen a year when he has sold less than a million dollars worth of insurance. He pioneered group insurance coverage and in 1930, when business was at its lowest point in the country, sold $58,000,000 worth of group insurance for the John Hancock Company alone.

As a result of a visit to Hawaii in 1936 he introduced the Macadamia nut to the U.S., where it became a leading gourmet item. Getting sole rights for this product he received $25,000 in commissions the first year. These have proved to be a valuable addition to the economy of Hawaii.

Elmer G. Leterman was made the only Life Honorary Mayor of Honolulu, a Life Honorary Senator from Hawaii and an Honorary Member of the Aloha Temple of Honolulu.

One of his great satisfactions was helping to organize the manufacture and merchandising of the Kahanamoku shirts, named after his great friend Duke Kahanamoku, Olympic swim champion, later sheriff of Honolulu and hero of the Hawaiian Islands.

Elmer Leterman has a great interest in clothes and designs his own. He believes clothes express the personality of a man as well as of a woman. "Clothes," he says, "help you get a job, a girl, the best table, and the order. Clothes are my self-assurance policy."

As an author, Elmer Leterman has had five books published on salesmanship — *The Sale Begins When the Customer Says "No," How Showmanship Sells, Commissions Don't Fall From Heaven, Personal Power Through Creative Selling* and *The New Art of Selling*, as well as countless magazine articles.

The New Art of Selling is used by the American University, Washington, D.C. as a text book in its salesmanship course, by the Prudential Insurance Company and by Trans World Airlines Inc. in their training programs. *The Sale Begins When The Customer Says "No"* is also used by Trans World Airlines Inc. in their basic training program.

One of Elmer Leterman's greatest qualities is his love of his fellow man. He has always found the time to give encouragement and counsel where needed, especially to the young. His basic philosophy is that anyone can achieve whatever he sets out to achieve, if he so will.

QUOTATIONS

A

ABILITY

The truth is that man's potential ability is always greater than his actual performance. You can always do better as long as you believe you can and put your belief to work. – L.F. McCOLLUM, Chairman, Continental Oil Company. (1)

ABILITY – Reliability

The best ability you have is reliability. – ELMER G. LETERMAN. (2)

ACCIDENTS

Most accidents happen to drivers with good records who have occasional lapses in attention or who make occasional errors in driving judgment. The great majority of these drivers are not criminals – and they are not deliberately careless. According to one safety expert, they are simply people with poor driving habits who, in effect, practice for their next accident every time they sit down behind the wheel. – L.L. COLBERT, Chairman of the Board, Chrysler Corporation. (3)

ACCOMPLISHMENT

Busyness is not necessarily accomplishment. Indeed, the opposite often seems to be true. The days spent at a frantic pace often yield little to recall with pride; and the days when, by accident or design, we find ourselves freed of the most intense pressure are those that are most productive. It is in a period of comparative tranquility that we face up to the real problems and follow up the flashes of insight that have come to us. – HAROLD MAYFIELD, *Supervisory Management*. (4)

Very little in this world has ever been accomplished through a passive attitude in the face of an organized and determined foe. – ARTHUR LANCKTON, Executive Vice President, Mobil International Oil Company. (5)

ACCOUNTANT – Future

The accountant of the future will require an educational program which will include more liberal education — education that enlarges the mind, that enables him to recognize new problems and generate new solutions. At the same time, his program will require greatly increased technical knowledge to enable him to cope with the demands of more sophisticated management problems. — JOHN W. QUEENAN, Managing Partner, Haskins & Sells.   (6)

ACHIEVERS
I think it's time we had a little less pity for those who refuse to help themselves and a little more respect for the doer, for the achiever. — RICHARD G. CAPEN, Jr, Director of Public Affairs, Copley Newspapers, La Jolla, California.   (7)

ACTION
You can be a success if you believe that progress and success come from action and are willing to use a little individual initiative to achieve it. You can't convert ideas and materials into units of greater value by sitting back and waiting for it to happen! — R.S. REYNOLDS, Jr, *Quote*.   (8)

ACTIONS
The man who observes how people act in exceptional circumstances will learn a lot he can use to advantage in all circumstances. — ELMER G. LETERMAN, *Personal Power Through Creative Selling* (Harper & Row).   (9)

ADAPTABILITY
It seems to me that the key to our future can be summed up in one word — adaptability. In a rapidly changing world it is often a matter of survival to change one's mind, one's attitude, one's way of thinking and doing things. Even when survival is not at issue, we should all know how to adjust to changed circumstances in order to capitalize on new opportunities. — ROBERT E. WILLIAMS, Executive Vice President, The Youngstown Sheet & Tube Company.   (10)

ADOLESCENTS
It is as if adult society regards adolescence as an unattractive extension of childhood that we must somehow put up with, until the magic of time has somehow transmuted that cute little baby of yesteryear into the adult of tomorrow. Most of us feel put upon by the very existence of the adolescent, annoyed with his presence, his unpredictability, his demands, his parasitic nature, and the like, as if

we were somehow the victim and he the aggressor. And as with any victim, the roads of appeasement and bribery are natural recourses. So we give them a car when they ask, or a new electric guitar, or an increase in their allowance — "anything, just get off my back and out of my way." — ROY W. MENNINGER, MD, President, Menninger Foundation. (11)

ADULTS — Examples

I think that our adult society, through its failure to set good examples, deserves a large share of the responsibility for one youth failure. — LEROY COLLINS, President, National Association of Broadcasters. (12)

ADVERTISING

Advertising is selling and selling is serious business. There is no place in it for knights on armored horses chasing dirt, tornadoes in kitchen sinks washing dishes, clothes so clean that they may safely be viewed only through smoked glasses, blacked eyes based on cigarette brand loyalty, etc. . . . My favorite recent headline in a magazine advertisement was, "How would you like an acid bath?", a question asked by a steel fabricator. The only possible answer I could think of was, "How would you like a punch in the nose?" — FAIRFAX M. CONE, Chairman, Exec. Comm., Foote, Cone & Belding, New York Advertising Agency, *Wall Street Journal.* (13)

Great advertising is compounded of great ideas and great execution. But . . . the secret ingredient is a great client who nods affirmatively and reaches for his courage and his wallet at the same time. — HERBERT STRAUSS, President, Grey Advertising, *Printer's Ink.* (14)

From 1950 to 1960 corporate gross income increased 72%. During this period profits increased only 4%, while advertising costs in measured media increased 108%. — WALTER P. MARGULIES, President, Lippincott & Margulies, Inc. (15)

Advertising creates and sustains mass consumption, and I know of nothing of greater importance to the health of the nation's economy than this. — V.E. BOYD, Vice President and Group Executive, Domestic Automotive, Chrysler Corporation. (16)

The American people have come to expect, and they demand, better and better quality in the products and services they buy, as well they should. Their demands keep us on our toes, to be sure, but that's where we ought to be anyway. And most of this appreciation of quality has come through advertising. — V.E. BOYD, Vice

President and Group Executive, Domestic Automotive, Chrysler Corporation. (17)

I am deeply concerned that we are turning out a nation of young people who are cynics — who might be said to know the slogan of every product, and to believe in the merits of none. — EDWARD H. WEISS, Chairman of a Chicago Advertising Agency, *Quote.* (19)

It (advertising) helps to lubricate the mental machinery that indirectly drives our vast and complicated industrial plant. It has helped to make this the richest and most affluent nation on earth. — CHARLES L. GOULD, Publisher of *San Francisco Examiner.* (19

Man does not live by bread alone. But it is comforting to know that if he should desire to do so there are seventeen different types at the corner grocer's. — ERNEST A. JONES, President, McManus, John & Adams, Inc. (20)

I regard it (advertising) as the first essential in any economy based on competition and freedom of choice. I believe that it brought the bathroom in from the back yard, put the medicine cabinet in the bathroom and put the toothbrush in the medicine cabinet. I believe it freed our women from drudgery and lifted all of our living standards beyond anything the world has seen — or is likely to see again. . . . And I believe that advertising and advertising alone furnishes the financial strength that keeps our free press free. — CHARLES H. BROWER, President, Batten, Barton, Durstine & Osborn, Inc, New York. (21)

Advertising is the background music of our times. It means that goods are moving . . . money is changing hands . . . people are working. — ERNEST A. JONES, President, McManus, John & Adams, Inc. (22)

When the critics of advertising advocate that advertising per se be sharply limited because it is confusing or because it creates demand that some consumers cannot reasonably afford, or because it gives an unfair advantage to the company that is wise enough to do more advertising, they hit at the basic concepts of freedom and practices of marketing that have contributed to the country's high standard of living. The system may not be perfect but it has surely placed the USA ahead of all other countries. — STANFORD SMITH, General Manager, American Newspaper Publishers Association. (23)

The real truth is that there is very little actual untruth to be found in advertising and promotion today. Enthusiasm, yes. Persuasion, yes. Provocative expression, yes. These are the elements of salesmanship — an institution as old as civilization. How insipid life would be without the age-old contest between salesmanship and sales resistance! How stifling it would be if the individual were denied the right to choose what he wants to buy. — RICHARD W. DARROW, Hill & Knowlton, Inc. (24)

By becoming one of the prime agents of competition, advertising has helped to bring about steady improvements in product quality and has been an instrumental force in new product development. Through such contributions, it has become a very necessary element in the creation of what we term our standard of living — which is far superior to that of any other country in the world, past or present. — JOHN E. SWEARINGEN, President, Standard Oil Company (Indiana). (25)

Many people don't understand about advertising. They think advertising means a page in a newspaper or an irritating interruption in their favorite television program. They don't understand that advertising of some breed or shade is being done all the time by all people, in all media, and for all purposes. A little Freedom symbol painted on the side of a stone wall can be an advertisement, too. — ARTHUR E. MEYERHOFF, President, Arthur Meyerhoff Associates, Inc, Chicago, Illinois. (26)

ADVERTISING — Art, Language

I believe advertising has raised the public taste in the intangible — in such things as art and language. Compare a magazine ad of fifteen years ago, or even ten, with one you can find today. And notice the differences in quality in the ads themselves — the better uses of color, of balance, of proportion, and line. . . . The man whose eye is caught by the balance and color of a good ad is certainly going to look with greater interest on an exhibit of the best modern painting, and vice versa. . . . The same thing applies to language. . . . By and large our language has been made leaner and more muscular by the people who are working under the pressures of writing good clean advertising copy with a minimum of bafflegab and gobbledygook and a maximum of good solid message. — V.E. BOYD, Vice President and Group Executive, Domestic Automotive, Chrysler Corporation. (27)

ADVERTISING — Government Control

The control of advertising by the federal government would be a catastrophe for free private enterprise of the first magnitude. — LAWRENCE H. ROGERS, II, President, Taft Broadcasting Company. (28)

ADVERTISING – Unethical
Just as Doctors and Lawyers and Bankers have established their own agencies for policing and correcting the excesses of associates, so, too, have the leaders of the advertising profession. No group is more critical of unethical advertising than those who are in the profession. And – they do take proper steps to correct the evils. – CHARLES L. GOULD, Publisher of *San Francisco Examiner.* (29)

ADVICE
The day you think you "have it made," quit, and give someone else a chance. You've started down the hill right then and there. – A. CLARK DAUGHERTY, President, Rockwell Manufacturing Company. (30)

AFFIRMATIVE THINKING
There are powerful new driving forces at work in our country, and most powerful is affirmative thinking. – L.F. McCOLLUM, Chairman, Continental Oil Company. (31)

AFFLUENCE
The only way to a truly affluent society is through savings. The welfare state may produce security, usually of a marginal kind, but it cannot produce affluence. – AUSTIN S. MURPHY, Managing Director, Savings Banks Association of New York State. (32)

AGE – Creativity
I believe that while youth is wonderful, maturity can be and ought to be magnificent – that, moreover, the young mind, the young heart, the young spirit have little or nothing to do with chronological age – and that the creativity they generate does not fade with the putting on of bifocals. – JO FOXWORTH, Vice President, Calkins & Holden. (33)

AGE – Indispensability
Try to overcome the thought that you are indispensable. Persistence in leading a strenuous life, after passing middle age, more often than not shortens life. So, bring yourself to relaxing your grip, to transferring some of your burdens to younger shoulders. Be your age! Take it easy! – B.C. FORBES, *Forbes.* (34)

AGE – of Man
The most urgent need in the world today is to make sure that the

coming age will be known as the age of man. — GUILFORD DUDLEY, Jr., President, Life and Casualty Insurance Company of Tennessee. (35)

If we can summon the will and the intelligence to use boldly and humanely the promising new tools in our possession, ours will be remembered not as the Computer Age or the Space Age or the Cybernetics Age — but as the Age of Man. — ARJAY MILLER, President, Ford Motor Company. (36)

AGE — Youth

When a man gets on toward fifty, I guess it's normal for him to worry more and more about what the younger generation is doing to the world he knew when he was young himself. — HENRY FORD, II, Chairman of the Board, Ford Motor Company. (37)

AGRICULTURE

The better we get at farming, the farther most people are away from it. We are getting pretty good at it, and the result is that we're heading for some real trouble, I think, if more people don't recognize and realize the accomplishments of our agriculture and what it means to our country as a whole. — RICHARD J. BABCOCK, President, *Farm Journal, Inc.* (38)

Agricultural advancement is essential if we want our future to be something other than a time in which most of the world starves. — GUILFORD DUDLEY, Jr., President, Life and Casualty Insurance Company of Tennessee. (39)

The future of agriculture in this country, I believe, will be a bright one. It is a growing, expanding industry. There will be fewer farmers tomorrow, but they will operate bigger farms; they will be more expensive farms, and still more efficient ones. — J.K. STERN, President, American Institute of Cooperation, Washington, D.C. (40)

Agriculture . . . is a keystone of our prosperity — not only through its own vast output of food, but through its supply of raw materials for other industry, and by virtue of providing itself a major market for such basic products as steel, oil, rubber, and machinery. This is often forgotten. — JOHN E. SWEARINGEN, Chairman of the Board, Standard Oil Company (Indiana). (41)

In the area of agriculture, America surpasses every other country in the world in its ability to secure the highest yeilds from an acre of ground. We are one of the few remaining surplus food producers in the world, and the American farmer deserves the lion's share of credit. — LESLIE B. WORTHINGTON, President, United States

Steel Corporation. (42)

Agriculture produces, efficiently and in volume, only under the private enterprise system. — RICHARD J. BABCOCK, President, *Farm Journal, Inc.* (43)

This is a nation investing three per cent of the gross national product in research and development. But in agriculture we are investing only six tenths of one per cent — including both private and public investment. — ROBERT R. SPITZER, President, Murphy Products Company, Inc, Burlington, Wisconsin. (44)

AGRICULTURE — Farmers

"Agriculture" in this country is a mighty diverse thing. We raise some 260 commercial crops. And "farmers" are all kinds of people. Big and little. Highly educated and poorly educated. Rich and poor. You can find farmers who are broke. You can find some driving Cadillacs., And if you look a little I suspect you could find some that are both broke and driving Cadillacs. One of the traps into which we seem to fall easiest is to speak of "farmers," and what they think, as though they were all of one kind and of one mind. Actually their opinions vary from pole to pole. — CARROLL P. STREETER, Editor, *Farm Journal.* (45)

AGRICULTURE — Food

The dramatic contributions made by agriculture to our national wellbeing have been largely overlooked by a public enjoying record prosperity. It has been calculated that we currently spend about $90 billion a year on food in this country — or less than one fifth of our national income — and we are the best fed nation on earth. Our household pets receive better nourishment than most humans elsewhere. — JOHN E. SWEARINGEN, Chairman of the Board, Standard Oil Company (Indiana). (46)

AGRICULTURE — Government

How long has the government been "helping the farmer?" It has been going on for more than 30 years. Today there are fewer farmers and there is some evidence to suggest that those who are producing crops in the government program are worse off than those who are not covered. We are paying out billions of dollars a year to maintain agricultural prices at a false level, yet the subsidized farmer's income is still falling. This is nationalization of farmers. It is expensive and it is morally wrong. — E.F. SCOUTTEN, Vice President, The Maytag Company. (47)

AIR POLLUTION — Automobiles

Madison Avenue has made deodorants popular by making people ashamed of their own odor. Perhaps, we can do the same thing with people and their autos (which pollute the air). — LELAND HAZARD, Director, Port Authority and Chairman, Pittsburgh Rapid Transit Committee, *Public Utilities Fortnightly.* (48)

AIR TRAVEL

Traditionally, the airline and aircraft manufacturing industry has concentrated on making their product faster and more comfortable for the passenger. But is the day not in sight when the thrust of aircraft development may be toward making the airplane a better citizen in the external environment in which it must live? There are major aircraft and engine designers today who believe that the greatest emphasis in aircraft development in the next decade or two will be toward making the jet engine more quiet rather than faster. — F.D. HALL, President, Eastern Airlines. (49)

AMERICA

We have not made America what it is today by thoughtless action — by saddling up and galloping off in all directions at once. We have made America with both words and deeds. — M.C. PATTERSON, Vice President, Chrysler Corporation. (50)

The factors that made this country great were faith in God, faith in oneself, hard work, thrift, self-denial, willingness to take great risks for that in which we believed. — J.K. STERN, President, American Institute of Cooperation, Washington, D.C. (51)

The United States has now come to the pinnacle of world power largely because her people have had the opportunity to develop this nation with its vast resources under a government and a Constitution that encourages initiative, enterprise, industry, thrift and inventive genius. They have cherished and held secure the blessings of liberty, and they have recognized the dignity of man. — HERBERT V. PROCHNOW, President, First National Bank of Chicago, Illinois. (52)

Our nation's founding brought hope to the down-trodden peoples all over the world. As a matter of fact, it is still doing so. — PRIME F. OSBORN, III, Vice President and General Counsel, Atlantic Coast Line Railroad Company. (53)

You can't measure America by the length of its highways or the heighth of its standard of living. The measure of America lies in its moral values, its political freedoms, and in the incentives behind our private enterprise economy. These are the foundations of our free society and the key ingredients in our progress as a nation. — T.F. PATTON, President, Republic Steel Corporation, Cleveland, Ohio.   (54)

The United States of America — with its will to work, its undergirding of moral values, and its human and economic freedom — is the most advanced industrial society in all history. — ARCH N. BOOTH, Executive Vice President, Chamber of Commerce of the United States.   (55)

We have become the most powerful nation on earth. We are the finest illustration in history of how a people enrich life and raise their whole level of economic well-being when they are given justice, liberty and incentive. — HERBERT V. PROCHNOW, President, First National Bank of Chicago.   (56)

Never before have I been so completely convinced that if we are to preserve those fundamental characteristics that made this country great, we must . . . find our way back to the path of our founders, the path laid out by the Declaration of Independence, the Bill of Rights, and the Constitution of the United States as conceived and written. — GUILFORD DUDLEY, Jr, President, Life and Casualty Insurance Company.   (57)

AMERICA — Abundance
As a nation, we now have more of everything — including new cars — than I would have dared to predict seven years ago. — HENRY FORD, II, Chairman of the Board, Ford Motor Company.   (58)

AMERICA — Americans
I have constantly fought the tendency of Americans to believe that our way-of-life, our heritage, and our commanding position in the world will continue for no other reason than we are Americans. Too many Americans seem to think that a democratic way of life, a free society, and moral-ethical individuals like ourselves can't go down the drain of history. This is not in the cards for us. We're different. We're special. Unfortunately, there's nothing inevitable about longevity as far as civilizations or progress is concerned. Of the 21 recorded civilizations, 19 no longer exist. We can only identify about two which are still surviving. — L.C. MICHELON, Director of Public Affairs, Republic Steel Corporation.   (59)

AMERICA — Beautification
The "Keep America Beautiful" project is an excellent example of enlightened self-interest which nevertheless is an outstanding public

service. Manufacturers whose products are likely to end up as litter along streets and highways finance this program in a frank effort to deter the littering that they might otherwise cause. It marks a gratifying acceptance of responsibility for the undesirable side-effects of their business. — LAURANCE S. ROCKEFELLER. (60)

AMERICA — Communists
Our forebears founded a system of government designed to advance freedom to protect the dignity of man. To call forth his noblest faculties. It is this freedom the Soviet Communists would destroy. They would subvert all other men to their absolute rule, to a condition of slavery, to the status of instruments of the state. For they are the state. — KARL R. BENDETSEN, President, Champion Papers Inc., Hamilton, Ohio. (61)

AMERICA — Crises
Since the year 1776 we have faced four great crises in our national life, the first when this nation was born, the second when it was preserved, the third when it came of age, and now when its maturity, wisdom, and common sense are being put severely to the test. — GUILFORD DUDLEY, Jr., President, Life and Casualty Insurance Company. (62)

AMERICA — Education
Now the United States is the envy of the world for its system of education, which has brought more educational opportunity within the reach of a greater percentage of population — and covering a greater variety of subjects and professional fields — than has ever been enjoyed by the people of any country at any time in history. — LYNN TOWNSEND, Chairman and Chief Executive Officer, Chrysler Corporation. (63)

AMERICA — Europe
We live in a world of many frightening divisions and we exist under a nuclear sword of Damocles. We are marching steadily towards dangerous confrontation between the rich and poor nations of this very small planet. The stork has outpaced the plow in at least two-thirds of the world, and famine, the first of the dreaded four horsemen, is at the starting gate. Together the United States and Europe can avert tragedy. But *without* the cohesion of the Atlantic region, the peace and prosperity — indeed the ultimate survival — of

mankind could be in dire jeopardy. — RUDOLPH A. PETERSON, President, Bank of America. (64)

AMERICA — Freedom

A man can achieve success here (in America) regardless of his background or his race or religion. The freedom to express whatever forces you may be endowed with or are able to develop is the most precious thing an individual can have. It is worth fighting for and dying for. — Gen DAVID SARNOFF, *Nation's Business.* (65)

AMERICA — Greatness

The greatness of this country is built on the outstanding fact that we, above everyone else, have the greatest and most solid middle-class which includes small businessmen. — MERRILL M. MITCHELL, Publisher, *American Furrier.* (66)

This country owes its greatness to men who are free to take chances — and who dare. — RAY R. EPPERT, President, Burroughs Corporation. (67)

The United States did not become a great nation by taking the easy way out, by being satisfied, by avoiding risks or evading controversy. We become great by aiming high, individually and collectively, and then surpassing our aims. We became great by recognizing our problems and responsibilities, by taking chances when chances were necessary, by facing up honestly to our disagreements and resolving them in free and open discussion. And this is the only way we can preserve our greatness. — HENRY FORD II, Chairman of the Board, Ford Motor Company. (68)

As you move along the inspiring pathway of American history, you quickly discover the reason for the greatness of this nation. It is the genius of the individual. It is the genius of the competent businessman who combines labor, capital and raw materials to produce a vast outpouring of goods to enrich the lives of the masses. It is the genius of the workingman, whose labor, self-discipline and thrift are vital to the creation and operation of modern industry. It is, and in great part, the genius of the devoted teacher who inspires youth to greatness. — ROBERT E. WILLIAMS, President, The Youngstown Sheet and Tube Company. (69)

AMERICA — Leadership

I sincerely believe that educated and responsible leadership is our country's most pressing need and our most vital national resource. — T.F. PATTON, President, Republic Steel Corporation, Cleveland, Ohio. (70)

AMERICA – Life

The "American way of life" is a characteristic society built upon the principles of a fundamental faith in God, a constitutional Republic, and a capitalistic economy. – NICHOLAS A. GEORGE, Vice President of Brunswick Corporation, Chicago, Illinois.   (71)

AMERICA – Obligation

America's obligation is not alone to lead Free World strategy in the decisive competition with communism. It is also to serve as a showcase of democracy, demonstrating the superior values of self-government, and hopefully inspiring the newly developing nations to embrace and advance these same ideals. – NEIL McELROY, Chairman, Proctor & Gamble Company.   (72)

AMERICA – President

No president can lead unless the people – and their representatives in Congress and the fifty state governments – are mentally equipped and ready to follow. – JOHN ALSOP, President, The Mutual Insurance Company, Hartford, Connecticut.   (73)

AMERICA – Problems

We shall prosper, and our way of life will be emulated by others, only so long as we meet our problems intelligently. – CHARLES E. WALKER, Executive Vice President, The American Bankers Association, New York.   (74)

AMERICA – Responsibilities

Realistically, the United States cannot be the sole contributor to the world's economic welfare and military security. And these people overseas that I spoke with understand this; furthermore, they don't expect the US to play such a role. What they do expect from us, though, is the kind of personal involvement that confirms that we as individuals recognize our responsibilities: first, as American citizens; and second, as world citizens. – GEORGE CHAMPION, Chairman of the Board, The Chase Manhattan Bank.   (75)

AMERICA – Strength

The strength of this nation was bred of free enterprise and catapulted to greatness on the fruits of private capital. – GEORGE A. NEWTON, President, Investment Bankers Association of America.   (76)

The strength of our nation depends upon the strength of our economy, which in turn depends upon the education of our businessmen. — JOHN A. BARR, former Chairman of the Board, Montgomery Ward & Company. (77)

Measured by almost any yardstick, the strength of the United States today is so impressive as to be the envy and aspiration of the world. — GEORGE CHAMPION, Chairman of the Board, The Chase Manhattan Bank. (78)

I doubt whether we really fully recognize our own strength. We Americans can pay better, build better, do more research and development, and sell on a larger scale than nearly any array of European companies which might be matched against us. Moreover, our ability is increasing. — THOMAS J. WATSON, Jr., Chairman of the Board, International Business Machines Corporation. (79)

AMERICA — The World

Within your lifetime and mine, our country has been transformed from a state of virtually no concern with our neighbors to one of daily, almost hourly, responsibility. Other nations of the Free World look to us to set the example. — GEORGE CHAMPION, Chairman of the Board, The Chase Manhattan Bank. (80)

In the almost twenty years since the end of World War II, we have seen the gradual deterioration of US prestige abroad. . . . On the basis of our skill in selling our products, we have built the most prosperous society in history. Yet we have not effectively applied our sales techniques to selling ourselves and our ideas to other countries. — ARTHUR E. MEYERHOFF, President, Arthur Meyerhoff Associates, Inc., Chicago, Illinois. (81)

We need to abandon the parasitic philosophy that has choked off our vigor and ambition. We need to dedicate ourselves to human values and human goals and to making a contribution to better living for others. This, I think, is the crux of our future relationship with the people of other countries. We are proud of our strength and our wealth and of the material benefits that these have brought. Out of our generosity as a people, we willingly share these benefits with others. Yet, at the same time, we tend to stress too often the materialistic side of our national wealth. — GEORGE CHAMPION, Chairman of the Board, The Chase Manhattan Bank. (82)

For a quarter of a century we have taken on the world's ills but it appears many of the varied infections we've been fighting have been contracted. In spite of our wealth, manpower, technical talents, scientific genius, creativity, social conscience and even economic muscle ... as a nation and as a people we've failed to earn love or respect. And that bitter truism is as true at home as abroad. — CHAYLIE L. SAXE, President, Saxe Bros. Inc.   (83)

AMERICA — World Leadership
There are many reasons why other nations expect so much of us, but the most important by far is that we are the richest and most powerful nation on earth. By the simple maxim that responsibility is proportionate to power, the burdens of world leadership are inescapably ours. — GEORGE CHAMPION, Chairman of the Board, The Chase Manhattan Bank.   (84)

AMERICANS
Americans by and large cling to the future, not the past. They have faith in perpetual progress, and dare to take a chance. They marry young, have children, and show no fear of debt, their own or their nation's. But in other ways they play it safe, for there is so much to lose: the home, the furniture, the car, the place in the community which goes with the job. They fear failure more than they crave success; hence many aim low, don't try very hard. Their life strategy is one of deterrence against the slings and smiles of fickle fortune. "Failsafe" becomes the dominant attitude of too many, not "Go west, young man," or "The sky's the limit." — GABRIEL HAUGE, Vice Chairman of the Board, Manufacturers Hanover Trust Company, New York.   (85)
Our children should be taught that it is not in our tradition for an American to leave his post because it is dangerous. We are not that kind of people. We do not scuttle; we do not abandon ship. In times of danger we go to our battle stations and await the orders of our Commander-in-Chief. — JAMES A. FARLEY, Chairman of the Board, The Coca-Cola Export Corporation, New York City.   (86)

AMERICANS — America
We do not need to be ashamed of our country. We do not need to say that we are in a competition for first place. We are not in the competition for first place or for second place, or for any place at all. We are what we are, and what we are is good and will be better as long as we are free. — GEORGE SOKOLSKY, Columnist.   (87)

APATHY
The problem of apathy on the part of our people is the most

serious challenge we face because with apathy our government and our foreign policy which ultimately express the will of the people are left without direction. – ALBERT J. NEVINS, M.M., Editor.   (88)

ARCHITECTURE
Too much of the urban scene is made up of buildings which toe the property line and shout their assertions of method and structure to their neighbors across the street. The cacaphony becomes a bedlam and we, the architect, little more than a huckster. Someone ought to "whisper" a building. – JAMES M. HUNTER, Six-State Western Mountain Regional Director of the American Institute of Architects, *Arizona Architect.*   (89)

What we need is a race of discriminating, 2-inch-high pygmies who can be rented out to architectural offices to wander through their 3-dimensional models and tell us how things look from down there. They may well observe: "Master, it may be breathtaking from up where you stand, but down here it's dull and tedious." – FRED SMITH, Vice President, The Prudential Insurance Company, Newark, New Jersey.   (90)

ARCHITECTURE – Industrial Design
Good architecture in insustrial design is finding increasing favor among all types of industries, and this is not because we are in a cultural explosion. This is because industry has found that it makes sound economic sense. Report after report proves that the new facility in pleasant surroundings substantially raises worker productivity. – FRANK L. WHITNEY, President, Walter Kidde Constructors, Inc., New York.   (91)

ARCHITECTURE – Modern
People get bored with too many modern buildings, stripped and stark and functional. They stay home when they might be window shopping, and tourists go elsewhere, and the city could be worse off than before. Experience has shown in city after city that the big standardized complexes that developers dream up because they represent advanced design, and demonstrate functionalism, and have a cost-to-cubic-content ratio to delight an investment banker, fail to have any particular magnetism for people. – FRED SMITH, Vice President, The Prudential Insurance Company, Newark, New Jersey.   (92)

ARCHITECTURE — Schools

One of the most encouraging signs of progress in our thinking today is the move by leading universities to revamp their architectural education programs. Our schools are recognizing that architecture must deal not simply with the physical design of structures, but with all the problems of the environment within which those structures must function. — FRANK L. WHITNEY, President, Walter Kidde Constructors, Inc., Engineers and Builders. (93)

ARTS

Too often the tendency is to regard the arts as something pleasing but peripheral. I feel the time has come when we must accord them a primary position as essential to the nation's well being. In our increasingly mechanized and computerized world, the arts afford a measure of consolation and reassurance to our individuality, a measure of beauty and human emotion that can reach and move most men. They are indispensable to the achievement of our great underlying concern for the individual, for the fullest development of the potential hidden in every human being. — DAVID ROCKEFELLER, President, Chase Manhattan Bank. (94)

ARTS — Business

The arts are a vital part of human experience, and surely our success as a civilized society will be judged largely by the creative activities of our citizens in art, architecture, music and literature. Improving the condition of the performing and visual arts in this country calls, in my judgment, for a massive cooperative effort in which business corporations must assume a much larger role than they have in the past. — DAVID ROCKEFELLER, President, Chase Manhattan Bank. (95)

ASIA

Asia has deep and highly developed social and cultural heritages, but they are unlike those that we take for granted in the industrial societies of the West. Until recently, there was little industrial development in Asia with, of course, the notable exception of Japan. The challenge in Asian nations today, therefore, is to develop a viable industrial economy within the framework of their own social and political structures. — R.A. PETERSON, President, Bank of America, *General Electric Forum*. (96)

27

ATTAINMENT

Every one of us is adequately equipped to attain all we can dream, but we achieve it only in proportion to the single-minded intensity with which we seek it. If any part of us remains unenlisted in the quest, it will not only be unemployed and unproductive, but worse, it will be a burden slowing down the rest of us. What in us is not working is not merely idle, it is a handicap. — ELMER G. LETERMAN, *Commissions Don't Fall From Heaven* (MacFadden-Bartell). (97)

ATTITUDE

When you take a job with a company, take it with this thought in mind: I have ability and I have knowledge and now I want to be of service. This attitude is the kind of attitude that will take you places, no matter what career you select. Too many people today feel the world owes them something. Consequently, they expect to receive without first making a contribution. It just doesn't work this way. — DON H. MILLER, President, Skelly Oil Company. (98)

The man who is content to get by is the man who will be passed by. — ELMER G. LETERMAN, *Personal Power Through Creative Selling* (Harper & Row). (99)

The day of the swearing, desk-pounding, autocratic boss is passed. We live too close together and are too sophisticated for this kind of relationship. The despot, the recluse, the sullen, critical individual has no place in modern-day business. I don't mean to say you must go around with a forced smile on your face and your hand ever extended in gratuitous friendship. Neither do I mean you must compromise your convictions simply for the sake of being agreeable. But I do mean that you must be pleasant, understanding, willing to listen, helpful to your fellow employees and positive in attitude. — DON H. MILLER, President, Skelly Oil Company. (100)

Every condition and every experience of your life is the result of your attitude. You and everyone else in the world do only what you think you can do. You can be only what you think you can be. — PAUL J. MEYER, President, Success Motivation Institute, Inc., *Specialty Salesman.* (101)

We are what we accept ourselves as being. We can be what we convince ourselves we can be. — ELMER G. LETERMAN, *Commissions Don't Fall From Heaven* (MacFadden-Bartell). (102)

We must *never* say that something — and everything, for that matter — cannot be improved. An attitude of *constructive discontent* should be developed by all firms. As soon as we improve something, we attempt to improve it even more. This is where as soon as we improve a manufacturing process, we begin immediately to make it even better. We should never be content with things as they are. — MARTIN J. CASERIO, General Manager, Delco Radio Division, General Motors Corporation, Kokomo, Indiana. (103)

Every one of us knows how to do more than he does. Every one of us knows how to do what he is doing better than he is doing it. Every one of us has brain power which he has not tapped. — ELMER G. LETERMAN. (104)

ATTITUDE — Skill

If a man does not have the right attitude, and all the skill in the world, he still isn't much good to his employer and his job. — Rev LEON H. SULLIVAN, Chairman and Founder, Opportunities Industrialization Center, Philadelphia. (105)

AUTOMATION

Although automation reduces the number of production workers, it does not necessarily reduce the number of employees. Sometimes — possibly due to Parkinson's Law — the number of people actually increases after automatic equipment is installed. What happens is that the color of the shirt changes from blue to white. — FRANK L. WHITNEY, President, Walter Kidde Constructors, Inc., New York. (106)

Automation is an economic necessity, a matter of national survival. We must grow economically if we are to meet foreign competition and take care of our increasing population. — EDMUND B. FITZGERALD, President, Cutler-Hammer, Inc. (107)

Automation is taking the drudgery out of work, eliminating the jobs no one ever liked to do — the jobs that degraded man to the status of a machine. But what price such liberation if the worker finds himself stamped "excess" in a society built on the dignity of toil, his emancipated talents unneeded and unwanted? — A.H. RASKIN, Assistant Editor, *New York Times*. (108)

The word and concept of automation have burst upon the national scene with a rapidity, force, and intensiveness, the likes of which we have never experienced before. Yet, unfortunately, automation is a dirty word in many quarters, and we all know that it will never become a respectable word until we . . . find a way of making it understood by the people who work for us. — ROBERT E. WILLIAMS, Executive Vice President, The Youngstown Sheet and Tube Company. (109)

Far from being the job destroyer many fear, automation is

actually a job creator that offers our best hope for greater productivity, a higher standard of living, and more effective competition in world markets. – GEORGE CHAMPION, Chairman of the Board, Chase Manhattan Bank. (110)

At the present state of development, automation does impinge primarily on simple, routine physical and mental tasks. Although automation continues to create more jobs than it destroys, the jobs it generates typically require better education, higher capability, more versatility. It reduces the need for the old fashioned, low-level entry jobs, both in the factory and office. – Dr VAN W. BEARINGER, Vice President and General Manager, Systems and Research Division, Honeywell, Inc. (111)

The experience of the past decade has validated the lessons of the past two centuries: that technological progress is completely compatible with high employment. Automation has made life easier for people in a variety of ways by providing services previously undreamed of. It has enabled factories to minimize waste and inefficiency, and turn out the better, more uniform products they need to compete effectively. – GEORGE CHAMPION, Chairman of the Board, Chase Manhattan Bank. (112)

Automation is not revolutionary, it is evolutionary. Seen in proper perspective, it is clearly identifiable as simply another of man's giant steps in the long history of discovery, development, and utilization of tools to help him meet his needs, satisfy his desire, and fulfill his high ambitions. – Dr VAN W. BEARINGER, Vice President and General Manager, Systems and Research Division, Honeywell, Inc. (113)

AUTOMATION – Computers

If the computer does not take over the world, it will at least have a very substantial hold on the American economy before too long. Private surveys indicate that within ten years the production of computer equipment and associated "software" materials will account for some 20 per cent of the gross national product. – ROBERT SILLECK, Vice President, First National City Bank of New York, *Computers & Automation.* (114)

AUTOMATION – Economy

I hate inefficiency, waste, featherbedding and fat, anywhere in our economy. They are, in the end, thefts from the hungry – from all of us. In their elimination, automation can be a sharp scalpel. – THOMAS J. WATSON, Jr., Chairman of the Board, IBM Company. (115)

AUTOMATION – Education

We should consider the creative power which automation puts at our disposal as a means to provide a more fruitful and abundant life for all of our people. And we ought to be moving toward a better education for all of our citizens so that they can reap these benefits. – RAY R. EPPERT, President, Burroughs Corporation.   (116)

AUTOMATION – Stagnation

I think we should not approach this matter of automating as if there were too much of a choice. Of course, there is a choice as to whether to automate, innovate, or change. But the choice is a bleak one. Either an industry automates, when technical feasibility is established, or the industry will stagnate, and a stagnant industry or company dies. – ROBERT E. WILLIAMS, Executive Vice President, The Youngstown Sheet and Tube Company.   (117)

AUTOMATION – World Trade

If we shrink from the challenge of automation, it will only be a matter of time before our position of leadership in world trade is whittled away. Other progressive nations are moving ahead with automation as quickly as their economies permit. We cannot strengthen or even hold our position in existing world markets, let alone penetrate the markets created by the developing nations, unless we commit ourselves to the productive power which automation and related technology makes possible. – RAY R. EPPERT, President, Burroughs Corporation.   (118)

AUTOMOBILES

I am particularly interested in the adaptation of the electric car for use as passenger taxicabs. In New York City, taxis account for about fifty per cent of all mileage driven, and most of this is done in highly congested areas. The introduction of this vehicle would therefore result in fifty per cent reduction of automobile pollution. – AUSTIN N. HELLER, Air Pollution Control Commissioner, New York City, *Public Utilities Fortnightly*.   (119)

AUTOMOBILES – Accidents

I believe that the vast majority of automobile accidents is not caused by automobiles; but by their drivers. – GUY E. MANN, Senior Vice President, Aetna Life & Casualty.   (120)

AUTOMOBILES – Driving

Mile for mile, American drivers have a safety record estimated to be six times better than that of drivers in the rest of the world combined – although it would be difficult to know this from reading the headlines, let's say, on the Tuesday morning following any Labor Day weekend. – L.L. COLBERT, Chairman of the Board, Chrysler Corporation, Detroit, Michigan. (121)

AUTOMOBILES – Safety

You can buy a safe American car, but only if you can combine the best safety features of each one. Where one car is safe in one area, it's lousy in another. – WILLIAM I. STEIGLITZ, former Special Consultant, National Traffic Safety Agency, *Quote*. (122)

As automobile manufacturers, we recognize the responsibility for building the safest cars possible is ours and ours alone. We accept that responsibility and intend to fulfill it. – BYRON J. NICHOLS, Vice President, Marketing, Chrysler Corporation. (123)

Automobiles have been subjected to much irresponsible and uninformed criticism. Too much effort has been devoted to assessing guilt, too little to the rational search for constructive solutions. The potential for improving safety through changes in vehicle design has been exaggerated, and the potential for major gains through improvements in highways, drivers and law enforcement has been played down. Too much emphasis has been placed on demands for tight regulations of motor vehicles, too little on the kind of regulation that is necessary to achieve maximum progress in safety without impeding the progress and efficiency of an important industry. – HENRY FORD, II, Chairman of the Board, Ford Motor Company. (124)

AUTOMOBILES – Safety Equipment

We can build the vehicles as safe and reliable as we know how, we can install the safety equipment called for under the new law, and we can make this equipment as appealing and as convenient to use as possible within the limitations imposed by this law, but we cannot make drivers and passengers use it. – BYRON J. NICHOLS, Vice President, Marketing, Chrysler Corporation. (125)

AUTOMOBILE INDUSTRY – Government

Had the automobile industry had its ear a shade closer to the ground during the past few years, it might have heard the rumblings about auto safety. It might then have taken some action in advance to make some of the changes that now are being forced on the industry by government edict. – JAMES M. PATTERSON, Director of Public Relations, American Oil Company. (126)

32

B

BALANCE OF PAYMENTS

As the balance of payments goes, so may go the prosperity of all American business. — EDWIN A. LOCKE, Jr, President, American Paper Institute. (127)

Governments with an immediate balance of payments problem on their hands have an almost incurable habit of looking at each item of the debit side of the balance of payments to see what can be cut without regard to the effect on items on the other side. It has to be recognized that action of this kind makes the longer-term balance of payments worse, and that therefore the longer such a policy is pursued the deeper we get into the mire. — PAUL CHAMBERS, Chairman, Imperial Chemical Industries, Ltd. (128)

BANKERS

No one is better positioned than the banker to help promote the policies necessary for healthy community and national growth. The banker possesses a unique capacity to articulate the intangible needs of a community and press the urgency of meeting those needs, constantly and forcefully, upon men and women who can do the most about them. — GEORGE CHAMPION, Chairman of the Board, The Chase Manhattan Bank. (129)

BANKING

The total investment in American agriculture is comparable to about three-fourths of the value of current assets for all corporations in the country. It represents three-fifths of the value of all stocks listed on the New York Stock Exchange. — ROBERT C. LIEBENNOW, President, Corn Refiners Association, Inc., *Banking*, Journal of the American Bankers Association. (130)

BANKING — Underdeveloped Nations

In my judgment, the time has now come for American private banking to discover ways to extend credit to underdeveloped countries that understand its importance and are willing to learn its most efficacious use. — LOUIS B. LUNDBORG, Chairman, Bank of America N.T. & S.A.. (131)

BANKS

A bank without money is like a doctor without pills. — GEORGE WOODS, President, World Bank, *Quote*. (132)

BEAUTY

One evening Keats was sitting writing in the same room with his friend, Leigh Hunt, who was reading. At one point, Keats looked up and said, "Hunt, what do you think of this? 'A beautiful thing is an unending joy.' " "Good," said Hunt, "but not quite perfect." There was silence for a while. Then Keats spoke again. "What about this? 'A thing of beauty is an unending joy.' " "Better," said his friend, "but still not quite it." Again there was silence, until Keats spoke again, "Now, what do you think of this? 'A thing of beauty is a joy forever.' " "That will live as long as the English language is spoken," said Leigh Hunt. — ELMER G. LETERMAN, Nylic Review, New York Life Insurance Company. (133)

BELIEF

I believe that courtesy is not corny, loyalty is not square and God is not dead — although He must get awfully sick. — JO FOXWORTH, Vice President, Calkins and Holden. (134)

BELIEF — Goals

I believe a man can do no more than he can. . . . Well, next, I believe that every human being must have a goal in life that is a constant challenge. As fast as a temporary goal is reached, I must move the boundaries and take a fresh start. I personally have never chosen goals so far distant as to be discouraging in their unattainability. . . . I believe in people. . . . I believe that people are innately good and that they want to be loved, respected, and remembered. They are often otherwise because of where they must live, and how, and with whom. — ARTHUR G. (ART) LINKLETTER, *Grit*. (135)

BERLIN WALL

To me, the Berlin Wall is — if anything — an economic shield . . . an admission that free choice and individual incentive must be walled out for the sake of East Germany's survival as a Communist state. — LOGAN T. JOHNSTON, President, Armco Steel Corporation, Middletown, Ohio. (136)

BIGOTRY

Bigotry can be effaced. . . . But it will be effaced more by

34

standing up for those politicians we admire than by lying down in the streets and public passageways. – JAMES C. HUMES, Executive Director, Philadelphia Bar Association. (137)

BILL OF RIGHTS
In intellectual terms the Bill of Rights is an invitation to disorder. It does not deny the possibility that man may be perfectible, but it assumes that he hasn't made it yet – and that the chance of his discovering truth depends upon his right to be wrong. – HARRY S. ASHMORE, Editor-in-Chief, Encyclopaedia Britannica. (138)

I contend that here, in the Bill of Rights, lies the real genius of the American system – here rather than in the economics of private property, the mechanics of the federal system, the separation of powers, representational democracy, or the happenstance of a continuing frontier to relieve the tensions of growth. These are important, of course, but they are important only as they complement or sustain the tradition of personal freedom. – HARRY S. ASHMORE, Editor-in-Chief, Encyclopaedia Britannica. (139)

BIRTH CONTROL
Six persons in every ten nationally think birth control pills should be supplied free to all women on relief of childbearing age. Significantly, persons in lower income and lower education groups are least receptive to this proposal, as well as being least likely to express an opinion. These are precisely the groups that are the particular target of efforts to encourage control of family size. America's lower income people have larger families than others, with less ability to support or raise them properly. A sizable majority (61%) believe birth control pills work, but fewer will vouch for their safety. Medical authorities claim the pills have proved to be highly effective when the proper program is followed. – GEORGE GALLUP, American Institute of Public Opinion, *Quote*. (140)

BOOKS
I think it is no exaggeration to say that next to people, books are the best ambassadors of international enlightenment and good will. – CURTIS G. BENJAMIN, Chairman of the Board, McGraw-Hill Book Company. (141)

In the area of international cultural understanding, the book is both basic and powerful. This is an obvious fact, but the need abroad for more knowledge and appreciation of the cultural achievements of America is not so obvious as it should be to many of our citizens.

35

Our books serve not only as direct evidence of our literary achievement but also as reflectors of our achievements in all other cultural areas — in music, in the representational arts, in the performing arts. We should not underestimate the critical nature of this particular battlefield of the cold war. — CURTIS G. BENJAMIN, Chairman of the Board, McGraw-Hill Book Company.   (142)

BOY SCOUTS
There is no better force than the Boy Scouts of America to strengthen America's Heritage. — PRIME F. OSBORN, III, Vice President and General Counsel, Atlantic Coast Line Railroad Company.   (143)

BRAINPOWER — Shortage
My personal opinion is that the most critical shortage facing our country today is the shortage of educated brainpower. — LYNN TOWNSEND, Chairman and Chief Executive Officer, Chrysler Corporation.   (144)

BRITISH POUND — Devaluation
The British pound was devalued simply because the metal that supported it had taken flight. Devaluation is simply the lowering of the currency's value to bring it into relationship with what's behind it. Having a printing press is not enough. — CHAYLIE L. SAXE, President, Saxe Bros. Inc..   (145)

BROADCASTING — Censorship
To do its job, broadcasting cannot carry on its back the handicap of censorship of news — whether that censorship is implied or direct, whether by government or by private interest. — LEROY COLLINS, President, National Association of Broadcasters.   (146)

BROTHERHOOD
The failure of the majority to think, act and live for the good of their fellow citizens makes men prey to rule by the power-minded minority. — GEORGE HAUER, Personnel Director, American Greeting Card Association, *Quote*.   (147)
The ideal of brotherhood is as old as civilization. It is a basic tenet of the Judeo-Christian ethic. This tenet affirms that all men, without difference or distinction, are brothers under the fatherhood of God. We believe in the essential, innate dignity of the individual. This belief is the very basis of our Western culture, and of our

American tradition and form of government in particular. – JAMES
M. ROCHE, President, General Motors. (148)

BUDGET – Government
If our economy is to remain healthy, the government must aim
over the longer run for a balanced budget. Surpluses in good years
should offset deficits in bad ones. We must realize that unbalanced
budgets are like trousers without suspenders; you can't keep them up
forever! – GEORGE CHAMPION, Chairman of the Board, The
Chase Manhattan Bank. (149)

BUREAUCRACY
Bureaucracy thrives on long corridors, many offices, many desks,
routine tasks, many carbon copies – and expanding power. – ARCH
N. BOOTH, Executive Vice President, Chamber of Commerce of the
United States. (150)

BUSINESS
Beware of the lure of the swivel chair! So easy is it to sink into
routine habits. One feels so much more at ease in the accustomed
office chair than in hurrying hither and thither, striving to overcome
barriers. Unless we are on guard, we are inclined to let others come,
if they wish, to see us. But the way to find business is, of course, to
go out after it. – B.C. FORBES, *Forbes.* (151)
For anyone who wishes to make it so, business is absorbing,
stimulating and challenging. The stakes are high, the dangers real, the
rewards commensurate with performance. – ELMER G.
LETERMAN, *How Showmanship Sells* (Harper & Row). (152)
Business is a means to an end for society and not an end in itself,
and therefore business must act in concert with a broad public
interest and serve the objectives of mankind and society or it will not
survive. – LAMMOT DU PONT COPELAND, President, E.I. du Pont
de Nemours, *Public Utilities Fortnightly.* (153)
Capital is a material thing, but capitalism is a method for
inspiring the maximum in imagination, ideas, and effort from free
men to fulfill a useful purpose. If business can't provide such non
material values along with material gains, then for what do we
labor? – J. WILSON NEWMAN, Chairman of the Board, Dun &
Bradstreet, *Public Utilities Fortnightly.* (154)
Business is a little bit of a crap game, and I think you have to
gamble. – A.C. DAUGHERTY, President, Rockwell Manufacturing
Company. (155)

Today more than ever, business is the stimulus of our national life. The vigor and growth of business are essential to the rising living standards of the American people and to the basic security of the Free World. — NEIL H. McELROY, Chairman of the Board, The Proctor and Gamble Company.   (156)

Of all the institutions shaping human life in the world today, none is more influential than business. — M.J. RATHBONE, Chairman of the Board and Chief Executive Officer, Standard Oil Company (New Jersey).   (157)

A business based on profit cannot thrive if its policies are controlled by men who are playing it safe. Top management knows this, and the record speaks for itself. The majority of individual companies among the top 100 today reached this position because they didn't play it "safe." They are the doers, the innovators . . . the companies that have staffed new industries, introduced new products and opened new markets. — R.S. REYNOLDS, Jr., *Quote.*   (158)

A business — any business — is first of all an idea. The nature and shape and character of the business will necessarily grow out of the fundamental thought that drives it. And there must be such a driving thought — some germinal, inspiriting, action-compelling concept — if the business is really to live and grow. — FREDERICK R. KAPPEL, *Michigan Business Review.*   (159)

Pharmacist E. Robert Feroli prescribes two over-the-counter remedies to ease the headache of doing business amid today's complex and ever-growing government controls, paperwork and regulations: "First," he says, "get yourself a good sense of humor. Then get yourself a damned good accountant." — *Nation's Business.*   (160)

Business must act in concert with a broad public interest and serve the objectives of mankind and society or it will not survive. — LAMMOT DU PONT COPELAND, Chairman of Du Pont, *Nation's Business.*   (161)

A business, like a plant, needs trimming back now and then, to give the roots a chance. — WILLIAM FEATHER, William Feather Magazine, William Feather Company.   (162)

Secretary of Commerce John T. Connor . . . said, "Business, far more often than government, must provide the solutions to satisfy human needs." I agree . . . America did not rise to its present heights by governmental fiat, but more accurately, by the freedom of our people to exchange their skills and energy for wages and income, and to direct the satisfaction of their needs through daily market-place decisions. — LESLIE B. WORTHINGTON, President, U S Steel

38

Corporation, *U S Steel Quarterly*. (163)

Only a free market can adequately test the validity of a product or a price. The free market may have its defects, but like our free government, it is far superior to any of the alternatives . . . the threat of a broader war in Viet Nam and growing inflationary pressure here at home puts additional burdens on our national leaders. Now, more than ever, the need to go that extra mile in cooperating with our government is obvious. — WILLIAM VERITY, President, Armco Steel. (164)

It (business) can bring you exciting opportunities. It can provide you an arena for creativity, for individualism. It can give you and your family comfort and pleasure. And what's more, it can provide you the chance to perpetuate our wonderful American economic system. — DON H. MILLER, President, Skelly Oil Company. (165)

In a world dedicated to improving the economic welfare of hundreds of millions of persons who are in poverty, business enterprise becomes a major center in a nation's life. — ROBERT E. WILLIAMS, President, The Youngstown Sheet and Tube Company. (166)

There are four significant things about American business. It has economic freedom, voluntary competition, consumer choice and a need to earn profits if it is to survive. — GENE C. BREWER, President, United States Plywood Corporation. (167)

Some unwholesome thinking is circulating throughout the business world today. To be sure, it comes from a minor element; but it needs to be dealt with, nevertheless. It is the fallacious concept that "business" is a dirty word. The word "business" connotes the many principles that are truly American — free enterprise, individualism, economic opportunity and the traditional and certainly true belief that a man can rise from rags to riches if he so has a mind to. — DON H. MILLER, President, Skelly Oil Company. (168)

Business has been the engine behind the great accomplishment of the American society in the past century. And I am convinced it holds the key to even greater accomplishment in the future. — E. HORNSBY WASSON, President, Pacific Telephone and Telegraph Company. (169)

BUSINESS — America

The business of business is America. — A.F. JACOBSON, President, Northwest Bell Telephone Company. (170)

BUSINESS – Control

I think that each time the President uses the presidential authority to hold down prices when they would naturally have gone up, it gives business the jitters. And the more frequently he does it, the more jitters they will have. – DAVID ROCKEFELLER, President, Chase Manhattan Bank, *Public Utilities Fortnightly.* (171)

BUSINESS – Economic Development

The skills and other human resources which the developing countries so desperately need must come largely from non-governmental sources. This means that business must of necessity assume a broader role in economic development. – GEORGE CHAMPION, Chairman of the Board, The Chase Manhattan Bank. (172)

BUSINESS – Education

There is a gap between business education and business' needs, and it is primarily in terms of more practical training. Specific steps are being taken by both business and education to bridge this gap. More businessmen are getting directly involved in education, companies are increasing their scholarship program, and they are urging personnel on every level to take advantage of educational facilities. – SUSAN J. HERMAN, *Administrative Management.* (173)

Business education cannot stop at either the undergraduate or the graduate school level; it must be a continuing, life-long process. – ROBERT E. WILLIAMS, President, The Youngstown Sheet and Tube Company. (174)

Business is placing high priority on education in its future plans for management. Businessmen expect employees to spend 25 per cent of employment time for further education. . . . Top business executives expect that within the next two decades they will work four days a week and study one day, probably using electronic consoles at home to advance their education. – HARRY R. HALL, President, Michigan State Chamber of Commerce. (175)

The world-wide importance of American business activities puts a heavy burden of responsibility on the shoulders of our industrial leaders. And our educational system, in cooperation with industry, must develop men and women who are able to carry that burden. – BYRON J. NICHOLS, Dodge General Manager and Vice President, Chrysler Corporation, Detroit, Michigan. (176)

We in the business world are beginning to realize that it is no longer possible for us to stay outside the educational world and participate only at a distance by making financial contributions or offering professional advice on how to stretch available funds. The

40

time has come for us to put our experience to use and to get involved in the job of helping young people prepare themselves for fuller participation in American society. — LYNN TOWNSEND, Chairman and Chief Executive Officer, Chrysler Corporation.   (177)

BUSINESS — Ethics
Business ethics, like God, country, motherhood and a clean shave, enjoys universal support. — ROBERT F. DRAPER, President, Schick, Inc., *Dun's Review*.   (178)

BUSINESS — Foreign Competition
To fight foreign competitive fire with fire-power of our own, labor must recognize the problem. Industry and the working man are riding in the same boat. If it is to be kept afloat in this country, the greatest cooperation is a matter of life and death. — E.J. HANLEY, President, Allegheny Ludlum Steel Corporation, Pittsburgh, Pennsylvania.   (179)

BUSINESS — Future
The American business economy is at the same time the most powerful and the most sensitive mechanism in the world today. It cannot grow by serving yesterday's wants. It can only exist today by anticipating tomorrow. It must continually stimulate the public to serve the public. — ERNEST A. JONES, President, MacManus, John & Adams, Inc.   (180)

BUSINESS — Generations
As a businessman, the basic conflict between your generation and mine that I can see is this: Your generation spends most of its waking hours worrying about things as mundane as running a business and making a profit. And my generation can't understand why your generation is as unconcerned as it appears to be about something as essential as running a business and making a profit. — MARVIN C. WHATMORE, President, Cowles Communications, Inc.   (181)

BUSINESS — Government
In our world of today and tomorrow, business has an equal responsibility with government — if indeed it does not have a greater one — for improving the quality of our society by acceptance of its social responsibilities. Our society, to a greater extent than any other society in history, is faced with great challenges, great decisions.

Since business is so dependent upon a healthy community, it behooves business to take up these challenges and participate in these great decisions. If it does, its public relations standing will improve also. — J. CARROLL BATEMAN, President, The Insurance Information Institute. (182)

The day is long past, however nostalgically we may look back on it, when American business can operate in an atmosphere free of government influence, or uninhibited by public policies. It might co-exist better with government if both knew more about the other's problems, if there was more flexibility in the movement of people and talent between the public and private sectors of the national economy. — JAMES P. MITCHELL, Vice President, Crown Zellerbach Corporation, San Francisco, California. (183)

If communism and other "isms" are to be contained, the U S must recognize the needs of other free world countries to export in order to maintain their own economic good health. Political considerations in addition to economic considerations are inevitable, and it is the responsibility of U S business to recognize our government's need for information and many other kinds of sympathetic help and understanding. As businessmen this is our obligation in the national interest. — FRED J. BORCH, President and Chief Executive Officer, General Electric Company. (184)

I believe that many of the basic disagreements between business and government are surmountable through better communication. — NEIL H. McELROY, Chairman of the Board, The Proctor and Gamble Company. (185)

Since the end of World War II, the relations between business and the federal government have been closer and perhaps more cooperative than ever before in our history. — J. CARROLL BATEMAN, President, The Insurance Information Institute. (186)

BUSINESS — Growth

Business and industry depend upon the institutions of higher learning for three important things: educated manpower, new knowledge, and the improvement of the economic, social and political climate. These are essential to the prosperity and growth of business. — DONALD L. JORDAN, Chairman, The National Association of Manufacturers. (187)

BUSINESS — Helpfulness

There are two ways to be helpful to others in business. One way is to help them to help themselves; the other, to pitch in and do some work for or with them. In either case, the "helper" needs special skills – be he boss, associate or subordinate. A kind heart isn't enough. Neither is willingness to give of himself. It's vital that he have something to give. – NORMAN G. SHIDLE, Consulting Editor, *Society of Automotive Engineers Journal.* (188)

BUSINESS – Ideas

Commerce and industry thrive on ideas. When the supply of ideas is cut off by the closed mind of a department head or a chief executive, the institution gradually droops like crops in a drought. One of the foremost problems of an executive is to keep open the paths to his office and to his mind, so that the institution will be nourished by new ideas and suggestions, and thus keep healthy and strong. – WILLIAM FEATHER, *William Feather Magazine*, William Feather Company. (189)

BUSINESS – Industry

Unless business and industry are encouraged to grow and prosper – and are able to attract enough talented people to make this possible – we may sacrifice the major force in the growth and prosperity of our nation and the world. – L.W. MOORE, President, American Oil Company. (190)

BUSINESS – Labor, Government

Only with the cooperation of these three (business, labor, government) can our nation shape social and economic change in a constructive way that will assure more abundant opportunities for all our citizens in a free society. – GEORGE CHAMPION, Chairman of the Board, Chase Manhattan Bank. (191)

BUSINESS – Letters

Writing effective business letters today demands, above all, a realization that the recipient is a human being, and that, therefore, the letter will arouse an emotional response. – ETHEL KAPLAN, *Commerce*, Chicago Association of Commerce and Industry. (192)

BUSINESS – Money

I believe that the businessman today must find a way to apply the profit motive of the spirit of competitive enterprise to the fulfillment of the new desires of society. Money, after all, has never been more than a measure of price and debt, though we have fallen into the habit of using it to express values for nearly everything. – J.

BUSINESS — Overseas
The overseas investor has no interest in driving the old-fashioned local firms out of business. On the contrary, he finds it to his interest to help in every way he can to strengthen and modernize them — because to do so will improve the climate of acceptance for *all* business including his own. Moreover, he knows that a country whose business community is modern and progressive will have a more dynamic economy in which his own markets are likely to grow faster. — DAVID A. SHEPARD, Director and Executive Vice President, Standard Oil Company (New Jersey).   (194)

BUSINESS — People
It is one of the supreme ironies of our society that business which depends on people for its success, should have allowed itself to become tagged as unconcerned with people. Yet too often in the past the tag has had some justification. — RICHARD J. ANTON, Manager, Business Education Service, General Electric Company.   (195)

BUSINESS — Politics
It is not easy to become involved in political affairs. The boss may object. Customers with different political viewpoints may be offended. You may be in direct political conflict with bankers, union leaders, or others whose good relationships with you are important to your business. Many businessmen are afraid that direct political involvement can lead to calamities ranging from a closer look at their tax returns to a loss of orders.... Fear of involvement in controversial issues keeps too many of our most energetic, capable, and effective business leaders on the sidelines. — HOWARD M. METZENBAUM, Chairman, Airport Parking Company of America, *Wall Street Journal.*   (196)

BUSINESS — Profit
Profit is not a dirty word, but the need of future growth for Americans of another generation. No single group of individuals in this nation is more totally involved in the issues that embroil us than the businessman. It is he, who must ultimately solve the civil rights problem. It is the money he produces that will create tomorrow's schools, hospitals, research institutes, the old age and child care centers, the more beautiful cities. — E.A. BUTLER, President, E.A. Butler Associates.   (197)

There is still somehow a taint of original sin connected with the very idea of profits. In the minds of a considerable number of people, instead of being recognized as the creative force of our economy, profit is equated with private greed. . . . Bargaining demands . . . seem to assume that profit is merely a dollar amount which shows on the books and should be divided between labor and management. Quite apart from the legitimate claim of stockholders to a share of profits as a return on investment and of customers to a share through lower prices, such factors as the company's need to reinvest profits in the business to insure the continued life of the organization appear to be, at best, dimly perceived. – JOHN E. SWEARINGEN, President, Standard Oil Company of Indiana, *Quote.* (198)

BUSINESS – Race
Few American business firms have any business executives at home or abroad who are empowered to make decisions – and who are of a different race from the "superior" North European. This is the root of much of the problem that we ourselves are creating for democracy throughout the world. – RAYMOND W. MILLER, President, Public Relations Research Associates, Inc., Washington, D.C. (199)

BUSINESS – Risks
There isn't an American business operating today which wasn't founded at the risk of somebody's personal fortune. Every large corporation has, at some point in its history, had to risk expansion which could have backfired into failure. – RAY R. EPPERT, President, Burroughs Corporation. (200)
Successful businesses don't talk of minimizing risk – they talk of minimizing opportunity. The role of the businessman is to take risks. The sure loss is the reckless investment. – PETER DRUCKER, *Personnel Administration.* (201)

BUSINESS – Schools
The business schools and the business community should work to develop a relationship comparable to that of the best professional schools and practitioners in other fields. – ROBERT E. WILLIAMS, President, The Youngstown Sheet and Tube Company. (202)

BUSINESS – Small; Big.
The small businessman – the ideal small businessman – has a

built-in resistance to managerial obsolescence. He keeps himself on the constant alert for change, fundamental change, because he knows he's fighting in a class in which the premium is on being lean, wiry, fast, up-to-date. He isn't wed to any preconceptions. He isn't shackled by any prejudgments. He's flexible long range as well as short. Much as I love big business . . . such significant flexibility is not an outstanding characteristic of big-business operation. Corporations take on a bureaucratic life of their own that seems at times to have almost nothing to do with the people who are in the Company. – WILLIAM C. MARQUIS, Manager of Industrial Marketing, Marketing Department, American Oil Company, Chicago. (203)

BUSINESS – Social Goals
To realize its full promise in the world of tomorrow, American business and industry – or, at least, the vast portion of it – will have to make social goals as central to its decisions as economic goals; and leadership in our corporations will increasingly recognize this responsibility and accept it. – SOL M. LINOWITZ, Chairman of the Board, Xerox Corporation. (204)

BUSINESS – Social Purposes
It is my opinion that American business should be engaged now in organized and searching dialogue with the other leadership centers of the country – the scientific and academic world, government, religion – to discover and develop new social purposes. If we wait for these goals to be imposed by time and politics, we may well become the managed rather than the managers. – J. PAUL AUSTIN, President and Chief Executive Officer, The Coca-Cola Company. (205)

BUSINESS – Stocks
One out of every six adult Americans owns a share of American business. – G KEITH FUNSTON, President, New York Stock Exchange. (206)

BUSINESS – Success
Broadway to the contrary, there is no way to succeed in business without really trying. – ROBERT E. WILLIAMS, Executive Vice President, The Youngstown Sheet and Tube Company. (207)

BUSINESS – Successful
When a business is truly successful, it has what might be called "economic elbow room." In other words, it becomes financially able

to devote some of its talents and resources to the long-range good of society. — A.F. JACOBSON, President, Northwest Bell Telephone Company. (208)

BUSINESS — Women

Women in business and industry constitute the largest single source of potential managerial talent that has been all but ignored by U S business. This is clearly evident from the fact that women make up about a third of our labor force, but only 4% of the nation's executives. — RALPH S. NOVAK, *Personnel.* (209)

BUSINESS — Youth

If I could convey only one idea to the younger generation of graduates and undergraduates, it would be that business and industry have always offered young people the values of growth, progress, and human betterment. And, if anything, this is more true today than ever before. Business provides the machinery for building a better standard of living — and, with it, the means of improving our social and cultural level. Business *is* challenging and personally rewarding. Business *does* seek new ideas, and prizes the man who has them. — FREDERICK J. CLOSE, Chairman of the Board, Aluminum Company of America, *Quote.* (210)

Business in its final analysis, is merely the organized action of people seeking to supply one another's wants. By its very definition, business is essential to the scheme of things. It is most essential to anyone, young or old, who wishes to multiply the impact upon mankind of his singular talents and energies. It is essential to American youth and to the future that youth is seeking to create in America and the world. — LESLIE B. WORTHINGTON, President, United States Steel Corporation. (211)

BUSINESS ABROAD

Today most of the larger companies of the United States are extensively involved in overseas operations; and many others are parties to joint ventures with the nationals of other countries. In a great number of instances, they can provide as good an appraisal of foreign relations as a diplomat, politician or statesman. Frequently, the businessman is a barometer who registers — sometimes with astonishing accuracy — the climate outside of our own shores. — SOL M. LINOWITZ, Chairman of the Board, Xerox Corporation. (212)

We can lower substantially the resentment against American business abroad by using local nationals in our managements. There

47

is nothing a European dislikes so much as an expert from overseas. With some effort and education I believe it is possible to staff our operations abroad entirely with the nationals of the countries in which we operate. Such action will go a long way toward making our presence more acceptable. – THOMAS J. WATSON, Jr., Chairman of the Board, International Business Machines Corporation. (213)

BUSINESS ABROAD – Ethics

It is essential that a company operate abroad with integrity. Few other nations have attached the importance we do to ethical principles of business, and it is very tempting, and sometimes very easy, to buy a given result. Playing by the rules, when others do not, often puts us at a disadvantage. But our practices have their advantages over the long haul. Our probity is respected and can become an important part of our capital. – CHRISTIAN A. HERTER, Jr., General Manager, Government Relations Department, Socony Mobil Oil Company, Inc. (214)

BUSINESS CORPORATIONS

The business corporation is a mirror of society. It exists at the sufferance of society to serve the broad purposes of society. It reflects at most times the prevailing ethical, moral, and even cultural values of society. More particularly, it tends to reflect the values of the people at the top levels of management. – HENRY FORD II, Chairman of the Board, Ford Motor Company. (215)

BUSINESSMEN

We all know the popular stereotype of the businessman – cold, ruthless, an uncultured conformist whose only interest is in making a fast buck. Like all stereotypes, it's not an accurate picture. But as you know and I know, it is not without some foundation in fact. . . . What I'm suggesting is that we pay more attention, both to the quality of our lives, and to the impressions we give others in casual, day-to-day encounters. – A.F. JACOBSON, President, Northwest Bell Telephone Company. (216)

If a man wants to move up in business today, he's got to move around. – VANCE GREENSLIT, President, Greyhound Lines, Inc., *Newsweek*. (217)

Contrary to opinion in some quarters, businessmen are human. They have both the faults and the ability to grow that are characteristic of all humanity. And the character of tomorrow's business leaders inevitably depends on the caliber of the young men

48

who choose business careers today. — A.F. JACOBSON, President, Northwest Bell Telephone Company.   (218)

Businessmen whatever their national allegiances share a common economic objective. — RUDOLPH A. PETERSON, President, Bank of America.   (219)

I know many very successful businessmen who lead full, rich lives ... who find deep satisfaction in their outside enthusiasms *as well as* in their business lives. Perhaps we should try harder to show this side of our lives in our casual encounters with others. The businessman who can do this is probably doing more to attract the sort of young people we need than anything else we might try. — A.F. JACOBSON, President, Northwest Bell Telephone Company.   (220)

BUSINESSMEN — Change

Tomorrow's businessman will have to be ready and able as never before to leap when he sees an opportunity. He cannot hope to store the new wine of change in the old bottles of today's time-worn methods. — M.J. WARNOCK, President, Armstrong Cork Company.   (221)

BUSINESSMEN — Education

Education ... will need to give the management leader of tomorrow a broader field of vision. He will need to view scientific, economic, political and social trends outside of his own business, his own markets and his own country. And he will need a knowledge of the people of other countries, their language, their customs, and their needs and wants. — BYRON J. NICHOLS, Dodge General Manager and Vice President, Chrysler Corporation, Detroit, Michigan.   (222)

BUSINESSMEN — Educators

I am fully convinced that a free exchange of ideas between businessman and educator can bring a multitude of benefits to the entire nation — and, for that matter, to the entire world. — BYRON J. NICHOLS, Dodge General Manager and Vice President, Chrysler Corporation, Detroit, Michigan.   (223)

BUSINESSMEN — Employees

Unlike most businessmen elsewhere, businessmen in this country adopted policies that made customers and investors out of their own employees. I am not being moralistic, but simply stating a fact. Hence we have an economy in which the whole population — not just a thin upper crust — participates as producers, consumers, investors, and voters. — RALPH J. CORDINER, Chairman of the Board, General Electric Company, New York. (224)

BUSINESSMEN — Foreign Language.
It is my firm conviction that by 1970 the successful industrialist and corporation executive will have to have some foreign language at his command and also be familiar with a sufficient number of foreign graces and cultures in order to be successful in his international operations. — DONALD E. KRAMER, Vice-President and General Manager, Tectum Corporation, Columbus, Ohio. (225)

BUSINESSMEN — Free Enterprise
Businessmen, contrary to a very popular myth, are just as interested in humanity and the humanities as anyone else. They are dedicated to the advancement of people and the fulfilling of people's needs, and the incentives of the free enterprise system have proved to be the most effective means of achieving these aims. — LESLIE B. WORTHINGTON, President, United States Steel Corporation. (226)

BUSINESSMEN — Future
What the future demands (of those who aspire to top management positions) is a man of values, vision and venture — a man of humanistic education, far better schooled than his predecessors, a man equipped to meet whatever challenge the future may bring. — GUILFORD DUDLEY, Jr., President, Life and Casualty Insurance Company of Tennessee. (227)

BUSINESSMEN — Government
Businessmen — and I mean anyone involved in the management of a business or industry, whatever their background may be — businessmen are going to have to learn to live successfully with government. It is closer to their lives now than ever before, and I see no signs that it won't be still closer in the future. — JAMES M. PATTERSON, Director of Public Relations, American Oil Company. (228)
Businessmen must realize that government — big government — is here to stay. They should make every effort to understand our political system and participate whenever feasible. Believe it or not, the old picture of businessmen's unrelenting antipathy toward government per se has faded. Businessmen today have a full realization of government's influence over their decisions, and many of them accept this as a fact of life. — GENE C. BREWER, President,

United States Plywood Corporation.   (229)

I am thoroughly convinced that a knowledge of government and a concern for governmental activities ought to be a part of every businessman's intellectual and educational equipment. This was important yesterday. Today and in the future it is absolutely essential. – JAMES M. PATTERSON, Director of Public Relations, American Oil Company.   (230)

BUSINESSMEN – Isolation

The businessman tends to be isolated within his occupation, and in his own way lives in an "ivory tower" more remote from realities than many an academic person. Part of the shift we need from the "specialist" to the "generalist" is getting the business man to "cross-pollinate," as it were, with the cultural community, the academic community, and the non-suburban community. – PETER G. PETERSON, President, Bell & Howell Company.   (231)

BUSINESSMEN – Politics

I believe wholeheartedly that businessmen – as individuals and human beings – should involve themselves in political action. – ARNOLD MAREMOUNT, President, Maremount Corporation, Chicago, Illinois.   (232)

BUSINESSMEN – Public Servants

I do believe – as a businessman – that we of the business community have a responsibility for raising the level of public understanding and respect for the demands these times are making upon our public servants. – BENJAMIN H. DEHLERT, Jr., Vice President, Coca-Cola Company.   (233)

BUSINESSMEN – Reading

Progressive business leaders recognize that they cannot afford not to read about business, business currents, business discoveries, business developments. The man, especially the young man, who conceitedly imagines he knows it all and that, therefore, there is no need for him to try to learn more, is doing his best, or the worst, to bring about his own undoing. – B.C. FORBES, *Forbes*.   (234)

BUSINESSMEN – Travel

In 1900, a man who traveled 300,000 miles in his lifetime was a world traveler. I have already traveled over 3,000,000 miles, and my travels do not compare to those of an airline hostess, to say nothing of an astronaut. Nor will they compare with the international businessman of tomorrow — and most of us will be basically international — traveling at a rate of 2000 miles an hour. — RALPH E. ABLON, Chairman and President, Ogden Corporation.   (235)

BUSINESSMEN — Tycoons

American businessmen today are more responsive to the total needs of our society. The day of the ruthless tycoon, whose attitude was "the public be damned," is gone. You still may hear stories about him, but the truth is that he departed from the business scene many years ago, never to return. There is no place for him in our society today because of the checks and balances within our political system, the enlightened self-interest of our modern businessman, and most important of all — public opinion. — GENE C. BREWER, President, United States Plywood Corporation.   (236)

BUSINESSMEN — Unions

I am convinced that if it hadn't been for the stupidity, the avariciousness and the plain short-sightedness of the businessman himself, particularly the businessman of yesterday who didn't give a damn about his workers' welfare, who cared not in the least whether his workers ate or slept, who provided abominable working conditions all around — that if it hadn't been for him, there would have been no need for workers to band themselves together in order to obtain economic justice. — MAURICE R. FRANKS, President, National Labor-Management Foundation, Chicago, Illinois and Editor of *Partners Magazine*.   (237)

C

CANADA — America

I think it is well recognized that the United States increasingly is dependent on Canada in much the same way as Canada is dependent on the United States. We are each the largest customer of the other. — NEIL McELROY, Chairman of the Board, Proctor & Gamble Company. (238)

CAPABILITIES

Each of us has unsuspected reserves of energy and power which we can call upon if only we dare believe they are there. We are capable of living, thinking, and working at a level of achievement and distinction far above anything we have yet attained. This is as true for the salesman as for the scientist, as true for the businessman as for the college professor. — ELMER G. LETERMAN, *Commissions Don't Fall From Heaven* (MacFadden-Bartell). (239)

CAPITAL

Capital might be simply defined as the tools of production, generated under the incentive of our profit system. Those who provide capital expect to share, and rightly should share, in the profits of business — just as he who provides the boat should share in the fisherman's catch. — CHARLES F. JONES, President, Humble Oil & Refining Company, *Quote.* (240)

CAPITALISM

With some justification it may be said that, for a time man served capitalism. Today, however, capitalism is man's servant. Prideful of their own progressiveness, proponents of ideologies opposing capitalism are dated in their expressed knowledge of capitalism. As the human being is the highest order of life, so is capitalism — as it has evolved — the highest economic order man has devised. Capitalism, synonymous with free men, means choice. It is the mother of initiative and the father of ingenuity and industriousness. A capitalist is merely a member of that society in which everyone profits. — CHARLES TALBOTT GARLAND, National President, American Society of Living History, Inc. (241)

Our North American system of capitalism centers around the profit motive. It permits the individual citizen to own land and property, productive equipment and resources — to work at a job of his own choosing — to take risks — to compete in the market place — and to keep as his own a fair share of what he earns. But this new capitalism is set up to meet human needs — to create jobs — and to contribute to the general good, as well as to enable employers and employees alike to make money. This system of capitalism recognizes values in life above and beyond economic security. — RAYMOND W. MILLER, President, Public Relations Research Associates, Inc., Washington, D.C. (242)

We need to dispel the most harmful of all the myths that have been handed down from the past — the myth which holds that conflict *must* exist between economic groups under capitalism. This belief is founded on another century's concept of capitalism. It utterly ignores the simple fact that what we have in the United States today is what has been aptly called a people's Capitalism. Ours is a system in which the savings of millions of men and women in all walks of life provide the capital for investment in the various industries and businesses of America. — CHARLES G. MORTIMER, Chairman, General Foods Corporation. (243)

Capitalism will not win out in the world unless capitalists make it win and that is all of us. — RAYMOND W. MILLER, President, Public Relations Research Associates, Inc., Washington, D.C. (244)

Communists say that capitalism is a decaying system. That is false. Capitalism is not suffering from decay but from immaturity. — EDWARD J. MEEMAN, Editor, *Memphis Press-Scimitar,* (245)

CAPITALISM — Communism

Capitalism has been more maligned than America. Communism has been "selling" communism, not Russia. It is time we told the world what capitalism is instead of leaving it to the communists to do for us. If we don't, they will; and they are and we aren't. It is for us to "sell" capitalism, putting the two *isms* in ideological competition in world markets. Competition is said to be our game, not theirs. — CHARLES TALBOTT GARLAND, National President, American Society of Living History, Inc. (246)

CAREER — Success

A man who yearns for success should spend money lavishly on his career, but he should hoard it like a miser when it comes to anything not directly contributing to his career. — ELMER G. LETERMAN, *How Showmanship Sells* (Harper & Row). (247)

54

CHAMBER OF COMMERCE

The Chamber of Commerce is no Johnny-come-lately. In America it was formed when the founders of this country were first breaking away from the shackles of a decadent Europe that provided little encouragement for individual thought or initiative. It prospered during the writing of the Constitution, the finest political document that has yet appeared to proclaim the rights of free people under law. And it flowered in an age when this country was advancing to a position of unprecedented prestige and power. – ROBERT G. WINGERTER, President, Rockwell-Standard Corporation Automotive Divisions. (248)

CHANGE

In this latter half of the twentieth century change is increasingly important because it is increasingly rapid. At one time the rate of change could be compared to the speed of a baseball thrown by a child in a sandlot game. Now change is so accelerated that it must be compared to a fastball hurled by Don Drysdale. More skill is required of the batter. – GUILFORD DUDLEY, Jr., President, Life and Casualty Insurance Company of Tennessee. (249)

In coping with the unpredictable variety of radical change, it seems to me that everyone, individuals and institutions alike, needs to combine firmness of purpose and principle with flexibility of mind and method. – RICHARD J. ANTON, Manager, Business Education Service, General Electric Company. (250)

The only constant factor in our frenetic era seems to be change – constant, never-ending change. – ROBERT E. WILLIAMS, Executive Vice President, The Youngstown Sheet and Tube Company. (251)

I believe in change – my profession is innovation – and innovation is change personified. – ROBERT ALAN CHARPIE, Director of Technology, Union Carbide Corporation, New York. (252)

Change is not new . . . it is not something born of the 20th century. History has recorded change since the beginning, and in our history we can find guideposts to help us in our task. – ROBERT E. WILLIAMS, Executive Vice President, The Youngstown Sheet and Tube Company. (253)

Our world is continually being bombarded with change, and we need a strong capacity to adjust to these changes. This calls for creativity, innovation and leadership. – GENE C. BREWER, President, United States Plywood Corporation. (254)

55

New ideas, new products, new markets and new methods will seem to destroy our world if we try to hold to the old and the familiar — if we lack vision of the new world that is being created. The change that growth brings is dangerous only if we stand in its way. We must navigate in the rushing river of change or drown. — HOWARD A. MOREEN, Senior Vice President and Secretary, Aetna Life & Casualty. (255)

It seems to me that the key to our future can be summed up in one word — adaptability. In a rapidly changing world it is often a matter of survival to change one's mind — one's attitude — one's way of thinking and doing things. Even when survival is not at issue, we should all know how to adjust to changed circumstances in order to capitalize on new opportunities. — DUDLEY DOWELL, President, New York Life Insurance Company, *Journal of Insurance Information*. (256)

Change is the essence of the future as it has been in the past. . . . We had better be better in anticipating change, preparing for change, accepting change, adapting to change. — HARRY R. HALL, President, Michigan State Chamber of Commerce. (257)

I am always slightly amused by those people who are perpetually alarmed by change. But I suppose it's only human to be disturbed by it. Adlai Stevenson once suggested that Adam and Eve might even have discussed it. He said that Adam, as he led Eve by the hand out of the Garden of Eden, may well have delivered what certainly would have been the first lecture on the significance of historical change — when he turned to her and announced: "We live in an age of transition." — LYNN A. TOWNSEND, President, Chrysler Corporation, *Quote*. (258)

CHANGE — of Mind

Don't be afraid to change your mind. Remember that any opinion, any judgment, is little more than a tentative approximation of the truth, subject to revision. It takes a wiser and stronger person to change his mind, to embrace new ideas, than it does to keep on thinking the same old thoughts. — ROSCOE DRUMMOND, Editor and Columnist. (259)

CHANGE — Progress

Most of us make the fundamental mistake of believing that all change is progress. I've heard many people say, "everything changes for the better." This is nonsense. Things don't always change for the better unless they are guided by intelligent individuals. – L.C. MICHELON, Director of Public Affairs, Republic Steel Corporation. (260)

CHANGE – Risk
Although all change involves risk, no organization can survive unless it embraces change and is prepared to manage its risk. – ROBERT E. WILLIAMS, Executive Vice President, The Youngstown Sheet and Tube Company. (261)

CHANGE – Security
Only by keeping abreast of change, I believe, can any nation maintain its security in this competitive world; and only by leading the race toward change can it increase its security and the well-being of all its people. Just keeping up will only perpetuate the problem. To solve it we must forge ahead. – ROGER M. BLOUGH, Chairman of the Board, United States Steel Corporation. (262)

CHARACTER
It is not by a man's purse, but by his character that he is rich or poor. – WILLIAM FEATHER, *William Feather Magazine*, William Feather Company. (263)

CHARITY
It is not time to scuttle the voluntary ship. It is a time, most urgently, to redefine the role of the voluntary agency. Governmental social services are essential in an industrial, urban society. The voluntary system has certain values, freedoms, and opportunities not available to the public agency. . . . In partnership, they do their part, along with other social forces, in building a better society. – ROBERT H. MacRAE, Executive Director, Chicago Community Trust, *Arkansas Methodist*. (264)

CHILDREN – Discipline
If a child does not learn discipline and responsibility in the home, he will not learn it elsewhere. The failure of some parents to meet this responsibility is the reason why we have problem children today. – JAMES M. ROCHE, President, General Motors. (265)

CHILDREN – Environment
It is not enough . .,. to ascribe the difficulties some young people get into today to the failure of parents to exercise adequate

responsibility for moral training. For, as changes come faster and faster, and life becomes more complex, the home environment frequently ceases to be the whole or even the major environment of a child. Other environments, other influences intrude — often to the extent that no amount of good intentions on the part of parents can meet all the requirements. — LEROY COLLINS, President, National Association of Broadcasters. (266)

CHILDREN — Obedience
Upon our children — how they are taught — rests the fate or fortune of tomorrow's world. — B.C. FORBES, *Forbes.* (267)

CHILDREN — Profit
The kids of today should know that profit is not a dirty word. They should know that profit is responsible for research, development, machine tools, and new factories, as well as rewarding shareholders for their faith in the business. They should know that without profit, business and industry would close its doors forever. — NICHOLAS A. GEORGE, Vice President of Brunswick Corporation, Chicago, Illinois. (268)

We must also teach our children to be contributors to the home, to the family and to society — not just acceptors of a standard of living that we supply. . . . Young people can wash cars and windows, mow and fertilize lawns, weed and edge beds, shovel snow, paint fences and garages, wash walls, iron, help serve at home dinner parties, wash dishes, baby sit and so on. What family does not have the need of all these services, and what better way to teach a family self-reliance, the dignity of worthwhile labor, the satisfaction of accomplishment, not to mention the learning of skills which will always be useful in later years. Children may do these things to merit an allowance, or be paid at a rate commensurate with their skill, but always with the knowledge that they are contributing as a family member to satisfy definite family needs, that their labors are dignified, and the habit of work becomes a part of their character. — ROBERT G. WINGERTER, President, Rockwell-Standard Corporation Automotive Divisions. (269)

CHRISTIANITY
It is 2,000 years since Christ commanded love of all men. And after 2,000 years there are 2 billion people in the world who do not know Christ. — ALBERT J. NEVINS, M.M., Editor. (270)

CHRISTIANS

Too many of today's Christians want Christ without the cross. — J.K. STERN, President, American Institute of Cooperation, Washington, D.C. (271)

CHURCH — Attendance

I feel sorry for the men and women who go to church on Sunday morning because they think it's the thing to do, and then forget about it for the rest of the week. Nothing in this world, and I mean that literally, is more deserving of enthusiasm than the salvation of your immortal soul. — EDWIN.M. CLARK, President, Southwestern Bell Telephone Company, St. Louis, Missouri. (272)

CHURCHILL, WINSTON

I sometimes think that Winston Churchill's magnificent leadership in wartime was his genius as a great communicator — not only to Britain but to all the nations in the Alliance. He conveyed not simply language and eloquence, but a spirit, purpose, and philosophy. — J. PAUL AUSTIN, President, The Coca-Cola Company. (273)

CITIES

Nobody really believes in the American city. We have lived so long with old, wornout, ugly places that we have become anesthetized to their condition. — JAMES ROUSE, Developer and Financier, Quote. (274)

People are fascinated and comforted by the garish signs and the store windows and the bustling sidewalks, and the lonely tree along the curb struggling to stay alive. Cities set the tempo for our civilization. — FRED SMITH, Vice President, The Prudential Insurance Company, Newark, New Jersey. (275)

The city is the birthplace of democracy, and today it is a testing ground for the effectiveness of the democratic process. Urban problems are immense, and the cultural pluralism of our cities represents both an asset and a challenge to making democracy work. — SIDNEY H. ALEXANDER, Jr., Executive Director, Wichita Urban League. (276)

The problem of the cities will not be solved until private industry takes its rightful role. The cities of the world have traditionally been not only the creators of art, science, literature, and civilization itself, but likewise the basic pool of creative and lucrative labor. They are no different today. — A.J. CERVANTES, Mayor of the City of St. Louis. (277)

Our cities will not reduce the level of crime by construction of public housing for people who remain unable to get jobs. They will not retain existing business and draw business by creating vast new highway systems that are immediately clogged with traffic. And they will not encourage the return or the retention of that vast tax base known as the middle class by isolating in ghettolike centers the cultural facilities that are a city's last remaining drawing card, no matter how magnificent in concept and execution those ghettos of culture may be. — FRANK L. WHITNEY, President, Walter Kidde Constructors, Inc., Engineers and Builders.   (278)

If the city is going down the drain, as many critics have said, then man is going down the drain. There is no alternative. Man wants to be where the action is. — STANLEY B. TANKEL, Director, Regional Plan Association, *Quote*.   (279)

The existence of slums, the migration of millions into the central cities, whether from farm or foreign shores, the middle class flight to the suburbs, are not new phenomena. Throughout history the advantaged have fled from the disadvantaged. The core areas of our major municipalities have long served as ports of entry and processing depots for migrants at the lower end of the economic ladder. — A.J. CERVANTES, Mayor of the City of St. Louis.   (280)

The United States — and most of the rest of the rapidly urbanizing world — is going to be a very strange country indeed if the problems of the city are not resolved within a reasonable period of time. The city is the heart and brain of an industrial society. — F.J. BORCH, President and Chief Executive Officer, General Electric Company.   (281)

CITIES — Crime

Until the Industrial Revolution, the European city existed for essentially one reason — protection. People had to come in from the fields at night to keep from getting killed. Today we leave the city at night for the same reason. — FRANK L. WHITNEY, President; Walter Kidde Constructors, Inc., Engineers and Builders.   (282)

CITIES — East

Today's big city, especially in the East, is running down, mostly worn out, and fundamentally is an uneconomic structure that has lost much of its original function and can't quite settle on what is to be its future significance. — FRED SMITH, Vice President, The Prudential Insurance Company, Newark, New Jersey.   (283)

CITIES — Money

Many people who have not worked closely with the new technology believe that the computer can solve all problems without realizing that the computer is a moron and if a man asks a silly question he will undoubtedly get a stupid answer, neatly printed out to be sure, but still meaningless. Similarly, there is a belief that money, or even better an appropriation, will cure the problems of our core cities. But money, like the computer has no life of its own — it is amoral. It will buy hospitals or destruction. It is up to us to devise the means and methods to channel the expenditure in a way that serves the common good. — WALTER B. WRISTON, President, First National City Bank.   (284)

CITIES — Suburbia

With the growth of suburbia, our cities are beginning to resemble a doughnut — a hole in the middle and all the dough around the outside. — STUART T. SAUNDERS, Chairman of the Board, The Pennsylvania Railroad Company.   (285)

CITIZENSHIP

If you would like to live in a community in which you may have pride, then dedicate yourself in a spirit of humility to your responsibilities in that community. These are practical ways in which to live the good life as a citizen. — HERBERT V. PROCHNOW, President, First National Bank of Chicago.   (286)

We must all be citizens first and businessmen or lawyers or doctors or whatever second. — THEODORE C. SORENSEN, Partner in law firm of Paul, Weisse, Rifkind, Wharton & Garrison, *Public Relations Journal.*   (287)

Too many people today regard citizenship as all take and no give. They accept all the benefits and take them for granted. But it does not occur to them to take an intelligent interest in the serious issues of the day. — JAMES M. ROCHE, President, General Motors.   (288)

CIVIC LEADERSHIP — Future

I believe that our schools and colleges are seriously at fault in not emphasizing more social sciences, particularly in the field of politics. We in business are perhaps equally at fault by not asking that the people they send to us have more academic credits in the social sciences. We should urge our schools to teach substantially more political science if we intend to have high caliber civic leadership in the future. — CHARLES R. BARR, Standard Oil Company (Indiana)
(289)

CIVIL DISOBEDIENCE

When rioters burn and loot our cities, that is *despair* in the fulfillment of democracy. When mass demonstrations try the methods of extorting instead of explanation that is *distrust* in the regular channels of democracy. When youths burn their draft cards instead of working for peace candidates, that is *disengagement* from the discipline of democracy. — JAMES C. HUMES, Executive Director, Philadelphia Bar Association. (290)

It seems to me the time has come, if indeed it is not long past due, for a strong stand to be taken by Government in this Country, at both the Federal and state levels, and by leading citizenry, against the toleration of civil disobedience and lawlessness, and that prosecution for alleged violations should be vigorous and without fear or favor, i.e., whether the alleged violation is committed by a member of the clergy, a radical or other professor, a civil rights leader or anyone else. — W.L. GRUBBS, Vice President-Law of Louisville and Nashville Railroad. (291)

The greatest danger in condoning civil disobedience as a permissible strategy for hastening change is that it saps our democratic processes. To adopt the techniques of civil disobedience is to assume that representative government does not work. To resist the decisions of our courts and the laws of our elected assemblies is to say that democracy has failed. — JAMES C. HUMES, Executive Director, Philadelphia Bar Association. (292)

CIVIL DISOBEDIENCE — Democracy

Those who advocate taking the law in their own hands should reflect that when they are disobeying what they consider to be a possibly immoral law, they are deciding on a possibly more immoral course. Civil disobedience may be above the law, but it is also against the law. Instead of ennobling democracy, it often erodes it. — JAMES C. HUMES, Executive Director, Philadelphia Bar Association. (293)

CIVILIZATIONS — Promises

Every civilization rests on a set of promises. If the promises are broken too often, the civilization dies, no matter how rich it may be, or how mechanically clever. Hope and faith depend on promises; if hope and faith go, everything else goes. — HERBERT AGAR, Author and Publisher, *Sunshine Magazine*. (294)

CIVILIZATIONS — Responsibilities

The only things that were ever swept under history's carpet were the fragments of those civilizations which, instead of facing up to their responsibilities, reacted by closing their minds and bringing upon them their own destruction. — KARL R. BENDETSEN, President, Champion Papers Inc., Hamilton, Ohio. (295)

CIVILIZATIONS — Survival

Our civilization cannot survive materially unless it is redeemed spiritually. — ANDREW R. CECIL, Executive Vice President, The Southwestern Legal Foundation. (296)

CIVIL LIBERTY

If we in the United States become careless of civil liberty, if we think of it as a liability rather than as an asset, if we put public safety above private rights, and the protection of the community above the protection of the individual, we shall end by making ourselves over into a mirror image of what we most abhor. And if we do that, we shall have betrayed and lost our richest inheritance. — ALAN BARTH, Editorial Board, *Washington Post*. (297)

CO-EXISTENCE

I detest the Russians and all forms of dictatorship with all my heart and soul and mind, yet I recognize that somewhere, without accommodation or appeasement, we must work out a way of living with them for a better world. — RICHARD H. AMBERG, Publisher, *The St. Louis Globe-Democrat*. (298)

COLLECTIVE BARGAINING

Public concern and disenchantment with collective bargaining as it now exists were especially vehement last year during the airline strike and earlier in the year during the New York City transit strike. While the public outcry has abated somewhat, my fear is that a new series of strikes will adversely affect enough citizens that the American public will say "A pox on both your houses," and insist upon mandatory settlement procedures such as compulsory arbitration. It will be a sad day for this country indeed if this comes about. — B.D. BILLMAN, Vice President, Armco Steel Corporation. (299)

We believe that management should approach bargaining with an open mind — but that its mind need not be so open as to be vacant. — VIRGIL B. DAY, Vice President, General Electric (300)

We in steel have been on the receiving end of a succession of massive power plays, supported and often initiated by the government. I fear that continuation of such tactics will endanger both collective bargaining and our competitive free enterprise system. — B.D. BILLMAN, Vice President, Armco Steel Corporation.   (301)

In one of my first ventures in collective bargaining I noted with concern the vigor of the language and table thumping but the virtual absence of discussion and persuasion based on relevant facts. It did not take too long to conclude that both the union and management negotiators were more concerned with satisfying what they thought were their constituents' demand for toughness than in reaching a fair and equitable settlement. — IRVING STERN, Director of Organization of the Amalgamated Meat Cutters & Retail Food Store Employees Union of Greater New York.   (302)

COLLEGES

College is no longer the sanctuary of the privileged. — PAUL C. HARPER, Jr., President, Needham, Harper & Steers, Inc.   (303)

When my little girl asked me one day at breakfast "What is a college?" I gulped a bit — I had not had my coffee as yet! — and then, as I recall, I told her, "It is a school you go to after high school to learn how to walk a bit taller in the world." — LEE HASTINGS BRISTOL, Jr., Director of Public Relations, Bristol-Myers Products Division.   (304)

COLLEGES — Degrees

The notion is too much about that the Ph.D, the Master's, or the Bachelor's degree is an immediate admission ticket to the highly publicized "ready-to-take-over" generation. The truth is that a degree — or two or three of them — is only an admission ticket — front row, if you will — to the most exacting of all universities, the university of life — sometimes called "hard knocks." There the seating — front row or back — will be determined by performance. — HENRY C. ALEXANDER, Chairman of the Board, Morgan Guaranty Trust Company of New York.   (305)

COLLEGES — Professors

A college professor is a necessity in our time. To have colleges and college professors is a must and not a luxury. — HENRY L. BOWDEN, Attorney.   (306)

College professors should realize that they hold exalted positions in the community. They are highly regarded. They are looked up to not only by their students but by a large segment of the informed public. Their utterances are given more credence than those of the man on the street. Therefore, their utterances should be more guarded and they should be more circumspect in making assertions than a small minority of them frequently seem to be. — HENRY L. BOWDEN, Attorney. (307)

COMMERCE — Government Control
Let our commerce continue to operate with the absolute minimum of government control and regulation. — LLOYD E. SKINNER, President, Skinner Macaroni Company. (308)

COMMITTEES
Throughout the history of the U S, when people want to get something done, they have banded together into associations and appointed committees. — WILLIAM C. MOTT, Executive Vice President, U S Independent Telephone Association, *Public Utilities Fortnightly*. (309)

Despite the protestation of the wit who once observed that the camel was a horse built by a committee, I believe the committee can have value as a management device. But it is often badly misused, horrifyingly inefficient, an enemy of decision-making, and a friend of vacillation. — LOUIS B. LUNDBORG, Executive Vice President, Bank of American N.T. & S.A. (310)

The philosophy of most committees: I came, I saw, I concurred. — Dr IRVINE H. PAGE, Director, Cleveland Clinic, *Quote*. (311)

COMMON SENSE
If there is one thing we businessmen pride ourselves on, it is common sense. Common sense is the basis for sound business judgment. And sound business judgment is the basis for a successful company. — PETER STEELE, Business Consultant. (312)

COMMUNICATIONS
Despite the vast augmentation of media and technology, one of our most pervasive problems today is the lack of genuine communication. The young don't trust anyone over 30, the hip put down the square, and whites and blacks pull further apart. There are generation gaps, credibility gaps, rich-poor gaps, racial gaps — it sometimes seems that there are more holes than cloth in the fabric of our

society. – HOYT AMMIDON, Chairman, United States Trust Company of New York. (313)

It is by communications that two individuals are able to reach an understanding of themselves and to agree upon their common purposes. In a mass society such as ours has become, we must utilize mass communications to accomplish the same understandings and agreements on a national scale. – LEROY COLLINS, President, National Association of Broadcasters. (314)

If there is one secret of successful communication it may lie in the ability to get the other person's point of view and to see things from his angle as well as your own. – LAWRENCE A. DYSART, Richfield Oil Corporation. (315)

At no time in history has a society had such a means for coping with its problems as ours has through modern means of mass communications. It is a resource we have only just begun to utilize. There is no visible limit on the heights to which it will allow man to soar. – LEROY COLLINS, President, National Association of Broadcasters. (316)

We have the habit of assigning a dollar cost to problems that beset society – a billion dollars for crime, hundreds of millions for traffic congestion, hundreds of millions for the common cold. For failures in communications – in companies, institutions, markets, communities and nations – we might estimate a cost of hundreds of billions of dollars, along with billions of years taken from people's lives. – J. PAUL AUSTIN, President, The Coca-Cola Company. (317)

This nation is not innately one of selfish and inconsiderate people. Its basic nature is one of generosity, understanding, compassion and selflessness. We need to communicate with outselves more in those terms. – LEROY COLLINS, President, National Association of Broadcasters. (318)

The intelligent people of the free world must communicate and communicate effectively, or we shall drown in a sea of ill-considered, unwise actions brought about by misinformation, confusion, and shortsighted snatching for the immediate benefit. – HAROLD BRAYMAN, Director, Public Relations Department, E.I. du Pont de Nemours & Company. (319)

Communication is a difficult thing. You must learn to listen carefully, because only if you listen carefully will people listen to you. – HERMAN C. KRANNERT, Chairman of the Board, Inland Container Corporation. (320)

For the nation, in an age of complexity, continuous change and tremendous pace of events, communications are literally the lifeblood of our free society. — ARTHUR R. MURPHY, Jr., President and Chief Operating Officer, McCall Corporation.   (321)

The world is in the midst of a communications explosion that may be fully as significant as the blast at Hiroshima. It would seem that we have at least the technical capability of making verbal fusion — a meeting of international minds through communications — as significant to mankind as nuclear fusion. — J.M. CLIFFORD, President, Curtis Publishing Company, *Quote*.   (322)

COMMUNICATIONS — Art

Modern communications and modern painting are alike in one respect. In each of them there is a first-class revolution going on. — FREDERICK R. KAPPEL, Chairman, American Telephone & Telegraph Company.   (323)

COMMUNICATIONS — English Language

We must rededicate ourselves to the beauties and the revelations of the English language and learn again how to write it, how to read it, and how to understand it — for it is the greatest communications tool of all. — ARTHUR R. MURPHY, Jr., President and Chief Operating Officer, McCall Corporation.   (324)

COMMUNICATIONS — Freedom of

You cannot strengthen the freedom to communicate without strengthening democracy. Nor can you weaken such freedom without weakening democracy. — LEROY COLLINS, President, National Association of Broadcasters.   (325)

COMMUNICATIONS — Government

Government at all levels has the responsibility to protect the freedom of communications and to help advance it. — LEROY COLLINS, President, National Association of Broadcasters.   (326)

COMMUNICATIONS — International

Ironically, some of the best international communications flow not through the medium of language or graphics, but through things and products. A can of soup, a package of powdered milk, or a bottle of coke can often say more than any number of carefully drafted words or pictures. Through exposure of the myriad products of the West, our merchants and traders may well be proving more influential as communicators than political propagandists. — J. PAUL AUSTIN, President, The Coca-Cola Company.   (327)

COMMUNICATIONS — Responsible

Responsibility is at the heart of genuine communication, on every level from the most intimate and personal to the gravest discourse between sovereign powers. Indeed, it is responsible communication that distinguishes men from beasts. — HOYT AMMIDON, Chairman, United States Trust Company of New York. (328)

COMMUNICATIONS — Youth

Many young people today frankly admit that they've plain given up on communicating with their elders — in fact, a sizeable number seem to have given up on communicating with *others*. A minority even argue that language itself is "a bag," and that the only valuable experiences are incommunicable. But like it or not, the future of the world really does depend in large measure on responsible communications between people. — HOYT AMMIDON, Chairman, United States Trust Company of New York. (329)

COMMUNISM

Communism, wherever it exists, is not there by the will or consent of the people; it is there because the people are enslaved prisoners of power and terror. — CHARLES NUTTER, The Hallmark Foundation, Kansas City, Missouri. (330)

We can unquestionably meet the economic challenge of communism successfully if we have the will to do it. No revolutionary new philosophy is required, no government bureaucracy spending more money is needed. We must work harder. We must produce more. We must save more. We must invest more. Work and thrift and investment are not social evils. They are the route by which economic growth is achieved. They are the route for the economic enrichment of man. They are the route to economic strength and power for men and nations. — HERBERT V. PROCHNOW, President, First National Bank of Chicago, Illinois. (331)

Communism is so parently specious, so brutally inhuman, so unsatisfactory economically, so jungle-like in its concept and so anti-Christ in its practice that if we believe in Christ, in peace, in the brotherhood of man and a world of law, order, and equal opportunity we *must* believe that Communism will fail. — CHARLES NUTTER, Managing Director, International House, New Orleans, Louisiana. (332)

Communism is an idea, a concept of man and his destiny, a philosophy of life, an ideology. And the ideology is this. All is matter. There is no God. Religion is the opium of the people. Man

68

exists without Creator and without divine assistance. His life is determined by economic forces. That which promotes the revolution is good; that which retards it is bad. The individual has no natural rights; rights are in the proletariat. Therefore communism liquidates individuals without scruple. Law, in the sense that we understand it, does not exist. Government exists by executive fiat; legislature and judiciary are nominal. — HAROLD R. McKINNON, Attorney, Bronson, Bronson & McKinnon, San Francisco, California.   (333)

"The Communist Manifesto" runs 27 book-size printed pages . . . it is something which I feel that every intelligent American should read, if for no other reason than to see what kind of thinking is back of the idea of communism — and what kind of appeal it took to set the whole chain reaction of communism into motion. — RAYMOND W. MILLER, President, Public Relations Research Associates, Inc., Washington, D.C.   (334)

I believe that Communism is the most cumbersome and oppressive system ever invented, and that it cannot forever stand up against the free, open society of the West if we really unleash our spiritual and physical energies. — LEE MILLS, President, American Society of Newspaper Editors.   (335)

Communism is the enemy of free men. — ROBERT H. HINCKLEY, former Vice President of the American Broadcasting Company.   (336)

Communism, in the first place, is a kind of blasphemous religion which is a standing threat to our whole way of life. In the second place, Communism is an armed revolution which threatens our very lives. Naturally, therefore, Americans want to defend themselves at both levels; the spiritual as well as the military. — EDMUND A. OPITZ, The Foundation for Economic Education, Irvington-on-Hudson, New York.   (337)

COMMUNISM — America
The difference between life behind the Iron Curtain and our way of life is essentially freedom. Freedom of choice, freedom to decide where to live and where to work. Friends who have visited in East Germany and Moscow all tell of sad faces and dejection — yes, the freedom to laugh and the freedom to use cream in a cup of coffee, or to drink it black. — LOWELL SCHMIDT, Senior Vice President, Sertoma International.   (338)

COMMUNISM — Class System
Communism, instead of abolishing classes, has brought the

sharpest class division the world has ever seen — on the one hand a handful of men who run the government and actually own everything — all means of production, all property, even the lives and bodies of the workers — and on the other hand millions of slaves without property or rights. — EDWARD J. MEEMAN, Editor, *Memphis Press-Scimitar*. (339)

COMMUNISM — Communists

It is very important to know the Communist peoples better. I spent two weeks in the Soviet Union and I believe that I understand the problems of the people better now. I feel that the best thing to improve relations with Communist countries is a great exchange of peoples. — DAVID ROCKEFELLER, President, Chase Manhattan Bank, *Quote*. (340)

COMMUNISM — Food

The greatest deterrent to the spread of Communism may not be the missile program, but the Communists' inability to satisfy their people's food wants. — W.B. MURPHY, President, Campbell Soup Company. (341)

COMMUNISM — Free World

The communist system is concentrating its great resources, its increasingly efficient and expanding production and the enormous energy of its people on the single objective of destroying the social and economic order of the free world and replacing it with communism. Such complete and total dedication can only be met successfully by the complete dedication of the genius, talent and resources of free men who cherish life in free societies. — HERBERT V. PROCHNOW, President, First National Bank of Chicago, Illinois. (342)

COMMUNISM — Russia

In forty-four years communism has spread to approximately one billion of the two billion nine hundred million people in the world. Simultaneously, Soviet Russia has been transformed from a backward agricultural country to an industrial nation, and from a nation with eighty per cent of its people illiterate to one where elementary education is compulsory. — HERBERT V. PROCHNOW, President, First National Bank of Chicago, Illinois. (343)

COMMUNISM — Underdeveloped Nations

Our struggle with Communism is taking place primarily among those uncommitted, under-developed nations of the world who hold, by sheer numbers, the potential, ultimate balance of power. If we hope to win them over to the side of freedom, we must demonstrate that our system, our individual freedom of action . . . is not something which works only in certain countries for certain people, but is something which can work anywhere for anyone. — RAY R. EPPERT, President, Burroughs Corporation. (344)

COMMUNISTS

Do you know what scares me about the Communists? It is not their political system, which is primitive and savage. It is not their economic system which works so badly that progress in a few directions is purchased at the price of progress in all the rest. It is their puritanism. It is their dedication and self-sacrifice. — JENKIN LLOYD JONES, Editor, *The Tulsa Oklahoma Tribune*. (345)

COMMUNISTS — America

To be lulled into any idea that the communists intend to do anything but overthrow this Nation is foolishness of the greatest magnitude. — R.L. SHETLER, General Manager, Defense Systems Department, General Electric Company, Syracuse, New York. (346)

COMMUNISTS — Propaganda

The Communists are the all-time masters of propaganda. They might well advertise that "Propaganda is our most important product," and it is often more effective than we realize. — LEE HILLS, President, American Society of Newspaper Editors. (347)

The principle weapon in the Communist arsenal is propaganda. Behind the mask of peaceful coexistence the Russians spread hate and subversion throughout the world. Having gained more territory than any other movement in history, their long-range propaganda war goes on unabated, without any major opposition. — ARTHUR E. MEYERHOFF, President, Arthur Meyerhoff Associates, Inc., Chicago, Illinois. (348)

COMMUNITY SERVICE

Everything begins with the individual — the awareness of community, the feeling of being responsible for it, the assumption of burdens of service and leadership in order to make it better, the willingness to meet its even more difficult challenges in the future. Some people do this. Most people don't. Those who do, however, discover an exciting thing. And it is this — community service, in time, is no longer an effort. It is a way of life. It is a way to build, to create, to open doors to people, and to transform ideas on paper into bricks and stone. It is also, in the best sense of the word, fun. — RALPH M. BESSE, President, The Cleveland Electric Illuminating Company. (349)

Unfortunately, one of the more important things Americans have learned to buy exemption from is service. Service to the community, to organizations, to causes. The checkbook has taken the place of personal service. Donation to a cause absolves one from working for that cause, and, at the same time, warms the conscience with a comfortable glow of satisfaction. The result is that more persons today are giving money; fewer persons are giving time and leadership; and because of the dwindling supply of workers and leaders, more and more responsibilities, long within the province of the community, are passing by default into the hands of federal government. — RALPH M. BESSE, President, The Cleveland Electric Illuminating Company. (350)

COMPANIONSHIP — Friendship

When people tell me that they are hungry for companionship, I think that they must be starved for friendship. And when they tell me that they do not have the time to make friends, I feel that they are rushing through life so quickly that they had better stop to catch their breath before they arrive at the other end and suddenly discover that they've missed the sweetest thing that human relationships have to offer. — ELMER G. LETERMAN, *The Sale Begins When the Customer Says "No"* (MacFadden-Bartell). (351)

COMPASSION

We learn compassion from the lessons of history. We see the rise and fall of empires and of nations and of peoples. The lessons of the past teach us the strengths and weaknesses of the present and light the way toward a better future if we are but wise enough to appreciate them. — RICHARD H. AMBERG, Publisher, *The St. Louis Globe-Democrat.* (352)

I do not see how we can be truly great citizens unless we have compassion, which is the opposite of intolerance. — RICHARD H. AMBERG, Publisher, *The St. Louis Globe-Democrat.* (353)

COMPETENCE

Competence is the hallmark of any profession. — JOHN W. QUEENAN, Managing Partner, Haskins & Sells. (354)

72

COMPETITION — Change

Competition is so keen today that if a company stands still for one year — changless in a changing world — it may never again be able to catch up. — Robert E. Williams, Executive Vice President, The Youngstown Sheet and Tube Company.　　　　　(355)

COMPLACENCY

The forces of mediocrity and complacency are strong today and are growing stronger. Too many people are still sitting it out instead of sweating it out. Too many don't have the guts to stand up straight and put their energy and talents to the test. Perhaps because they fear failure or are simply satisfied with low success. But this situation cannot endure if America is to remain strong and grow stronger. — GUILFORD DUDLEY, Jr., President, Life and Casualty Insurance Company, *Journal of Insurance Information*.　　　　　(356)

In both education and government we should have learned one lesson: Complacency leads to destruction. — WILLARD M. WILSON, Secretary, American Petroleum Institute.　　　　　(357)

COMPLETE MAN

The person who lives for himself and selfishly, no matter how successful, leads a cold and narrow life. The man of compassion, of humility and action, of unselfish virtue, of sharing God's blessings with those less fortunate and well-endowed is the complete man. — RICHARD H. AMBERG, Publisher, *The St. Louis Globe-Democrat*.　　　　　(358)

COMPLIMENTS

It's ironic, but the toughest thing to take gracefully is a compliment. — MALCOLM S. FORBES, Editor, *Forbes*.　　　　　(359)

COMPUTERS

Over the next twenty years computers will touch off an explosion in the social sciences comparable to that which we witnessed during the last half-century in the physical sciences. — DAVID SARNOFF, Chairman of the Board, Radio Corporation of America, *Quote*.　　　　　(360)

I would like to advance the thesis that the whole world of computer people is one of the most socially significant elements of our time. This pool of talent may be our most potent weapon for national survival. These creative minds can surely help contribute solutions to our national and international problems with the same zeal and intelligence that went into establishing this dynamic industry in the first place. — DAUSE L. BIBBY, President, Remington Rand Division, Sperry Rand Corporation. (361)

As a manufacturer of computers, I feel both shocked and alarmed whenever I hear the prediction — and I hear it often — that one day "the machines will take over" and give us the answers to everything. A computer is a machine and a machine is a tool — a means to an end — nothing more. — THOMAS J. WATSON, Jr., Chairman of the Board, International Business Machines Corporation. (362)

One of the best things about the computer is that it forces us to think through our problems logically before we can even turn it on. In order to program a computer, we must have clearly in mind what it is we are trying to accomplish and the various means by which we can achieve our goals. — ARJAY MILLER, President, Ford Motor Company. (363)

COMPUTERS — Human Brain

It is as true of computers as of the human brain: They are only as good as the uses to which they are put. — DAUSE L. BIBBY, President, Remington Rand Division, Sperry Rand Corporation. (364)

COMPUTERS — Man

Personally, I have no fear that computers will ever do away with their programmers. They may have the electronic ability to store and digest a lot of information, but they lack one essential ingredient — the ability to communicate with one another and to work out agreements, computer to computer, based on the facts they have on hand. — LESLIE B. WORTHINGTON, President, United States Steel Corporation, Chicago, Illinois. (365)

The danger of the computer is not the science-fiction fear that machines will begin to think like men, but the more realistic apprehension that men will begin to think like machines. — PETER G. PETERSON, President, Bell & Howell Company. (366)

The computer is logical but not perceptive. Man is perceptive but not particularly logical. They can be an effective combination. — RALPH E. ABLON, Chairman and President, Ogden Corporation. (367)

COMPUTERS – Schools

Soon every respectable institution of higher education will have a computer center as naturally as it has a library. – LAUNOR CARTER, Systems Development Corporation, *Phi Delta Kappan.*
(368)

CONFORMITY

A degree of conformity in manners and little things is sometimes essential to the free and effective exercise of originality of thinking. – HAROLD BRAYMAN, Director of Public Relations, Du Pont Company, *Quote.* (369)

CONGRESS – Actions

Take time to learn as much as you can about what Congress is doing, and thinking about. Make yourself an authority of what new laws and programs are being planned and promoted. Settle for nothing less. Ignorance is bondage. – ARCH N. BOOTH, Executive Vice President, Chamber of Commerce of the United States. (370)

CONGRESSMEN

Throughout our history, as a nation, generations of Americans have harbored and nurtured the attitude that, as someone once expressed it, "politics is the last refuge of the incompetent." Whether we are businessmen, professionals, farmers, workingmen, or whatever, we take satisfaction – a very perverse satisfaction – from believing that our own occupations are hard and demanding while the jobs of public servants are soft and easy. This is peculiarly and particularly true of our attitudes toward Congress. – BENJAMIN H. OEHLERT, Jr., Vice President, Coca-Cola Company. (371)

Members of Congress find themselves under almost intolerable pressure from their voters to get more and more federal handouts – apparently in the belief that somebody else is paying for them. Make no mistake these pressures impair the effectiveness of our Congressmen and Senators to the point where they have less and less time to give adequate attention to our real national interests and the national problems involved. – EDWIN P. NEILAN, President, Chamber of Commerce of the United States. (372)

The life of the Congressman or Congresswoman – the life of the Senator or the Representative – is the most demanding and least appreciated in our system and society. In fact, I know of only two callings, other than President of the United States – the medical and legal professions – in which the demands can even be compared to those placed on Senators and Congressmen – and upon analysis they, too, pale into significance. — BENJAMIN H. OEHLERT, Jr., Vice-President, Coca-Cola Company. (373)

CONGRESSMEN — Congress

The members of Congress, if not the institution of Congress itself, have been — and, all too many places, still are — looked upon as fair targets for our ridicule, disrespect, even sometimes contempt. — BENJAMIN H. OEHLERT, Jr., Vice-President, Coca-Cola Company. (374)

CONGRESSMEN — Education

The educational level of our representatives is rising, and younger people, despite the attitude of their parents, are going into politics. The educational level in Congress, especially in the Senate, is among the very highest in the country. A majority of Senators and around half the members of the House have been through post graduate work of considerable intensity, principally but by no means exclusively in the law. — JAMES P. MITCHELL, Vice President, Crown Zellerbach Corporation, San Francisco, California. (375)

CONSERVATION

Today, man and his environment, the condition of his environment and its effect on man, are not only of deep interest to all but of vital necessity to our well being. Our environment is a part of us. How we care for our environment and live with it, utilize and enjoy it, determines the kind of people we are and will be. So, we have joined together in this common cause. This common cause is not new, for in the past our separate organizations have been dealing with various phases of the overall concept of parks and recreation at the various levels of government. What we are now doing is unifying our efforts and helping each other. — LAURANCE S. ROCKE-FELLER, *Parks and Recreation Magazine.* (376)

We should all believe in conservation and we should all practice it. — OWEN R. CHEATHAM, Chairman, Georgia-Pacific Corporation, Portland, Oregon. (377)

No doubt we are making some progress in protecting or restoring the whole range of our resources — but not nearly enough. The problems are growing faster than our current efforts to meet them. — MILLARD E. STONE, Chairman, Committee on Public Affairs, American Petroleum Institute; Vice President and Director, Sinclair Oil Corporation. (378)

Sound conservation demands not only that we take care of

76

current needs, but also that we provide for the future. — MILLARD E. STONE, Chairman, Commitee on Public Affairs, American Petroleum Institute; Vice President and Director, Sinclair Oil Corporation. (379)

CONSERVATION — Air, Water
Society must come to grips with the problem of air and water conservation. We must not do this, however, in a mood of panic. We must develop a reasoned and effective response to the challenge. To be specific, industry must act responsibly — government must act fairly — the public must act with understanding. The time for decision is here. — M.A. WRIGHT, President, Chamber of Commerce of the United States. (380)

CONSERVATION — Research
Research is the lubricant of dynamic conservation. It results in more and more profitable use of each harvest, integrates production facilities with the forests, and accelerates the growing of new trees. — OWEN R. CHEATHAM, Chairman, Georgia-Pacific Corporation, Portland, Oregon. (381)

CONSTITUTION
A good constitution . . . is no small accomplishment, but let me point out that it is no more than the best thoughts of good men committed to writing, a mere document unless it is generally subscribed to by people with the intellectual and moral qualities necessary to make it operative. — LEONARD E. READ, President, The Foundation for Economic Education, Inc., Irvington, New York. (382)

CONSTRUCTIVE ACTION
Public relations, no matter how skilled, can never be a substitute for integrity; pretty words, no matter how smoothly fashioned, can never be a substitute for constructive action. Images, no matter how carefully molded, will always yield to reality. — HARVEY C. JACOBS, Under Secretary, Rotary International, Evanston, Illinois. (383)

CONSUMER SPENDING
For the first time in history, the American consumer is spending more to satisfy desires than needs. — HERBERT D. SMITH, Vice President of Sales, US Carbonated Operations, Canada Dry Corporation. (384)

CONVENTIONS

The reason most (people attending) business conventions are bored to death is because they're hearing a recital of what they already know — without a single opinion expressed. — GEORGE C. WHIPPLE, Vice President and Director of Public Relations, Benton & Bowles, New York, *Public Relations Journal.* (385)

COOPERATIVES

Freedom is most secure in those countries which use cooperatives as a basic part of their capitalistic economy. Communism, on the other hand, finds a toehold and grows among the population in those areas where cooperatives are either non-existent or very weak. — RAYMOND W. MILLER, President, Public Relations Research Associates, Inc., Washington, D.C. (386)

CORPORATE CITIZENSHIP

Corporate citizenship, like individual citizenship, carries certain clear responsibilities. I think you will agree that, in the long run, the interests of our government and of American business abroad must be mutually responsive, although they may be by no means identical. — CHRISTIAN A. HERTER, Jr., General Manager, Government Relations Department, Socony Mobil Oil Company, Inc. (387)

CORPORATIONS

Almost imperceptibly over the past several years, the modern corporation has evolved into a social as well as an economic institution. Without losing sight of the need to make a profit, it has developed ideals and responsibilities going far beyond the profit motive. It has become, in effect, a full-fledged citizen, not only of the community in which it is headquartered but of the country and indeed the world. — DAVID ROCKEFELLER, President, Chase Manhattan Bank. (388)

Like all living things, a corporation must adapt itself to changing environment. Its survival depends upon its fitness to survive, and fitness for a corporation means growth ability. — RALPH E. ABLON, Chairman and President, Ogden Corporation. (389)

CORPORATIONS — Profit

The real objective of corporate management should . . . be to become not necessarily the largest company but certainly the most profitable. — A.C. DAUGHERTY, President, Rockwell Manufacturing Company. (390)

CORPORATIONS – Youth

For those of our young people who have the necessary intellectual capacity, the determination – and the vision that is called for – there are very few careers in life which can match the opportunity and the challenges to be found within today's corporation, nor are there many which involve as great a contribution to society, both directly and indirectly. – LAWRENCE A. KIMPTON, Vice President, Standard Oil Company (Indiana).   (391)

COURAGE

Without courage, whether it is an individual's or a nation's, there can be no success, whatever the other virtues one possesses. – RICHARD H. AMBERG, Publisher, *The St. Louis Globe-Democrat.*   (392)

Any other virtue is unavailing without courage for it is the implementation of every good deed and every good desire. Courage, in part, is a knowledge of virtue and a willingness to implement it. Courage is knowing right from wrong and following the course of right. Courage is taking the part of the underdog when the underdog is right. Courage is also not being deterred from speaking for the majority when the minority wrongly assails it – a virtue too frequently forgotten in these days. – RICHARD H. AMBERG, Publisher, *The St. Louis Globe-Democrat.*   (393)

CRAFTSMEN

The craftsman is a worker of a special kind; he is skilled in the mechanics of his craft. He has taken the time to familiarize himself with what is required. He has almost certainly spent a painstaking apprenticeship, and what he does in so easy and apparently casual a manner now is the result of long practice. The craftsman, then, brings to bear on a job talent, knowledge and practice, these three – and I guess if you had to choose, you would say that the greatest of these is practice. This is not to say that knowledge and talent are not important. They are essential; in fact, all three are closely interrelated. – CHARLES F. MOORE, Jr., Vice President, Public Relations, Ford Motor Company, Dearborn, Michigan.   (394)

CREATIVITY

The ability to see or discover the positive side of any situation is the hallmark of true creativity. – GORDON SMITH, Vice President, Remington Rand Division, Sperry Rand Corporation.   (395)

Usually it is assumed that a creative person must be an artist of

79

some sort — a painter, sculptor, writer or, perhaps, an architect. . . . Not necessarily so. . . . In essence, creativeness is nothing more or less than applied imagination; not to be confused with intelligence, expertise or skill. There are able men, learned even, who have not been blessed with a creative faculty. Fortunately, in the sense that would be unfair if all the talents would be vested in the same people, there are men, women and children not much above average in their intellectual accomplishments, who possess a strong creative faculty. — Commander EDWARD WHITEHEAD, OBE., President, Schweppes (USA) Ltd., *Salesman's Opportunity.* (396)

Unlike talent, birth does not insulate you irrevocably from becoming creative. Creativity is yours for the effort. — GORDON SMITH, Vice President, Remington Rand Division, Sperry Rand Corporation. (397)

We think of creativity, and we think of bearded artists, struggling authors, and far-out scientists who can't find their way home from the laboratory. It's an image we'll have to shake. — A.C. DAUGHERTY, President, Rockwell Manufacturing Company. (398)

Creativity is not a matter of birth, but a matter of worth — what you make of yourself. — GORDON SMITH, Vice President, Remington Rand Division, Sperry Rand Corporation. (399)

The common tendency is to think of creative people as somewhat dreamy, and not concerned about details. It may or may not be true that they lose their wallets or lock themselves out of their houses more than other people. Some of them may not be too prompt for appointments. But if they're good, if they're real professionals, the details they overlook are never those of their craft. — CHARLES F. MOORE, Jr., Vice President, Public Relations, Ford Motor Company, Dearborn, Michigan. (400)

The creative person is someone who sees more clearly than others. His product, whether concept, aria, building, book or painting, is merely evidence of the clarity of his vision and the quality of his credentials. — RALPH E. ABLON, Chairman and President, Ogden Corporation. (401)

CREATIVITY — Sewing

Women don't sew because they have to — that era died in the thirties. There's a culture boom of monumental proportions in America, and home sewing is part of it. It's the in thing to do, like taking French lessons, or studying Etruscan pottery. Everyone wants to *do* something, be creative . — JAMES J. SHAPIRO, President, New York's Simplicity Pattern Company, *Forbes.* (402)

CREDIT

The use of credit is now regarded as a birthright — as a fundamental freedom — even as a way of life by the average American citizen. — SHEFFIELD BOARDMAN, Cincinnati Zone Manager for B.F. Goodrich Tire Company. (403)

There can be no doubt that the increased use of consumer credit through the years has been a very big factor in developing our high American standard of living. It was credit that created the vast markets that put science and mass production to work. And today, more than ever before, credit is enabling the vast majority of Americans to enjoy the products of our technical skills. — SHEFFIELD BOARDMAN, Cincinnati Zone Manager for B.F. Goodrich Tire Company. (404)

CRIME — Cities

Crime in our big cities has become so serious that we may soon be forced to take the extremely radical step of beginning to deal with its causes, instead of just dabbling helplessly at its consequences. — ALAN BARTH, Editorial Board, *Washington Post*. (405)

CUBA

Today Cuba is a well-developed Communist state and a glaring worldwide symbol of United States' indecision, weakness, unpreparedness, and lack of purpose; it is the result of a series of ghastly American diplomatic, political, and journalistic mistakes. — CHARLES NUTTER, Managing Director, International House, New Orleans, Louisiana. (406)

CULTURE

The power of the word is at the very core of human culture. When that word is a smutty word, that culture becomes a smutty culture. — JAMES J. CLANCY, Lawyer of Burbank, California. (407)

While massive force-feeding has been used successfully in promoting pate de foie gras, it is a useless technique for raising the taste and cultural or educational sights of a society. — ROBERT W. SARNOFF, Chairman of the Board, National Broadcasting Corporation. *Quote.* (408)

CURRENCY

Debasement of currencies has contributed to the fall of empires. — JOHN EXTER, Senior Vice President, First National City Bank, New York. (409)

81

CURRENCY – Dollar

The dollar is far and away the world's strongest currency – strong enough to withstand even the great financial strain imposed by our commitments in Vietnam. But we must work constantly at keeping it strong through sound fiscal and monetary policies. – GEORGE CHAMPION, Chairman of the Board, The Chase Manhattan Bank. (410)

CURRENCY – Gold

I am confident gold will prevail and will continue to command respect far beyond any other commodity or device that might conceivably serve as the basic monetary unit of the world. It alone provides the world with a common money, indestructible and accepted everywhere – a function of inestimable value in the turmoil of depreciating currencies competing for nationalistic ends. – DONALD H. McLAUGHLIN, Chairman, Homestake Mining Inc. (411)

CYNICISM

I am alarmed at the extent to which cynicism has wormed its way into our national attitude. Tearing down has always been easier than building up. – CHARLES G. MORTIMER, Chairman, General Foods Corporation, White Plains, New York. (412)

D

DEBT
Debt is an essential element of the modern world. True, it can grow too fast or too slowly. Its uses can be badly distributed, or its quality impaired, with sad consequences for the Nation. Basically, however, under the conditions which prevail today, debt must grow in order for the economy to prosper. — RUDOLPH A. PETERSON, President, Bank of American N.T. & S.A. (413)

DECISIONS
To my mind, decision-making is an art — not a science. It is a serious error even to think of decision-making as a science. Such thinking envisions a fool-proof formula of some kind that will guarantee a high batting average of right decisions. There is no way to insure a good decision. We can do no better than to know and understand all the various alternatives, assess the advantages and disadvantages of each and decide on the one we think will work best. — CHARLES G. MORTIMER, Chairman, General Foods Corporation. (414)

Indecision is one of the greatest occupational hazards of the executive function. But if you can't make a decision, then you will never be able to fulfill the primary role of the manager in industry. — WILLIAM T. INGRAM, Vice President, Executive Sales, Reynolds Metals Company. (415)

It is my . . . opinion that decision making will continue to be one of the most important, demanding, exciting, and rewarding activities to be found in the changing world ahead. — JOHN E. SWEARINGEN, President, Standard Oil Company (Indiana). (416)

DECISION — Indecision
Decision making is the executive characteristic that separates the men from the boys. Indecision is one of the greatest occupational hazards of the executive function. — WILLIAM T. INGRAM, Vice President, Executive Sales, Reynolds Metals Company. (417)

DEMOCRACY
When we help eliminate poverty, unfair employment practices,

deceptive marketing practices and labor management strife we are not only *telling* the world that American capitalism and American democracy work; but we are *showing* them that they work. — JOHN I. SNYDER, Jr., Chairman of the Board and President U.S. Industries, Inc. (418)

A little noted feature of democracy is that it is the only form of government that permits inactivity. Fortunately, not many people want to be parasites. And not many who fail remain failures. To fail, you must be trying to do something. If you try once, ordinarily you will try again. — EDWIN M. CLARK, President, Southwestern Bell Telephone Company, St. Louis, Missouri. (419)

Only an educated, enlightened, self-disciplined citizenry is capable of exercising the judgments and making the decisions necessary in a lasting democracy. — CHARLES G. MORTIMER, Chairman, General Foods Corporation, White Plains, New York. (420)

DEMOCRACY — Education

Just as education has made it possible for democracy to flourish in this country, so has our democracy made it possible for education to flourish. In no other country are there so many colleges and universities or so high a proportion of young people in attendance. — CHARLES G. MORTIMER, Chairman, General Foods Corporation, White Plains, New York. (421)

DEMOCRACY — Equality

No political thinker of any stature in all history has ever interpreted democracy as necessarily meaning equality in all things. When the founding fathers incorporated into the Declaration of Independence the phrase, "All men are created equal," they referred only to equality before the law and equality of opportunity to each individual to fulfill his highest potential. This is the American ideal. — E.F. SCOUTTEN, Vice President, The Maytag Company. (422)

DEMOCRACY — Political

We are so busy with our own personal and business affairs we fail to realize that our national problem could be solved better — and the world would be more stable — if we took time out to strengthen and advance economic democracy, educational democracy, and judicial democracy, so that political democracy could survive. — RAYMOND W. MILLER, President, Public Relations Research Associates, Inc. (423)

DEMONSTRATIONS
It seems to me that the demonstration has become a part of the American scene. – ELMER W. LOWER, President, A B C News.

(424)

DEPRESSIONS – Recessions
It is my opinion that depressions or recessions are brought about by underconsumption rather than overproduction. Underconsumption creates inventory recessions which result when stocks are not moved and production cannot be curtailed quickly enough to avoid accumulation. – JACK I. STRAUS, Chairman, R.H. Macy & Co. Inc. (425)

DESTINY
Your personal destiny is not a matter of chance, but a matter of choice. Fate is not the hunter in our lives. We fashion our own destiny by what we do! – T.F. PATTON, President, Republic Steel Corporation, Cleveland, Ohio. (426)

DEVELOPMENT – Human, Economic
We need to equate human development with economic development. We need to understand that these broad, social, economic and political issues of today and tomorrow are inter-related, interdependent, inter-reacting. None of the major issues today with which we must concern ourselves exist in isolation. They are inextricably interwoven. Each is intractibly a part of the other. As knowledge becomes more specialized, as society becomes more complex, problems become more interdependent. They require a more studied sense of general direction in the larger framework of total effect on the total community – the total society. – HARRY R. HALL, President, Michigan State Chamber of Commerce. (427)

DICTATORSHIPS
In a modern communist state, a minority obtains control of the army, the courts, the means of communication and the means of production. With ruthless discipline, secret police, various types of incentives and strict controls, the minority group regiments the nation to compel the people to attain certain economic goals. This type of centralized dictatorship which subordinates man to the state and compels him to seek the one objective of economic growth may

for a time go far in achieving this goal. However, it will finally fail if it does not assure the greater goal of human freedom and the dignity of man. — HERBERT V. PROCHNOW, President, First National Bank of Chicago, Illinois. (428)

DISARMAMENT

Up to now we have been looking on disarmament with much the same mixture of feelings with which we have viewed automation. Instead of seeing in it an avenue of enrichment and ennoblement, we have worried about whether our economy could withstand the impact of cancelled defense employment along with the technological displacement that already is causing us such anxiety. — A.H. RASKIN, Assistant Editor, *New York Times* Editorial Page. (429)

DISCIPLINE

Discipline is most often lacking when the person considers the group as a "they" group; a situation in which a person is being moved without knowing where he is going, why he should go, or the goal he is being headed toward. When a person refers to the group as "we," this choice of words is often evidence of a genuine discipline over himself in the group situation. He sees purpose in his efforts. When we have a driving purpose and desire to help, we have achieved "discipline." — WALTER MACPEEK, Consultant, American Humanics Foundation. *Quote*. (430)

Discipline is too often tagged as conformity. Webster defines it as teaching and instruction, but it is far more than this. Discipline, in the broadest sense, is the training of the mind, the willingness to take the hard right instead of the easy wrong — to resist the blandishments of cheapness in favor of goodness for the sake of goodness. — RICHARD H. AMBERG, Publisher, *The St. Louis Globe-Democrat*. (431)

DISCOUNT STORES

I do not believe . . . that the discount store in any sense replaces the full-line department store with its breadth of assortments and services. — JACK I. STRAUS, Chairman, R.H. Macy & Co. Inc. (432)

DISSENSION — Riots

No fair-minded citizen minimizes the significance of the right to dissent and to petition for the redress of grievances. These are essential elements of a free people. But rioting, looting, burning and killing — deliberate crimes — are outrages spawned under the banner

86

of civil disobedience, a dangerous philosophy based on shallow reasoning. – FELIX R. McKNIGHT, Executive Vice President and Editor, *The Dallas Times Herald*. (433)

DISTRESS– Relieving

Spending money to help people to help themselves is a far better investment than spending money to relieve the distress of those who are unable to help themselves. – HENRY FORD II, Chairman of the Board, Ford Motor Company. (434)

DISTRIBUTION

We owe a great deal in this country to the fact that the distribution system of the United States is an immensely skillful consumer service. It does a complex job in a vigorous dynamic society like ours. What the American consumer wants the consumer gets. – JACK I. STRAUS, Chairman, R.H. Macy & Co. Inc. (435)

DRINK – Drinking

Booze is beautiful. Through booze I met two Chief Justices, fifty world champs, six Presidents and DiMaggio and Babe Ruth. – TOOTS SHOR, Restauranteur, (436)

E

ECONOMIC EDUCATION

Economic education should be made a required course in high school and in college. . . . There can be nothing voluntary about it from the point of view of citizenship. Science, mathematics, and other subjects to the contrary notwithstanding, we've got to make sure that our students — all of them — understand the economics of a free society. This is a minimum requirement for citizenship in a rapidly changing world. — L.C. MICHELON, Director of Public Affairs, Republic Steel Corporation. (437)

ECONOMIC FREEDOM

Our history proves that our greatest advances have always been made under the banner of economic freedom. That is still the banner of hope for this country, and so long as we carry it forward, we cannot fail. — EDWIN A. LOCKE, Jr., President, American Paper Institute. (438)

Years of human experience tell us that the greatest good for the greatest number is achieved with economic freedom. — LELAND I. DOAN, Chairman, Executive Committee, The Dow Chemical Company, Midland, Michigan. (439)

A free market society and not government is the most fair and impartial arbiter of economic freedom. Under this system every purchase is a vote. No one is disenfranchised for any reason. Every day is election day. Moreover, minorities count. I know of no example of any society which has maintained great political freedom that has not also had great economic freedom evidenced by a free market or its reasonable substitute. — LELAND I. DOAN, Chairman, Executive Committee, The Dow Chemical Company, Midland, Michigan. (440)

ECONOMIC INTERNATIONALISM

From the time of Alexander the Great to the time of Napoleon and right down to our own century, men have tried to force countries into lasting and prosperous federations by military conquest. They failed. I believe we are now entering a period when the sliderule may help the human race to realize the benefits of economic internationalism in a way that could never be accomplished by the sword. — LYNN A. TOWNSEND, President, Chrysler Corporation. (441)

ECONOMIC PROGRESS — Education
The economic progress that has been made in this country would not have been possible without the general rise in the educational level of its people. Education does influence the values, the judgment and the behavior of our people, and is a most essential factor in making our free-choice system work. — CHARLES G. MORTIMER, Chairman, General Foods Corporation, White Plains, New York.
(442)

ECONOMIC STRENGTH
For America, the challenge in the next 10-15 years will be to remain a strong and vigorous contender in the world economic race. Only by succeeding, can we in the long term contribute to real progress in the standard of living of all our friends in the world. For successful trade rests on the much more solid foundation of mutuality, than does aid alone. — FRED J. BORCH, President and Chief Executive Officer, General Electric Company. (443)

ECONOMICS
Clemenceau once said that war was too important a matter to be entrusted to the generals. In like vein I would submit that economics today has become too important a matter to be left to the economists. It has become a personal, over-riding concern for everyone. — G. KEITH FUNSTON, President, New York Stock Exchange. (444)

The economic face of America is changing, but its principles will remain the same. Broadly based private ownership of the means of production is the basis for initiative and growth. The profit system is the incentive for progress. And individual freedom is the life blood of the system. A violation of any one of these principles weakens the other. — CHARLES H. PERCY, President, Bell & Howell Company, Chicago, Illinois. (445)

In our own country we speak of "the economy" as if it were a machine and we chart its "growth" in dollars of "gross national product," which are as fictional in meaning as they are diluted in real value by inflation. We ignore the reality that the economy is not only products — even more it is people — and economics is not statistics but rather the material manifestation of human action and the

89

satisfactions underlying freedom of choice. — BAY E. ESTES, Jr., Vice President, Marketing, United States Steel Corporation.   (446)

Our economic system rests on six fundamental concepts: dignity of man; private property; free market; profit motive; competition, and limited government regulation. — NICHOLAS A. GEORGE, Vice President of Brunswick Corporation, Chicago, Illinois.   (447)

The silliest myth in the folklore about our economic system is the all-too-prevalent contention that our powerful and creative economy needs massive transfusions of defense money to stay healthy and grow. — LYNN A. TOWNSEND, President, Chrysler Corporation,   (448)

In the field of economics the individual reigns supreme with us. In all history no other form of organization for production has ever been conceived which gives greater significance to personal decisions than ours. — CLARENCE B. RANDALL, Retired Chairman, Inland Steel Company.   (449)

We need not so much to be "educated" in economics as to be "reminded." We need to be reminded that every single one of us has a role to play in making the economic process work for our best national interests as well as our individual interests. Above all, we need to be reminded that the economic process is inexorable — that it goes on whether we are aware of it or not. — CHARLES G. MORTIMER, Chairman of General Foods Corporation.   (450)

Ours is an economy of diverse and seemingly separate and independent elements. But they are bound together with emotional mortar of consumer faith. — CHARLES L. GOULD, Publisher of *San Francisco Examiner*.   (451)

By combining the technical and managerial skills of the more advanced countries with the human energies and aspirations of the developing nations, it would be possible to create an entirely new economic way of life. — GEORGE CHAMPION, Chairman of the Board, The Chase Manhattan Bank.   (452)

ECONOMICS — Politics

Our economic system is the design for efficiency and economic equity; our political system is the engine of equality. How we utilize each to complement and not obstruct the other will critically influence our strength at home and our posture in the world. — GABRIEL HAUGE, Vice Chairman of the Board, Manufacturers Hanover Trust Company, New York.   (453)

ECONOMISTS – Politicians

Economists should make recommendations, politicians should carry them out. That's the way it should be. But the way things are going now, the politicians make the recommendations and the economists are merely called in to justify them. – PIERRE RINFRET, Chairman, Lionel D. Edie & Company, *Forbes*.   (454)

ECONOMY

I am a great believer in the fundamental strength of the American economy. – ROSS D. SIRAGUSA, Chairman of the Board and President, Admiral Corporation.   (455)

Ours is a system which rests on consumption. If we are to keep our heads above water, we must continue not only to provide work for the millions engaged in our industries, but we must also continue to pioneer industriously, with new inventions, new services, new opportunities. We cannot afford to tell our research scientists to slow down their researches, our inventors to stop inventing, our investment agencies to curtail their efforts to keep our money-wealth and our credit working for us. Nor can we afford to deter our persuaders from trying so hard to persuade us. This would bring on stagnation – and mighty fast, too. – CHARLES G. MORTIMER, Chairman, General Foods Corporation, White Plains, New York.   (456)

Our government must come to the realization that, strong and powerful as we are, we cannot do everything at once without courting disaster. Specifically, we cannot fight what has become a major war, serve as the world's banker, rebuild our cities, cure environmental problems, render massive aid to foreign nations, dramatically upgrade the quality of our education, increase welfare programs, and solve the racial problems all at once. Strong as our economy is, it simply is not that strong. – RUDOLPH A. PETERSON, President, Bank of America.   (457)

The health of the U.S. economy is essential to the security of the entire Free World. – E. SHERMAN ADAMS, Vice President, First National City Bank, New York.   (458)

ECONOMY – Federal Government

Every day the Federal Government is a more important factor in our daily lives and because of the fact that from a dollar standpoint it gets bigger and bigger and because we are able to see every day of the week that what it does has meaning to us not only as a nation but as individuals, there has been a natural turning toward Washington for economic forecasts. And more and more people look to the Federal Government to say what they think is going to happen

91

in the American economy. — PIERRE A. RINFRET, Chairman of the Board of Directors and Head of the Economics Division, Lionel D. Edie & Co. Inc.   (459)

ECONOMY — Free, Controlled
No economy can remain half controlled and half free for long. If wages and working conditions are to be determined by politicians, in some bargaining disputes, they will soon be determined in all bargaining disputes. If wages and working conditions are to be dictated, then prices and, hence, profits must be dictated. If freedoms in respect to labor contracts are removed, then so will be freedoms in respect to commercial contracts. The corporate state will have arrived in short order. — R. HEATH LARRY, Administrative Vice President, Labor Relations, United States Steel Corporation.
(460)

ECONOMY — Profits
We all know that the food the human body requires must contain a balance of certain basic nutrients if good health is to be maintained. When we fail to get enough of any important one, the result is ill health. The economic body cannot survive without a balance of nutrients any more than the human body can. Profits are the protein of our national economy. Profits revitalize our economic body and insure its future growth. We must bring about public understanding that a healthy growing economy requires a balanced diet of competitive prices, good wages, fair profits and sound investment. — CHARLES G. MORTIMER, Chairman, General Foods Corporation.   (461)

ECONOMY — Small Business
When the economy trembles, the first boat rocked is the one containing small business. — CHAYLIE L. SAXE, President, Saxe Bros. Inc.   (462)

EDITORS
All editors have insomnia. They read late, and they know that the factory of the mind never stops working. — EDWARD WEEKS, Editor, *Atlantic Magazine*.   (463)

EDUCATION
Education is not a cultural nicety; it is the cutting edge of civilization. We must have it for survival. — CHARLES H. PERCY,

President, Bell & Howell Company, Chicago, Illinois.   (464)

These four qualities — the ability to decide, the ability to relate, an abiding faith and an unquenchable curiosity — are the products not of training alone, but of education in its truest, broadest, and most important sense. — CHARLES G. MORTIMER, Chairman, General Foods Corporation, *Quote*.   (465)

Education gives a man a great opening wedge; there is no question about that. But there is always the fellow who had to go to work, who never had the college education, who seems to shinny up between these fellows just the same. Good basic education is a very important thing. If I had had it, I might not be where I am. I might be twice as far ahead. — HOWARD JOHNSON, *Nation's Business*.
(466)

Education about our way of life is needed . . . not education that is aimed at making happy citizens in a comfortable country — but education whose purpose is the development of an active, responsible, participating member of a free society. — L.C. MICHELON, Director of Public Affairs, Republic Steel Corporation.   (467)

The main object of education is to tap human potential. Whether education is for specific jobs or for broad tasks, it should be geared so that the individual has a wide-open future. — BYRON J. NICHOLS, Dodge General Manager and Vice President, Chrysler Corporation, Detroit, Michigan.   (468)

Too often in the past, education has been designed to prepare young people for college. We are beginning to learn that education of this kind fails to meet the needs of great masses of our people. As a result, it leaves many of them outside our society, unemployed and discouraged. We are only beginning to understand how to cultivate all our human resources through education. — LYNN TOWNSEND, Chairman and Chief Executive Officer, Chrysler Corporation.   (469)

We must take an even greater interest in education. We must help make education more universal and see that it is closely geared to the needs of our times. — L.C. MICHELON, Director of Public Affairs, Republic Steel Corporation.   (470)

Education is the most important source of human enrichment in both an economic and a broader sense. Education increases our ability to enjoy more things more, to live more richly, more creatively, and in greater harmony with ourselves, our environment, and our fellow man. — ROBERT E. WILLIAMS, President, The Youngstown Sheet and Tube Company.   (471)

Without more and better schools, more an; better colleges, more and better paid teachers, we will never achieve the greatness that is so clearly within our power — nor will we do much that is meaningful about wiping out the blots of racial discrimination and large-scale joblessness. — A.H. RASKIN, Assistant Editor, *New York Times* Editorial Page. (472)

Education cannot stop with the diploma. Each man must seek to grow in knowledge, in intellect, and in wisdom from this day forward. — ROBERT ALAN CHARPIE, BS., MS., D.Sc., Director of Technology, Union Carbide Corporation, New York. (473)

We have learned through the years that economic growth and social progress are both inseparable and interrelated, that such things as hope and enthusiasm, skill and knowledge, curiosity, vision, and wisdom are no less important than steel, cement, sand and machinery.... Economic growth must be rooted in educational development. — GEOFFREY M. WILSON, Vice President, World Bank and International Development Association, *Quote*. (474)

Education is no longer the province of the rich and wise. In the industrialized society, wherever it may be, education is the touchstone to survival. — ROBERT ALAN CHARPIE, BS., MS., D.Sc., Director of Technology, Union Carbide Corporation, New York. (475)

Today our educational system is confronted by two major crises. One is the expanding hard core of young people in urban ghettos who have dropped out and passed beyond the years of formal schooling. The other is the expanding student population, and the continuing growth of knowledge to be communicated to them. — ROBERT W. SARNOFF, President, Radio Corporation of America. (476)

While the quality of American education as superior to that of other societies may be argued, there is a clear superiority for American education as to quantity. — RALPH E. ABLON, Chairman and President, Ogden Corporation. (477)

In a generation, this country has changed from a nation whose preponderate number of citizens worked at dull, repetitive, unskilled jobs in factories to one of automated manufacture. Each year a greater proportion of our people sit at desks manipulating pencils, around conference tables figuring out questions for electronic brains to solve. Modern, prosperous America is the product of our parents' unquenchable worship of education. Every educated man makes his country richer and, if you please, makes the institution with which he works more prosperous. — LYLE M. SPENCER, President, Science Research Associates, Inc. (478)

94

EDUCATION — College   (483)
Every ten years we are failing to provide a college education for well over a million of our best prospects for the critically important professions. This is a waste of human resources that our country simply cannot afford. — LYNN TOWNSEND, Chairman and Chief Executive Officer, Chrysler Corporation.   (479)

EDUCATION — Continuing
Your education is not ending today any more than it did when you were graduated from college or high school. It cannot — because 10 years from today the total amount of scientific and technological knowledge will have doubled. And that knowledge will affect the way you live and work. Continuing education has become a competitive necessity. — HOWARD A. MOREEN, Senior Vice President and Secretary, Aetna Life & Casualty.   (480)

EDUCATION — Curiosity
Education can encourage in a man an unquenchable curiosity that will stay with him throughout his life and assure that he will continue his education far beyond the day of his graduation. — CHARLES G. MORTIMER, Chairman, General Foods Corporation, White Plains, New York.   (481)

EDUCATION — Europe
I believe that educators and men of business and men of government and the professions in a great arc of the western world from Alaska to Athens must begin to think and talk and act together in new ways to bring the advances of education within reach of young people throughout that community of countries. We must speed the oncoming of the day when the educational differences that divide us are no more. — THOMAS J. WATSON, Jr., Chairman of the Board, International Business Machines Corporation.   (482)

EDUCATION — Gifted Children
We must educate all of our children to the maximum limitation of their individual capacities. But as we provide for the handicapped, physically, mentally and emotionally, as we provide for the multitudes of our so-called average people, we must *now* also give attention to the education of our intellectually talented. From their ranks will come the leaders, in the professions and in the art and science of politics which is so essential to the preservation of freedom. — JOHN ALSOP, President, The Mutual Insurance Company, Hartford, Connecticut.

EDUCATION – Liberal

The man who can establish and guide the corporate vision of the future will need breadth and a world view far more expansive than has ever been required in the past. Toward this end, I believe that American industry will have to give a new emphasis to the importance of a liberal education in the preparation of its business and industrial leaders. – SOL M. LINOWITZ, Chairman of the Board, Xerox Corporation. (484)

EDUCATION – Life-long

In our age of rapid change and innovation, the life-long view of education is a necessity rather than a luxury. We must retain an up-to-date fund of knowledge and maximum adaptability if we're going to be successful and take our rightful place in society. – T.F. PATTON, President, Republic Steel Corporation, Cleveland, Ohio. (485)

EDUCATION – Radio, Television

It is axiomatic that television and radio can inform. To my mind they are the universal teaching machines, available in every home. It is incomprehensible that they have not been better used as teaching machines to create the "educated society" – a society which has the capability of rising to undreamed heights of literacy, unattained levels of income, where each member of that society has available to him complete equality of opportunity of education. – RALF BRENT, President, Radio New York Worldwide (WRUL). (486)

EDUCATION – Religion

The basis of any education, transcending knowledge and learning, is the Christian religion. This is our great Judeo-Christian heritage, based on the Ten Commandments, the Sermon on the Mount, and the Golden Rule. – RICHARD H. AMBERG, Publisher, *The St. Louis Globe-Democrat*. (487)

EDUCATION – States Responsibility

I am among those who believe that our states have the responsibility of providing an education for every boy and girl to the full extent that he or she is capable of benefiting from it. But the fact is that our states have demonstrated a persistent inability or unwillingness to meet the whole of their responsibility for public education, and the nation unquestionably is seriously weakened thereby. — LEROY COLLINS, President, National Association of Broadcasters. (488)

EFFORT — Reward
Today's employer is yesterday's employee who found opportunity waiting for him at the end of the second mile. — Dr NAPOLEON HILL, *American Salesman.* (489)

ELECTED REPRESENTATIVES
When we have a good man in office, let's give him warm moral support, and fight to keep him there. It's easier to keep a good man in than to get a bad man out. Let's not be too critical of an official because he does something we don't agree with, as long as he is conscientious. The American people are sometimes too impatient with their elected representatives, fail to see that it is more important to be for someone or something than to be against someone or something. — EDWARD J. MEEMAN, Editor Emeritus *The Memphis Press-Scimitar* and Conservation Editor of the Scripps-Howard Newspapers. (490)

ELECTION DAY
The responsibility of voting ought to be associated not with a crushing inconvenience, but with a special day dedicated nationally to the most fundamental act of democratic life. — FRANK STANTON, President, Columbia Broadcasting System, Inc., *Quote.* (491)

ELECTION DAY — Legal Holiday
The national uniform voting day should also be a national legal holiday. This would free thousands to vote at their convenience, rather than attempting to squeeze it in before work or at lunch time or on the way home. Absentee balloting could be standardized and made easy for those who cannot be at home on election day. — FRANK STANTON, President, Columbia Broadcasting System, Inc. (492)

ELECTIONS
Elections are not just simple matters of victory or defeat. They are, essentially, times of stocktaking, of review and of reappraisal. They are times when — despite all the extravagant talk — we *think.* — G. KEITH FUNSTON, President, New York Stock Exchange. (493)

ELECTIONS — National

For national elections, we need and ought to have an interstate, permanent registration, making full use of modern electronic equipment. Moreover, we need to make voter registration easier, more automatic and more systematically inclusive. — FRANK STANTON, President, Columbia Broadcasting System, Inc.　　　(494)

ELECTIONS — Time Zones

The differences in time zones add to the chaos that has become a characteristic of our election day. If we had a common opening time everywhere, regardless of the clock hour in any one place, and a common closing time everywhere twenty-four hours later we could have the real advantages both of nationwide, simultaneous balloting and of results becoming available on a nationwide rather than a regional or local basis. — FRANK STANTON, President, Columbia Broadcasting System, Inc.　　　(495)

ELECTRIC POWER — Federal Encroachment

There is no field, I think, in which federal encroachment and federal domination are being achieved, quite so studiously and callously, through secrecy, subterfuge and indirection, as in my own field of electric power. — HARLLEE BRANCH, Jr., President, The Southern Company, Atlanta, Georgia.　　　(496)

ELECTRONIC DATA PROCESSING

Today, the management man who lays claim to well-rounded understanding of business practice must have a basic working knowledge of electronic data processing in all its myriad commercial and industrial applications. — GORDON SMITH, Director of Marketing, Univac, Remington Rand Corporation, New York City. (497)

EMPLOYEE PUBLICATIONS

Employee communication through employee publications has become big business in this nation. . . . Billions of words are directed to employees. A vast array of communications channels and revolutionary techniques have been developed with the objective of influencing the thinking, the attitudes, and the actions of employees. — HARRY R. HALL, Executive Vice President, Michigan State Chamber of Commerce, Lansing, Michigan.　　　(498)

EMPLOYEES

The days are lost and gone forever when a manager, or just a few management personnel, will be the key to success for a firm. The utmost help from *all* employees must be obtained. And to obtain that help, they must be aware of the problems, they must know what is going on in their business. — MARTIN J. CASERIO, General Manager, Delco Radio Division, General Motors Corporation, Kokomo, Indiana.											(499)

EMPLOYEES — Leadership
The success of a business — yours or mine — depends on the actions of employees who accept leadership. Who adopt as their own policies and objectives of the firm. Who carry out the jobs to which they are assigned in the best way they know how. — E.M. CLARK, President, Southwestern Bell Telephone Company, St. Louis, Missouri.											(500)

EMPLOYMENT
The job of meeting the increasing demand for qualified people at every level of our society is in my opinion the most important single task facing the nation — and the success of all our other undertakings will depend on how well we do this job. — LYNN TOWNSEND, Chairman and Chief Executive Officer, Chrysler Corporation.	(501)

EMPLOYMENT — Displacements
We have exhibited enormous imagination in the design of space ships to go to the moon, and in the shape of next summer's peek-a-boo bathing suits. Yet, we have not learned to plan for, and cope systematically with, even the most easily anticipated employment displacements such as the miner, the foreman, the welder, and the small farmer. — ROBERT ALAN CHARPIE, BS., MS., D.Sc., Director of Technology, Union Carbide Corporation, New York.
											(502)

EMPLOYMENT — Future
The whole broad outline of employment is shifting. Tedious, unskilled labor is fading from the picture. The majority of workers in the next decade will hold white-collar jobs or highly-skilled blue-collar jobs that require solid training and the ability to make sound decisions. — BYRON J. NICHOLS, Dodge General Manager and Vice President, Chrysler Corporation, Detroit, Michigan.			(503)

It is said that today's skills will not hold tomorrow's jobs; and we must recognize that as true in a remarkably high percentage of cases. — ROGER M. BLOUGH, Chairman of the Board, United States Steel Corporation.									(504)

ENGINEERS

In a very literal sense, the engineer is going to be the architect of a new world. He is going to be privileged to be among the most important makers of history in our time. — LYNN A. TOWNSEND, President, Chrysler Corporation. (505)

ENTERPRISE — Thought, Creativity

As history has so often shown, enterprise, thought, and creative expression thrive in the same climate — one of freedom and openness. — ROBERT W. SARNOFF, Chairman of the Board, National Broadcasting Company, Inc. (506)

ENTHUSIASM

Enthusiasm is the greatest business asset in the world. It beats money and power and influence. Singlehanded the enthusiast convinces and dominates where a small army of workers would scarcely raise a tremor of interest. — ELMER G. LETERMAN, *Nylic Review,* New York Life Insurance Company. (507)

A writer once said "Nothing great has ever been done without enthusiasm." That can be changed to "Nothing worthwhile has ever been done without enthusiasm." The enthusiasms of an individual don't have to be directed only toward greatness. Every person can't hope to be great. But neither can they feel that life has cheated them by withholding greatness. Everyone needs something to be enthusiastic about, no matter how commonplace it might seem to another person. — EDWIN M. CLARK, President, Southwestern Bell Telephone Company, St. Louis, Missouri. (508)

ENVIRONMENT

Americans are becoming increasingly concerned about how we are treating the air and the water and the land about us. They are becoming convinced that the quality of the environment we are creating for our children and grandchildren may be just as important as the quantity of our gross national product. — LAURANCE S. ROCKEFELLER. (509)

Only man, of all the creatures on earth, was given the godlike power to change his surroundings to fit him. The man is not the reflection of his environment as are the creatures of the woods; the environment is the reflection of the man. Neighborhoods ... whether we like it or not ... are the reflections of the people who inhabit them. – EARL NIGHTINGALE, Chairman of the Board, Nightingale Conant Corporation. (510)

Movements of population to urban areas, combined with accelerated industrial activity, have intensified peoples' concern with their environment. Rising incomes and increased leisure time have stepped up demands for better recreation facilities. And with it all is a general upgrading of quality standards. Today's Americans find unacceptable any number of conditions our grandparents tolerated in the name of progress. – MILLARD E. STONE, Chairman, Committee on Public Affairs, American Petroleum Institute; Vice President and Director, Sinclair Oil Corporation. (511)

EQUALITY
The demand for equality cannot be converted into a fight for superiority. We must be for equality under the rule of law. – MORRIS I. LEIBMAN, Chairman, ABA Standing Committee on Education Against Communism. (512)

EQUAL OPPORTUNITY
We believe that all men are created equal and should have equal opportunity regardless of race, creed or color. But I also believe that this right of opportunity is not accomplished by the right to riot in the streets, destroy property and disrupt the life of the entire communities. – ROBERT G. WINGERTER, President, Rockwell-Standard Corporation Automotive Divisions. (513)

ERRORS – Mistakes
An error becomes a mistake only when you refuse to correct it. – ELMER G. LETERMAN, *Gold Book,* New York Life Insurance Company. (514)

ETHICS
I often wonder why business ethics are given so much attention when so little is devoted to exploring ethics in other aspects of our national life. – EDWARD MAHER, Vice President, National Association of Manufacturers. (515)

EUROPE – America
We must use every effort within our power to encourage the forging of new bonds – intellectual, educational and economic, of the heart and of the hand and of the mind – between ourselves and our friends across the Atlantic – ties, in the words of Edmund Burke

"which though light as air, are as strong as links of iron." — THOMAS J. WATSON, Jr., Chairman of the Board, International Business Machines Corporation.   (516)

EXCELLENCE

If adversity were all that were needed to produce excellence, the Eskimos and Africans would possess the most advanced civilizations. If change were the only requirement, the Chinese Communists would be marching vigorously forward. — ROBERT C. KIRKWOOD, President, F.W. Woolworth Company.   (517)

The pursuit of excellence is the cornerstone of our American heritage. Without excellence, we cannot fulfill the promise of this heritage. Without excellence, we cannot achieve our national purposes. Without excellence, we cannot fulfill the precious privileges, rights and responsibilities of American citizenship. What the Declaration of Independence calls the pursuit of happiness is really the pursuit of excellence. — BRENDAN BYRNE, Executive Director, The American Heritage Foundation, New York.   (518)

No longer is excellence of performance a sought-after goal. We seek to have a leveling type of society. In our schools the curriculum is neither demanding nor rewarding of excellence. It is designed so that the poorest student can fare as well as the best. Pride in one's accomplishments is no longer an admired characteristic. Let me assure you that when one loses the desire to perform in an outstanding fashion, he loses the spark of life which was so important a part of the make-up of our forefathers. — PRIME F. OSBORN, III, Vice President and General Counsel, Atlantic Coast Line Railroad Company.   (519)

EXECUTIVES

Executive: A man who can make a decision and stick to it — no matter how wrong he is. — ELMER G. LETERMAN.   (520)

If a man has an office with a desk on which there is a buzzer, and if he can press that buzzer and have somebody come dashing in response — then he's an executive. — ELMER FRANK ANDREWS, *Administrative Management.*   (521)

Developing an executive is like developing an athlete. It not only takes time and patience but requires the perfecting of a number of characteristics. — DON H. MILLER, President, Skelly Oil Company.   (522)

EXECUTIVES — Confidence

Every executive has to have confidence. You can almost feel it in the air around them. It spills over to those associated with them. I don't think anyone is born with it. It has to be developed — the hard way. — A. CLARK DAUGHERTY, President, Rockwell Manufacturing Company. (523)

EXECUTIVES — Junior

An executive doesn't need to know the ins and outs of a business. In many situations you have an advantage if you don't know how something is supposed to be done. That's why we put so much stress on hiring young people who are willing to make decisions and take risks. We don't want conformers. We'd rather have angry young nonconformers. Sure, they make a lot of noise, but they're also alive and vital. — MYRON M. CHRISTY, President, Western Pacific Railroad, *Forbes.* (524)

EXECUTIVES — Knowledge

There is no such thing as a completed education in this complex, changing world. We hear a great deal about high school and college dropouts, but not enough about executive dropouts. The manager who stops learning stifles his personal growth and the profit growth of his company. It is a prime responsibility of the president to act as a kind of academic pacesetter and to establish in the company an environment of healthy respect for the accumulation of knowledge. — W.F. ROCKWELL, Jr., *Dun's Review.* (525)

EXECUTIVES — Successful

The really successful executive, it seems to me, has above all the ability to imagine and do the unexpected. — PETER G. PETERSON, President, Bell & Howell Company. (526)

EXECUTIVES — Training

It seems to me that in order to develop the kind of business leaders we must have, promising young men should be rewarded with jobs in increasing responsibilities and different functions — a progression which would be neither lateral nor vertical but *diagonal.* This would give a man scope, sustain his interest and curiosity, challenge his ability and — most importantly — equip him far better with the diversified knowledge necessary for executive leadership in the company of tomorrow. — SOL M. LINOWITZ, Chairman of the Board, Xerox Corporation, *Quote.* (527)

EXPERIENCE

The great trouble with the school of experience is that the course is so long that the graduates are too old to go to work. — HENRY FORD, *Quote*. (528)

Experience, the right kind, is priceless. It gives you not only knowledge, but confidence. — DON H. MILLER, President, Skelly Oil Company. (529)

EXPORTS

We have moved a long way from the days when exports were only the drastic necessity forced upon us by our overproduction; or when our export managers had to beg, borrow, and steal from the domestic sales groups to get products to sell. Today the whole world is one market, inseparable from the purely domestic market, and exports are an important segment of a company's overall sales effort. — KENNETH RUSH, Executive Vice President, Union Carbide Corporation, New York. (530)

F

FAILURE

A man may fail many times ... but he isn't a failure until he begins to blame somebody else. – L.F. McCOLLUM, Chairman, Continental Oil Company. (531)

I can take any group of young people any place, and teach them to be inventors, if I can get them to throw off the hazard of being afraid to fail. You fail because your ideals aren't right. You shouldn't be afraid to fail, but you should learn to fail intelligently. By that I mean, when you fail, find out why you failed, and each time you fail it will bring you up nearer to the goal. – CHARLES F. KETTERING, *Quote*. (532)

FAITH – Fear

Never forget that faith, not fear, built this country. I never knew the hour in our history when fear should have replaced reason and courage as the helmsman of our ship of state. – ROBERT H. HINCKLEY, Former President of the American Broadcasting Company. (533)

FAMILIES

In the feverish pace of personal life – in the intense desire to get ahead – we sometimes forget the many unrewarded things our families have done, and continue to do, for us. – T.F. PATTON, President, Republic Steel Corporation, Cleveland, Ohio. (534)

FARMERS

Farmers still are the most conservative group of people in this nation, and I believe they have more of the homely virtues on which this nation was founded, than any other segment of our society. Perhaps I am prejudiced on this, but this is my honest conviction. – J.K. STERN, President, American Institute of Cooperation, Washington, D.C. (535)

FARMERS – Government Aid

It is hardly an exaggeration to say that the more successful a farmer becomes, the more he stands to receive from the government.

Over the years, the Agriculture Department has increased its costs, its personnel and its services — but it has done little about trying progressively to lower price supports and reduce controls so as to promote the kind of freer competition that would be most beneficial to the farmer himself, the consumer and the nation at large. If we assume depression as a normal condition — as the farm program does — then the farmer will always need help and so will almost everybody else. — GEORGE CHAMPION, Chairman of the Board, The Chase Manhattan Bank. (536)

FARMERS — Government Subsidies
Farmers distrust the Big State. They always have, in any land and at any time. They highly prize their liberties. They will take government money if it's being handed out, but they have no wish to become wards of the State. — CARROLL P. STREETER, Editor, *Farm Journal.* (537)

FARMERS — Wives
Don't overlook the importance of the farmer's wife in the major decisions having to do with the business of farming. She knows the business. She's part of the business. And she'll participate in the business — as a sales instigator or as a sales obstacle. — RICHARD J. BABCOCK, President, Farm Journal, Inc. (538)

FARM FAMILIES — Freedom from Controls
Of all the people in America, none cherish their freedom from restraint and control more than our farm families. — RICHARD J. BABCOCK, President, Farm Journal, Inc. (539)

FARMING
Farming is a way of life with its own vernacular, its own customs, its own kinds of neighborhoods, its own hazards, its own standards, and its own outlook. It is not just another occupation. It is a social entity, having an independent genius of its own which distinguishes it in kind from other callings. It is compact of the soil, the sun, the winds, the rain, and the seasons. It measures time not by clocks but by the rising and setting of the sun, and knows its roads not by direction of right and left, but by east, west, north and south. That it has a quality of greatness in it which becomes a part of those who practice it is attested by the fact that, alongside the homes of clergymen, it produces more of those who are included in *Who's Who* than any other group proportionally. — ELMER G. LETERMAN,

Commissions Don't Fall From Heaven (MacFadden-Bartell).   (540)

Farming is an exciting occupation when the farmer has good education and training and when the farm has the potential to be profitable. This means a sizeable acreage, his production, modern farm machinery, funds for fertilizing and spraying and ample water supply. But it's no fun being a break-even or loss farmer and so over the last several decades there has been an evolutionary change entailing large, year-after-year reductions in small farms. This will continue, in all probability, until there remains a hard-core of well educated, high income farmers. – W.B. MURPHY, President, Campbell Soup Company.   (541)

I regard farming as an occupation apart from which there is none more basic, more useful, more noble, or more rewarding in the enduring satisfactions of life. – EDWARD J. MEEMAN, Editor Emeritus *The Memphis Press-Scimitar* and Conservation Editor of the Scripps-Howard Newspapers.   (542)

Farming in this country is coming into a new day. Not only is it a growth industry, but it is moving into stronger hands every day. There will be ups and downs, as there always have been, but if we can avoid a depression, a calamitous drought, serious inflation, or a major war the future is brighter than it ever has been for farmers who have the intelligence and the capital to stay in the game. – CARROLL P. STREETER, Editor, *Farm Journal, Quote.*   (543)

FASHIONS

I believe that any knee over 40 is better off covered, except Marlene Dietrich's – and so are all the knobby knees of any vintage. – JO FOXWORTH, Vice President, Calkins & Holden. (544)

FATHERS-IN-LAW – Arguments

Arguing with your father-in-law is, I guess, a little like testifying before Congress; you never have the last word, you never really say things as conclusively as you intend. – EDWARD WEEKS, Editor, *Atlantic Magazine.*   (545)

FEAR

The fear of the unknown is one of the most powerful emotions in our human nature. – RICHARD J. ANTON, Manager, Business Education Service, General Electric Company.   (546)

FINANCE – World Leadership

When we lose our world financial leadership, we also lose our strength as a world power; and the representative form of government we have known may well suffer a defeat from which recovery will be difficult if not impossible. — HENRY T. BODMAN, Chairman of the Board, National Bank of Detroit.   (547)

FISH — Protein
    Fish, which are highly effective protein builders, will be the predominant source of man's protein needs in the years to come. — Dr. THEODOR F. HUETER, General Manager, West Coast Operations Ordnance Division, Honeywell, Inc.   (548)

FLEXIBILITY
    Increasingly in years ahead, the greatest premium will be placed on those individuals who can demonstrate this priceless quality of flexibility. — ROBERT E. WILLIAMS, Executive Vice President, The Youngstown Sheet and Tube Company.   (549)

FOLLOWERS — Leaders
    Active partisans are the lifeblood of any enterprise. Without them, there would be no enterprise. Without followers, there are no leaders. — E.M. CLARK, President, Southwestern Bell Telephone Company, St. Louis, Missouri.   (550)

FOOD
    When the Master of all men suggested the prayer which includes, "give us this day our daily bread," He was suggesting something that was uppermost in the minds of everyone, every hour of every day, except the few wealthy rulers of the land. — J.K. STERN, President, American Institute of Cooperation, Washington, D.C.   (551)

FOOD — Transportation
    When we worry about all those hundreds of millions of people in other parts of the world who are hungry most of the time, we would do well to remember that one reason for their hunger is that much of the land capable of growing food is out of reach. Moreover, it has been estimated that one-third of all the food that is grown rots in the fields because there is no way to move it to market. — LYNN A. TOWNSEND, President, Chrysler Corporation.   (552)

FOREFATHERS — Courage
    This nation was built by men who took risks, pioneers who were not afraid of failure, scientists who were not afraid of truth, thinkers

who were not afraid of progress, dreamers who were not afraid of action. If our forefathers had not had the courage to stand up for right, to fight for right and to risk their all in so doing, there never would have been a U.S.A. — GUILFORD DUDLEY, Jr., President, Life and Casualty Insurance Company. (553)

FOREIGN AID
It is time that we look realistically into this business of giving our aid all over the world. We cannot buy friends. And often the recipients of aid become resentful. Were we to give our food as was done under Herbert Hoover after World War I, where Americans supervised the actual distribution of our food to those who were to eat it, then it would be different. — WILLIAM H. SMITH, President, Threadmiller Corporation, New York City. (554)

Clearly the whole process of development in the emerging nations requires a considerable measure of outside assistance, if it is to move with adequate speed. Our foreign aid program is intended to help meet this need, and we are serving our own best interests in providing such assistance. — DAVID ROCKEFELLER, President, Chase Manhattan Bank. (555)

No amount of money will solve the problem of people who do not want to help themselves. — GEORGE CHAMPION, Chairman of the Board, The Chase Manhattan Bank. (556)

Take a map of the world. Close your eyes and place a pin in any inhabited area and you will find some people who have benefited as a result of the generous heart of the American taxpayer. — CHARLES L. GOULD, Publisher, *San Francisco Examiner*. (557)

FOREIGN AID — Latin America
When the history of Aid to Latin America finally comes to be written, I suspect that the balance of payments form of assistance may be seen to have done more harm than good. — GEORGE CHAMPION, Chairman, The Chase Manhattan Bank, New York City. (558)

FOREIGN TRADE
The strength of the U.S. economy and our world leadership position will largely be determined by the worldwide competitive effectiveness of American business. — RAY R. EPPERT, President, Burroughs Corporation. (559)

While other nations of the world draw closer together through ties of trade ... many people in our country are still not convinced that foreign trade is even important. — B.K. WICKSTRUM, President, General Time. (560)

It is my conviction that U.S. success in continuing to lead the way toward free world economic growth must be contingent on American business becoming much more international minded. — RAY R. EPPERT, President, Burroughs Corporation. (561)

FREEDOM

The surest way to lose freedom to own a home of one's choosing is to attempt to deny that freedom to another. The surest way to lose the free access to learning and education is to deny that freedom to someone less powerful than oneself. The surest way to lose the freedom to run my business is to run it on contempt of the general interest. — J. IRWIN MILLER, Chairman of the Board, Cummins Engine Company, *Quote*. (562)

Freedoms are lost only through disuse. No people ever lost their freedoms when they exercised them. — ARTHUR H. MOTLEY, President, Parade Publications. (563)

You and I have long reaped the blessings of freedom. The time has now come to actively support it. — RALPH M. BESSE, President, The Cleveland Electric Illuminating Company. (564)

Freedom demands eternal vigilance, but that vigilance must be based on economic and political understanding. — L.C. MICHELON, Director of Public Affairs, Republic Steel Corporation. (565)

Let's remember that freedom always has two sides — free for better or free for worse . . . free for good or free for evil . . . free to sin or free to seek God. — WILLIAM I. NICHOLS, Editor and Publisher, *This Week Magazine*. (566)

Take away freedom from business, and it is likely that not far behind will be the loss of religious, political and academic freedom. Once any part of the fabric of freedom is torn, that fabric is finished. — GENE C. BREWER, President, United States Plywood Corporation. (567)

It is an axiom of history that no major activity of a society can long remain free unless all major activites remain free. And freedom is not indestructible. Freedom is a strong, beautiful, gothic arch rising stone by stone to a towering height. Anchored properly, buttressed properly, it can defy time. But one faulty stone, one crumbling stone, sets up a chain reaction of shifting stresses and balances, until the entire arch is affected and crashes. When freedom is threatened or lost or relinquished in any major activity of society — the chain reaction spreads out until the great fundamental activities of political freedom and freedom of economic enterprise is affected. — RALPH M. BESSE, President, The Cleveland Electric Illuminating Company.   (568)

Freedom has a great future if we level our guns and our efforts at the enemy instead of at ourselves. — ROBERT R. SPITZER, Businessman.   (569)

Freedom is an indivisible garment which cannot be successfully cherished at home if the right of others to freedom is allowed to be suffocated abroad. — ROSCOE DRUMMOND, Editor and Columnist.
                                                                         (570)

Unfortunately, freedom can be too easily confused with license. We are not free to do anything we wish. Our own acts must be balanced against the needs and the rights of our fellow men. — EDWIN M. CLARK, President, Southwestern Bell Telephone Company, St. Louis, Missouri.   (571)

To have freedom we must understand what it is. We must work for it and, if necessary, fight for it. It is a great heritage and our most precious possession. — LELAND I. DOAN, Chairman, Executive Committee, The Dow Chemical Company, Midland, Michigan. (572)

We rarely think we ought to be free, or think about it at all, until something shows us we are not free. — LEONARD E. READ, President, The Foundation for Economic Education, Inc., Irvington, New York.   (573)

Today, the word "freedom," means not just the abolition of the institution of slavery, but the absence of all manner of artificial restraints upon the ability of each and every American to acquire for himself and his family, the blessings and the obligations of a free society and an abundant economy. — LEROY COLLINS, President, National Association of Broadcasters.   (574)

Freedom, of course, cannot be absolute, for absolute freedom is anarchy, a chaotic, undesirable state, which seemingly in the law of nature is abhorred, as nature abhors a vacuum, and a state which is often followed by severe repression and intolerable loss of freedom. — LELAND I. DOAN, Chairman, Executive Committee, The Dow Chemical Company, Midland, Michigan.   (575)

Freedom is a commodity beyond price ... the most valuable thing that man has ever produced. — CHARLES H. BROWER, President, Batten, Barton, Durstine & Osborn, Inc., New York. (576)

FREEDOM — Laughter

It is well to remember that one hallmark of freedom is the sound of laughter. — HARRY S. ASHMORE, Editor-in-Chief, Encyclopaedia Britannica. (577)

FREEDOM — of Choice
Freedom of choice is our most essential freedom. Take away freedom of choice, and all freedoms are undermined — almost automatically. — CHARLES G. MORTIMER, Chairman, General Foods Corporation, White Plains, New York. (578)

The entire American private enterprise system is an outgrowth of the traditional democratic principle of individual freedom of choice. As a citizen, the American has free choice in the matter of political representation. As a consumer, he has free choice of what he will or will not buy. We must keep it that way — in both respects. — CHARLES G. MORTIMER, Chairman, General Foods Corporation, White Plains, New York. (579)

FREEDOM — of Press
The press endures because it is free, and it is free only to make other freedoms endure. — PEDRO G. BELTRAN, Peruvian Publisher, *Journalism Quarterly*. (580)

If the doors are going to be closed to the press in its search for legitimate news, if the people's business is going to be conducted in secret, we must not simply sit down outside and wail. We must use the power of the press to kick the doors open. — CLIFTON DANIEL, Managing Editor, *New York Times, Quote*. (581)

Restrictions on any part of the press threaten the principle underlying the vitality of all parts of the press. — ROBERT W. SARNOFF, Chairman of the Board, National Broadcasting Company, Inc. (582)

I think if we do not use the freedom of the press to participate in issues it will wither away like an unused muscle. — RALPH McGILL, Publisher, *The Atlanta Consitution*. (583)

Freedom of the press is an American shibboleth. And although not everyone who uses it knows precisely what it means, most Americans would fight for it and, perhaps, even die for it. — ALAN BARTH, Editorial Writer, *The Washington* (D.C.) *Post*. (584)

FREEDOM — of Speech
If you demand free speech, you must not suppress it in others, or use violence to deny the right of free speech to those with whom you disagree. — HERBERT V. PROCHNOW, President, First National Bank of Chicago. (585)

FREEDOM — Personal Credit

The Bill of Rights of the Constitution guaranteed us four freedoms — the freedom of assembly, freedom of expression, freedom of worship and freedom of privacy. During World War II President Franklin Roosevelt enunciated a Fifth Freedom — freedom from Want and Fear. And now the American people are declaring a new freedom — freedom to exercise the personal credit which they regard as their natural heritage as free and economically independent citizens. — SHEFFIELD BOARDMAN, Cincinnati Zone Manager for B.F. Goodrich Tire Company. (586)

FREEDOM — Strength

Freedom . . . is the only state of man that does require strength. It takes none to do whatever you're told, without complaint. It takes none to accept whatever comes, without trying to make changes. It takes none to believe whatever you're told, without seeking the truth. To preserve the freedom of America for future generations, there are four kinds of strength we need to exhibit now, and need to develop in our children: Physical. Moral. Spiritual and Intellectual. — E.M. CLARK, President, Southwestern Bell Telephone Company, St. Louis, Missouri. (587)

FREEDOM — to Fail

Communism or any other planned economy is by definition so carefully hedged against failure that any success an individual attains must be small. Our individual freedom to fail, which gives us our freedom to succeed, is the great weapon which has brought the United States its role of world leadership, and if we continue to exercise it, will keep us there. — RAY R. EPPERT, President, Burroughs Corporation. (588)

FREEDOMS

When the Founding Fathers wrote into the Bill of Rights guarantees of freedom of speech, press and religion, it was not in any casual or haphazard manner, that they acted. Nor were they acting in a vacuum — making rules in a sea of tranquility and hoping they would stand up under pressure 200 years later. On the contrary, issues of free speech, religion and assembly were as pertinent and as hot then as they are today. — STANFORD SMITH, General Manager, American Newspaper Publishers Association. (589)

FREEDOMS – Preservation

Preservation of our freedoms depends on the average citizen. It not only depends on every single one of us; but this is one responsibility we can never delegate. – WILLARD M. WILSON, Secretary, American Petroleum Institute. (590)

FREE ECONOMY – Competition

I sometimes have the feeling that the imposition of 90 per cent of the rules and restrictions applied to a free economy to assure competition is like breaking a man's leg to make him run faster. – LELAND I. DOAN, Chairman, Executive Committee, The Dow Chemical Company, Midland, Michigan. (591)

FREE ENTERPRISE

Our free enterprise system – or, as I prefer to call it, our free opportunity system – does a better job of producing goods and services than any other system in the world. It is the only system which guarantees true freedom. It is built on the basis that one must produce more than his needs if he is to contribute to the general well-being. It has a built-in drive for improvement, and a built-in fear for falling behind in the race where individual progress is measured by the fairest judge of all, the market place. – GEORGE CHAMPION, Chairman of the Board, The Chase Manhattan Bank. (592)

Free enterprise is becoming more and more a phrase to which we all subscribe, but which we are not practicing with the enthusiasm that our beliefs would normally induce. – L.C. MICHELON, Director of Public Affairs, Republic Steel Corporation. (593)

Free private enterprise is not really free. The price we all must pay . . . and it's the greatest bargain in the world . . . is the constant vigilance and effort on all our parts to keep it alive and flourishing. – LAWRENCE H. ROGERS, II, President, Taft Broadcasting Company. (594)

In many ways, America's free enterprise business system is literally "the goose that lays the golden eggs." Almost anything that Americans are doing anywhere depends to a considerable extent on the productiveness, the efficiency, the creativeness and the individual initiative that our economic system encourages. – A.F. JACOBSON, President, Northwest Bell Telephone Company. (595)

I am completely convinced that the fountainhead of our affluent society is not the Federal Government. The mainspring of our capacity to produce more . . . spend more . . . and share more than ever before is our free enterprise system. And – equally important — the faith of our people in this system. — CHARLES L. GOULD, Publisher of *San Francisco Examiner*.   (596)

The free enterprise system has achieved greatness for our people because it brings out the best of our abilities through voluntary competition. It assumes that people want to obtain more than security or a bare existence and are willing to work as individuals for better lives when given the opportunity and incentive. And free enterprise does give every individual opportunity and incentive, is sharp contrast to political systems in other parts of the world. — GENE C. BREWER, President, United States Plywood Corporation.   (597)

In every facet of our economy you will find some elements that are shady or shoddy and subject to censure. But those who pursue these paths do not long survive. One of the great strengths of competitive free enterprise is its ability to purge most of the poisons from its own system. The practicing physicians who administer the purge are the men and women of the consuming public. — CHARLES L. GOULD, Publisher of *San Francisco Examiner*.   (598)

The worst thing that could happen to us . . . is the loss of our unique enterprise system — the system that permits us to invest risk capital, and to manufacture goods or perform services at a profit. — DONALD I. ROGERS, Business and Financial Editor, *New York Herald Tribune*.   (599)

If the United States is to maintain its economic leadership in the critical years ahead, the private enterprise system must be permitted to function freely. — ROBERT C. KIRKWOOD, President, F.W. Woolworth Company.   (600)

The American enterprise system may be criticized by some people for having given us more pizza parlors than we care to see lining our highways. But it is also a system that can devote years of research and millions of dollars to finding the causes and the cures for crippling childhood diseases. — LESLIE B. WORTHINGTON, President, United States Steel Corporation.   (601)

It is my strong conviction that our personal and political liberties, our spiritual and moral values, our entire way of life, are dependent upon the preservation of a free economic system. Without it, in my opinion, all other freedoms would be in jeopardy. — JOSEPH L. BLOCK, Chairman, Inland Steel Company, Chicago, Illinois.   (602)

One of the great needs in our economic system is for the continuous and increasing availability of venture capital. . . . Such capital is the lifeblood of our Free Enterprise system. Without it — without people who have saved money from their earnings and who are willing to risk it on new ventures — Free Enterprise, as we know it, could not exist. — E.F. SCOUTTEN, Vice President, The Maytag Company. (603)

Free enterprise is not a system which is the outgrowth of a plan. It is a plan which is an outgrowth of a system — and the system, though couched in some of the noblest and most meaningful phrases of all time, simply provides for as much human freedom as possible. — WARD L. QUAAL, Executive Vice President and General Manager, WGN, Inc., Chicago, Illinois. (604)

This thing we call free enterprise means the freedom of every man to have a dream, then put it on sale in the market place in competition with the dreams of other men. — ROBERT R. GROS, Vice President, Pacific Gas & Electric Company, San Francisco, California. (605)

This country has grown and become strong because it has relied on private initiative and enterprise for its economic development. Many another nation has benefited from our example. We must not stray from the path we have traveled with such success. — EDWIN A. LOCKE, Jr., President, American Paper Institute. (606)

If the free enterprise system goes, our country as we know it will go too. — MARTIN J. CASERIO, General Manager, Delco Radio Division, General Motors Corporation, Kokomo, Indiana. (607)

Our free enterprise system has given us the greatest growth, with the gains broadly shared by all groups, in the history of mankind. — ARTHUR H. MOTLEY, President, Chamber of Commerce of the United States. (608)

I believe that the strength of our free enterprise system lies, not in what the government can do for people, but rather in what millions of Americans can and will do for themselves. — FRANK G. BINSWANGER, Chairman of the Board, Binswanger Corporation, Philadelphia, Pennsylvania. (609)

Free enterprise is not a mere slogan. It is the heart and soul of economic freedom for all. It maximizes human freedom and minimizes force and coercion. It avoids monopoly. It enlarges free choices on a broad front. — ARTHUR H. MOTLEY, President, Chamber of Commerce of the United States. (610)

FREE WORLD — Communism

We in the free world must do everything in our power to bring an end to the communist deception, and help the nations of the world build the foundations for strong, free, self-reliant and responsible societies. — RALPH J. CORDINER, Chairman of the Board, General Electric Company, New York. (611)

FREE WORLD – Universities
Mankind's most profitable potential for progress and for peace is in the universities of the free world. — JOSEPH H. McCONNELL, President, Reynolds Metals Company. (612)

FRIENDS
There is only one thing better than making a new friend and that is keeping an old one. — ELMER G. LETERMAN. (613)

FRIENDSHIP
The remarkable thing about friendship is that it is an endless chain and those who benefit most are sometimes people we do not even know. — ELMER G. LETERMAN, *The Sale Begins When the Customer Says "No"* (MacFadden-Bartell). (614)

FUTURE
Startling as it may seem, it is a plain fact that even without a radical acceleration in our productivity, by the year 1985 we shall have a choice which past ages would never have believed possible. We could ... choose to work only 24 hours a week, or 27 weeks a year, or let everybody retire at the age of 38, and still produce enough to give every American the standard of living he has today. — THOMAS J. WATSON, Jr., Chairman of the Board, International Business Machines Corporation, *Public Utilities Fortnightly*. (615)

The future belongs to those who prepare for it. — HERBERT D. SMITH, Vice President of Sales, U.S. Carbonated Operations, Canada Dry Corporation. (616)

The future of any of us is unknown. As we look to tomorrow we can be sure of only one thing. Tomorrow will yield its prizes only to the man who has the courage to face it without fear, and the preparation to meet its demands. — ELMER G. LETERMAN, *Personal Power Through Creative Selling* (Harper & Row). (617)

Wonder drugs, jet aircraft, nuclear fission and space travel have radically altered our ways of doing things and our outlook. We tend to think of the future not just as a modified extension of the past but more and more as an amazing phenomenon we can hardly imagine. — ROBERT E. WILLIAMS, Executive Vice President, The Youngstown Sheet and Tube Company. (618)

Perfect prophecy may be impossible, but all of us — educators and businessmen alike — must attempt to imagine the shape of things to come. And the more accurately we do so, the better our chance to shape the future closer to what we would like it to be. — M.J. RATHBONE, Chairman of the Board and Chief Executive Officer, Standard Oil Company (New Jersey). (619)

If present trends continue, by the year 2000 it is predicted that there will be over 7 billion people in the world — nearly twice today's population and four times that when I was born. Most of them will be hungry, half of them starving, many of them dying for lack of adequate food. — ROY L. ASH, President, Litton Industries, Inc. (620)

Don't docilely accept myths that say the future pattern of society — a pattern you don't want — is fixed by technological advance. Regardless of your field of endeavor, consider it part of your duty to participate in and to force the social advance you want for yourselves and your children. — Dr. SIMON RAMO, Vice Chairman of the Board, T.R.W. Inc. (621)

Men have never known anything like the challenges that will confront the world during the remaining third of this century. The size of the world's population alone will assure that we will be faced with richer opportunities — and more critical problems — than we can possibly foresee at this time. — M.J. WARNOCK, President, Armstrong Cork Company. (622)

Today must always be taken care of, today's job always be done. But the gravest sin of omission that business leadership can make is to fail to *try* to see the future and prepare for it. — FREDERICK R. KAPPEL, Chairman of the Board, American Telephone and Telegraph Company. (623)

Everyone is interested in the future, in what lies ahead, and particularly is this true in business. Peering into the crystal ball to discern the future can be interesting, frustrating, tedious, sometimes even humorous, but at all times it is an important phase of business leadership. Forecasting has been described as an educated guess. — WAYNE A. JOHNSTON, President, Illinois Central Railroad, *Quote*. (624)

The future rests on a foundation established in the past and present. — JOSEPH J. ELEY, President, Public Affairs Counsellors, Inc. (625)

A future that is planned and managed for growth is the most exciting and rewarding kind. In fact, a future spent in calmly admiring something that has stopped growing is really no future at all. — OWEN R. CHEATHAM, Chairman, Georgia-Pacific Corporation, Portland, Oregon. (626)

I believe that in the cybernetic era, in which we now live, we make our own future: it is our dreams and nightmares which determine the course of history. — ROBERT THEOBALD, Economist. (627)

FUTURE — History

It is my conviction that the future is shaped largely by man, not by natural or supernatural causes. Nor is it just the work of a few individuals who are remembered in the history books. History is a composite, shaped both by the outstanding few and many millions of others. — M.J. RATHBONE, Chairman of the Board and Chief Executive Officer, Standard Oil Company (New Jersey). (628)

FUTURE — Past

Although there are some who allege that you cannot predict the future by observing the past, I, for one, know of no other reliable method. — E.F. SCOUTTEN, Vice President, Personnel, The Maytag Company. (629)

FUTURE — Present

My own deep conviction is that we need never fear the future when we are willing to face the present. — ROSCOE DRUMMOND, Editor and Columnist. (630)

FUTURE — Youth

The future of the nation and the destiny of the individual depends upon the wisdom of decisions of young people entering our colleges and universities. — ANDREW R. CECIL, Executive Vice President and Educational Director, The Southwestern Legal Foundation, Dallas, Texas. (631)

G

GETTING – Giving
We have allowed ourselves, as a society, to listen to those among us who place above all else a purposefulness to *get* rather than to *give* in life. You can find this kind of philosophy in every phase of our society and national life. This is the lush soil in which greed, lust, envy and the disregard of the rights of others, flourish. This philosophy is, indeed, the sure harbinger of delinquency. – LEROY COLLINS, President, National Association of Broadcasters.   (632)

GIRLS
I hope we never run out of little girls. It does every heart good to see them dressed up in the spring of the year. When one bunch of little girls grow up, they promptly and beneficiently produce another crop of little girls. Between the ages of 3 and 8 the little girl is the best example of the human race. – HARRY GOLDEN, *Carolina Israelite*.   (633)

GIVING
The one great trouble with this old world today is not the acts of legislatures, but the want of a more friendly, kindly spirit. We have not learned how to give, many of us. We have wanted too much, the thought is – if I give, how is it going to benefit me? If we do learn how to give, then much of the world's discord and strife and unhappiness will be eliminated. – J.C. PENNEY, *Christian Herald*.
     (634)

Giving is the secret of a healthy life. Not necessarily money, but whatever a man has of encouragement and sympathy and understanding. – JOHN D. ROCKEFELLER, Jr., *Quote*.   (635)

GIVING – Voluntary
Voluntary giving is more than an expression of compassion or a demonstration of democracy's ideals. It is a frame of mind that is essential to democracy itself. A people who are willing to turn all their problems over to government have lost the will to govern themselves. – HENRY FORD, II, Chairman of the Board, Ford Motor Company.   (636)

GOALS

Most of us serve our ideals by fits and starts. The person who makes a success of living is the one who sees his goal steadily and aims for it unswervingly. — CECIL B. DE MILLE, *Personnel Administration*. (637)

The goal toward which we move is that which our secret thoughts have set us — "as a man thinketh in his heart, so is he." — ELMER G. LETERMAN, *Nylic Review*, New York Life Insurance Company. (638)

Goals give meaning to life. If your motive is strong enough, you can attain great heights. — BRENDAN BYRNE, Executive Director, The American Heritage Foundation, New York. (639)

A person without a goal toward which he is consciously and daily striving is like a ship without a rudder, drifting aimlessly at sea. And yet it is conservatively estimated that less than five per cent of all the working people in this country have goals toward which they are working. — EARL NIGHTINGALE, Chairman of the Board, Nightingale-Conant Corporation. (640)

GOALS — Purposes

Men and institutions are not evaluated and adjudged solely by the fruits of their labors, but by the high purposes of their goals. — W. HOWARD CHASE, Chairman, Howard Chase Associates, Inc. (641)

GOD

God gets credit for all the bad things in the world, flood, famine, disease and death. These are the things people discuss with Him at length. But business, science or government gets credit for all the good things. — E.M. CLARK, President, Southwestern Bell Telephone Company, St. Louis, Missouri. (642)

GOD — Belief

Ours is a society based on the belief in God. Without it, nothing avails us. — RICHARD H. AMBERG, Publisher, *The St. Louis Globe-Democrat*. (643)

GOD — Good Society

We all agree that "Only God can make a tree" and I am ready to concede that only God can make a good society. — LEONARD E. READ, President, The Foundation for Economic Education, Inc., Irvington, New York. (644)

GOD – Man

Man is not a beggar or pensioner at the court of heaven. He is the son and heir, reigning over the world with the Father, who shares all things with the son, even his very dominion. He is the expression of God's being. He is as necessary to God as God is to Man; without Man, God would not be completely expressed. Therefore Man has a sure place in the Universe and is of course, immortal. – EDWARD J. MEEMAN, Editor, *Memphis Press-Scimitar*. (645)

GOLD

When gold speaks, men listen. When gold moves, men watch. – HENRY C. ALEXANDER, Chairman of the Board, Morgan Guaranty Trust Company of New York. (646)

Until we can depend on governments to impose on their countries the discipline of necessary monetary and fiscal restraints to provide stability, or until nations are willing to transfer their wealth to support the economic needs of their neighbors, it seems to me that the world's economic system needs the discipline of gold. – GEORGE S. MOORE, Chairman, First National City Bank. (647)

GOLDEN RULE

There is gold in the golden rule for the man who does not estimate others by the rule of gold. – ELMER G. LETERMAN. (648)

GOOD – Bad

There is always something useful in most happenstances we regard as bad, that is, the useful is present if we can but discern it. – LEONARD E. READ, President, The Foundation for Economic Education, Inc., Irvington, New York. (649)

GOOD DEEDS

We must at all times ... remember that a good deed done in a bad way destroys the doer and the deed. – ROBERT G. WINGERTER, President, Rockwell-Standard Corporation Automotive Divisions. (650)

GOVERNMENT

When government is limited to well defined and well understood functions and duties in society, men have plenty of elbow room to go about their creative and productive tasks. This is the meaning of freedom in human affairs, and such freedom as we have enjoyed in

America is the result of keeping government within its proper bounds. – EDMUND A. OPITZ, The Foundation for Economic Education, Irvington-on-Hudson, New York.   (651)

Good government is a "do-it-yourself" project. – WILLARD M. WILSON, Secretary, American Petroleum Institute.   (652)

The force of government is now directed more fully toward the security of the weak than the encouragement of the strong. – CHARLES H. BROWER, President, Batten, Barton, Durstine & Osborn, Inc., New York.   (653)

When you stand off and look at the American system of representative government from any distance, it seems rather remarkable that a country as large and complex as ours can govern itself and periodically renew its political leadership without coming apart at one seam or another. – JAMES P. MITCHELL, Vice President, Crown Zellerbach Corporation, San Francisco, California.   (654)

I think our form of government depends on the people controlling the government. It has to begin on the lowest level. If you destroy the contact of the citizen with the forms of government that established the nation, the communities and states – you have permanently taken away from him one of the essential forms of democracy in a republic. – ALLAN SHIVERS, President, Chamber of Commerce of the United States, *Nation's Business*.   (655)

Government has become the dominant single factor in our economy. It buys, sells, competes, regulates, protects, subsidizes, manufactures, lends and borrows. And of course the money it spends is not its money but yours and mine – because that's the only money government has, ours. – ROBERT R. GROS, Vice President, Pacific Gas and Electric Company, San Francisco, California.   (656)

Self-government is most cautious and most economical where people are most directly affected by governmental expenditure. Anyone who has watched a New England town meeting wrestle over whether to reshingle a school house or replank a bridge understands this. – JENKIN LLOYD JONES, Editor and Publisher, *Tulsa Tribune*.   (657)

I am continually amazed to hear my friends in business talk about government as "they." "They" do this, and "they" think this, and "they" ought to be curbed. . . . Government is *not* "they"; it is "you" and "I," and we should never forget that. Government won't improve unless we improve our participation in it. – GEORGE CHAMPION, Chairman of the Board, The Chase Manhattan Bank.   (658)

The philosophical structure of American society is based on citizen participation in that society. When citizens become too bored, or too concerned with other things, to participate, Washington is forced to assume additional responsibilities — and the additional powers that go with them. And this, carried to its ultimate conclusion, can alter drastically the entire character of our American form of government. — RALPH M. BESSE, President, The Cleveland Electric Illuminating Company. (659)

We the people are the government, and we will get as good a government as we are willing to work for. — JOHN D. HARPER, President, Aluminum Company of America. (660)

GOVERNMENT — Broadcasting

The executive branch of our federal system has made great use of broadcasting for communicating with the people. From the days of the fireside chats to the present live presidential news conferences, the people have developed a far better understanding of the executive than of any other branch of government. And unquestionably, radio and television have made this possible. — LEROY COLLINS, President, National Association of Broadcasters. (661)

GOVERNMENT — Business

There are few major problems that can be solved by government alone, without business, or by business alone, without government. — HENRY FORD, II, Chairman of the Board, Ford Motor Company, *Public Utilities Fortnightly*. (662)

We can function productively as businessmen only if we recognize that government and business must be partners. — RICHARD V. SCACCHETTI, Director of Administrative Services Life Association of America. (663)

There really isn't any such thing today as minding one's own business. There are few, if any, business or professional enterprises left which government doesn't help to manage; there are few industries in which the interferences are not assuming bold new forms and purposes, all of which could, with similar logic, be imposed on every man's business depriving us all of the right to manage. — ALLAN SHIVERS, President, Chamber of Commerce of the United States. (664)

During the past three decades, this nation has completed its divorce from Locke's concept of government as an instrument intended solely for the preservation of property. In its place, we have evolved a new relationship based upon growing cooperation between

124

government and business in the achievement of national goals. – ROBERT W. SARNOFF, President, Radio Corporation of America. (665)

When government action affecting business is motivated by political tactic, there is real damage to the confidence of managers of business, who must guide their enterprises through enormously complex problems. And when actions of public servants undermine public confidence in American business, the whole nation is the loser. – NEIL H. McELROY, Chairman of the Board, The Proctor and Gamble Company. (666)

It is now generally recognized that government and business share a common interest in maintaining a climate for economic expansion, and that each has a part to play in the process. It is also recognized that some of our vital national needs can be met only with efforts so large that the active partnership of industry and government is essential to their success. – ROBERT W. SARNOFF, President, Radio Corporation of America. (667)

GOVERNMENT – Businessmen

By indicating a willingness to advise with the Government and to work *within* its framework, the businessman has already found that he is able to make his views known more clearly and with more influence. As a result, the voice of the business community can become increasingly more effective in Government deliberations. – SOL M. LINOWITZ, Chairman of the Board, Xerox Corporation. (668)

GOVERNMENT – Careers

No one expects a government career to offer wealth. It has its other valued compensations. Like teaching or the ministry, it is a dedicated service. It can offer satisfactions in personal accomplishment and fulfillment for which, for many, there is no substitute. – NEIL McELROY, Chairman, Proctor & Gamble Company. (669)

GOVERNMENT – Centralized

The Declaration of Independence indicted the British Government for maintaining here "swarms" of officials "to harass our people and eat out their substance." Today the swarm of federal employees is almost as large as was the entire population of all the thirteen colonies in 1776. There can be no doubt that a people who once demanded independence from centralized government have now come, on the whole, to welcome dependence on centralized government. – FELIX MORLEY, Author. (670)

GOVERNMENT – Citizens
When the central government tries to do too many things for the citizens of the country, it creates a sense of irresponsibility on the part of the citizens. It leads the people to feel that they no longer need to do things for themselves. – ARCH N. BOOTH, Executive Vice President, Chamber of Commerce of the United States. (671)

GOVERNMENT – Controls
When the government becomes involved in the market place, the inevitable result is pressure on the marketing and communications system of the manufacturer. This can result in disastrous expenses for a small firm. – LLOYD E. SKINNER, President, Skinner Macaroni Company. (672)

GOVERNMENT – Economic Freedom
If we have men afraid of standing up to the government, then we have the strongest indictment of "Big Government" that could ever be imagined. When that happens, economic freedom in our country will be dead. – GEORGE CHAMPION, Chairman of the Board, The Chase Manhattan Bank. (673)

GOVERNMENT – Expenditures
I'm very much concerned that unless we bring government expenditures under control through an intelligent ordering of national priorities, we face a continuing budget crisis with periodic tax increases and persistent inflation. We cannot solve our fiscal problems by preaching economy and practicing extravagance. – GEORGE CHAMPION, Chairman of the Board, The Chase Manhattan Bank. (674)

GOVERNMENT – Federal
Too many people have become accustomed to looking toward Washington every time a problem arises. We must, instead, look to our own communities. We shouldn't expect the federal government to do a job in our own city that the people of the city can do for themselves, through voluntary contributions, tax payments, bond issues or other local means. – E.M. CLARK, President, Southwestern Bell Telephone Company, St. Louis, Missouri. (675)

126

GOVERNMENT — Foreign Trade

I view the steps the government has taken so far to spur foreign trade, especially with underdeveloped countries, as inadequate. — B.K. WICKSTRUM, President, General Time. (676)

GOVERNMENT — Industry

The services of government now account for a quarter of all industrial activity, and this far exceeds the government share in such an avowedly socialist state as India, and considerably exceeds that in the social democratic countries of Sweden and Norway. Actually, it's commensurate only with Poland, a communist country. — CHAYLIE L. SAXE, President, Saxe Bros. Inc. (677)

The case of the government that thinks it knows more than the marketplace about how to run the economy is nothing new in history. This was one of the root causes of the American Revolution. — GEORGE CHAMPION, Chairman of the Board, The Chase Manhattan Bank. (678)

GOVERNMENT — Intervention

I know no antidote to spreading government intervention in our society like being anxious to apply ourselves as industrialists to every facet of that society's improvement before government has to move in to correct a grave deficiency. — Colonel BARNEY OLDFIELD, U.S.A.F. (Ret.) of Litton Industries, Inc. (679)

GOVERNMENT — Labor, Management

Businessmen, labor leaders and educators talk primarily to themselves — that is, to members of their own group. And most of them seldom, if ever, come face to face with government spokesmen. There is a crying need for a better cross-fertilization of ideas, for members of each group to listen to other points of view and to seek common ground in behalf of the nation's welfare and the preservation of our free society. — JOSEPH L. BLOCK, Chairman, Inland Steel Company, Chicago, Illinois. (680)

I am not suggesting that the government *never* has the right to intervene in the affairs of labor or management — there are times when the overriding public interest or the security of the nation must take precedence over the interest of any segment of our economy. I *do* suggest, however, that intervention must be used more sparingly if our free collective bargaining process is to survive. — B.D. BILLMAN, Vice President, Armco Steel Corporation. (681)

Better government, labor and management cooperation is essential for our survival as a free nation. — JOSEPH L. BLOCK, Chairman, Inland Steel Company, Chicago, Illinois. (682)

It seems clear to me what the relationship between government, labor and management should be. While each must represent its respective interests, they must also endeavor to work in tandem in the public interest. Indeed, this is essential if we are to survive as a free nation. — JOSEPH L. BLOCK, Chairman, Inland Steel Company, Chicago, Illinois. (683)

GOVERNMENT — Law

Government and law are made for man and not man for government and law. — KENNETH IRVING BROWN, Executive Director, Danforth Foundation, St. Louis, Missouri. (684)

GOVERNMENT — Officials

No persons in our society have more solemn and vital responsibility than those who make up our government. — NEIL McELROY, Chairman, Proctor & Gamble Company. (685)

The broad dissemination of authority in government, which demands team play rather than brilliant personal performance, is the hard lesson which those must learn who suddenly leave private life to assume posts in Washington. The man who at home has been accustomed to think a tough problem through on his own, then promptly make a decision, and get the job done in forthright fashion, finds it cumbersome first to consult those holding parallel authority. Conferences are galling to him, but nevertheless must be accepted, for they are part of our system of checks and balances. — CLARENCE B. RANDALL, Retired Chairman, Inland Steel Company. (686)

From my own experience in government, I know that the vast majority of the men and women in government are conscientious public servants. Few really want to be unreasonable. Most are not doctrinaire. Most are receptive to facts properly presented to them; and most are readily approachable. — NEIL H. McELROY, Chairman of the Board, The Proctor and Gamble Company. (687)

We'd better learn — and learn soon — that government officials represent people. Elected officials, of course, depend for their survival on responding to the wishes of their constitutents. But more than that — the administrative officers in agencies and bureaus, whose job is to carry out government policy, must also respond at least indirectly to what the majority of American people want. — JAMES M. PATTERSON, Director of Public Relations, American Oil Company. (688)

GOVERNMENT – People

We Americans have an abiding faith that we can solve our problems by electing the right men to run our government. It is of course true that incompetence or ignorance in government has always led to disaster. But we are still a democracy, and the greatest leadership we can find will achieve little or nothing if the people through lack of knowledge or education fail to heed their summons. – JOHN ALSOP, President, The Mutual Insurance Company, Hartford, Connecticut. (689)

GOVERNMENT – Politics

In government and politics there is nothing that can substitute for on-the-job training. – JAMES P. MITCHELL, Vice President, Crown Zellerbach Corporation, San Francisco, California. (690)

GOVERNMENT – Power

It is not unusual to encounter in Washington and on our college campuses people who would like to sweep away the whole concept of state and local powers. A centralized domination, with states and localities reduced to mere administrative units, they argue, would be far more efficient. They seem to forget the lesson of history that such centralization flouts basic rights, weakens the moral fiber of the people, restricts individual decision-making, and, in the long run, would destroy the incentives that have made our country and our economy the envy and aspiration of the world. – GEORGE CHAMPION, Chairman of the Board, The Chase Manhattan Bank.
(691)

The power of the government derives from the people. But the people lose this power the moment they permit it – or encourage it – to be thrust into the hands of officeholders and lawmakers, who feel that they themselves are the source of the power, rather than merely public officials designated to direct it. – ARCH N. BOOTH, Executive Vice President, Chamber of Commerce of the United States. (692)

GOVERNMENT – Programs

It has been well said that if a monument were erected in Washington to every government program that has been discontinued in the past three decades, the landscape of the nation's capital would not be perceptibly altered! – GEORGE CHAMPION, Chairman of the Board, The Chase Manhattan Bank. (693)

GOVERNMENT – Restrictions
My philosophy rejects undue restrictions on our liberties by paternalistic government. If continued to their extreme, we could end up like Russia – where all that is not forbidden is compulsory. – ROBERT R. GROS, Vice President, Pacific Gas and Electric Company, San Francisco, California. (694)

GOVERNMENT – The Press
Nothing expresses more clearly the essential difference between a totalitarian society and a free society than the relationship in each of the press to the government. Among the totalitarians, the press, like every other institution, is an instrumentality of the state; it is used to propagate support for official policies and to promote official doctrines. In a free society, however, the function of the press is, rather, to oppose the government, to scrutinize its activities and to keep its authority within appropriate bounds. – ALAN BARTH, Editorial Writer, *The Washington* (D.C.) *Post*. (695)

The truly great are seldom recognized in advance by their own generation. – CLARENCE B. RANDALL, Retired Chairman, Inland Steel Company. (696)

All of the great men of history have had to answer the same critical questions. Each had to choose between the safe protection of the crowd and the risk of standing up and being counted. And you can find no truly great men who took the easy way. For their courage some suffered abuse, imprisonment, or even death. Others lived to win the acclaim of their fellow men. But all achieved greatness. – THOMAS J. WATSON, Jr., Chairman of the Board, IBM Corporation. (697)

Greatness in a great society stems from individuals achieving to the maximum of their ability and accepting responsibility to perform in their chosen fields – housewife, lawyer, barrister, educator, religious leader – but *accepting* that responsibility, not *abdicating* it. – ARTHUR H. MOTLEY, President, Parade Publications. (698)

GREATNESS – Faith
A man can become great by expecting the probable if the probable be great enough. But the man who expects the impossible will become the greatest of all, for in him is faith, and faith stands at the beginning of all creative thinking and work. – ELMER G. LETERMAN, *Commissions Don't Fall From Heaven* (McFadden-Bartell). (699)

GREAT SOCIETIES — Building

You cannot build great societies with nothing more than the flimsy fabric of men's dreams. The gap between what is and what should be can only be bridged with the realities of money, men, methods and machines. — LESLIE B. WORTHINGTON, President, United States Steel Corporation. (700)

GUARANTEED INCOME

The guaranteed income establishes the most fundamental human right of all; the right to life regardless of whether the individual can find a job or not. As such, it is an extension of the civil rights — or more accurately human rights — movement of recent years. If we are to provide dignity to man, his right to an income must be absolute and not postulated on the administrative rules of any organization of the generosity of any individual. — ROBERT THEOBALD, Economist. (701)

The minimum step which we must take if we are to eliminate the poverty which exists in the United States is to introduce the guaranteed income. — ROBERT THEOBALD, Economist. (702)

There is ... a strong possibility that the guaranteed income would become a *supplement* for the current welfare programs rather than — as has been proposed — a *substitute* for these programs. — M.A. WRIGHT, Chairman of the Board, Humble Oil & Refining Company. (703)

Basic economic security can be provided most easily through the guaranteed income. This proposal for making a basic income available as a matter of right is rapidly moving toward the center of the political stage. — ROBERT THEOBALD, Economist. (704)

Those who work closely with the poor maintain ... that freedom from want is more than freedom from hunger and exposure — it is being allowed the opportunity of earning a decent living, of enjoying economic security, and of recognizing one's potential. To be meaningful, freedom from want must, they insist, include hope — hope for a better life and a more fulfilling life. It is this element of hope that has been overlooked by the social engineers of the guaranteed income. — M.A. WRIGHT, Chairman of the Board, Humble Oil & Refining Company. (705)

H

HABITS — Changes

Let's make a real effort to force changes in our habit patterns, so that we do not become so deeply committed to them that we limit our ability to accept new ideas rapidly. — M.J. WARNOCK, President, Armstrong Cork Company. (706)

HAPPINESS

True happiness comes from a sense of high purpose and striving to achieve that purpose. — BRENDAN BYRNE, Executive Director, The American Heritage Foundation, New York. (707)

HAPPINESS — Duty

It is my observation over a lifetime and in many countries that no person has found his happiness very far from his path of duty and I believe that those who wander from that path of duty lose their rights, their freedom and their happiness. — JAMES A. FARLEY, Chairman of the Board, Coca-Cola Export Corporation. (708)

HIGH SCHOOLS — Colleges

The lack of liaison between high schools and colleges is one of the stark facts of the American educational system. About the only place where there has been good liaison between colleges and high schools is found in the relationship between private preparatory schools and the quality colleges to which the preparatory schools ' hope to send their graduates. — RALPH M. BESSE, President, The Cleveland Electric Illuminating Company. (709)

HIGHWAYS

The highway system is a vital part of our national life and our national economy. It is now suffering severe growing pains manifested in such problems as traffic safety, air pollution, traffic congestion and the restructuring of our cities. With goodwill, understanding and cooperation between government and industry, these problems can be solved and the American people can continue to enjoy the benefits of increasing mobility. — HENRY FORD, II, Chairman of The Board, Ford Motor Company. (710)

132

HIGHWAYS — Beautification

In the course of constructing urban freeways in various parts of the country, engineers have sometimes relied too much on computers and have failed to make proper allowance for such factors as beauty or esthetic value. In some cases, a technically correct freeway network has threatened to lessen unnecessarily the attractiveness of the communities it is meant to serve. — ARJAY MILLER, President, Ford Motor Company.   (711)

HISTORY

The history of any great company is the history of the great men in that company. — LEE S. BICKMORE, President, National Biscuit Company.   (712)

HOME LIFE

The influence of the family and environment on a child is enormous, almost overwhelming. Virtually everything of an emotional and life-shaping nature is learned in the home, not in school. In school we learn the nuts and bolts of living, the technical aspects of education, reading and writing and arithmetic . . . the technical tools of life. But it is in the home and the home's environment that we form our attitudes, our deeply held beliefs. It is in the home that hope is fostered or destroyed. — EARL NIGHTINGALE, Chairman of the Board, Nightingale-Conant Corporation.   (713)

HOME RULE

Home rule is a valuable tool of government which once thrown away will be hard to ever find again. — EDWARD F. TAYLOR, Taylor, Smith and Williams, City Attorney of Redlands, California.   (714)

HONESTY

Regardless of how educated, confident and ambitious you are, you will not realize your potentialities for success in business, or your personal relations, without simple, basic honesty. And the first person you have to be honest with is yourself. — L.F. McCOLLUM, Chairman, Continental Oil Company.   (715)

HOUSING

The day is fast approaching when our Government will compel cities to house their needy citizens properly, just as cities are now required to educate all children. — CHARLES F. PALMER, President, Palmer, Inc., Atlanta, Georgia.   (716)

HOUSING – Peace

Slum clearance and rehousing is the greatest force for peace in the world today. Good housing makes contented families. Contented families are not restless. "Isms" do not attract them. – CHARLES F. PALMER, President, Palmer, Inc., Atlanta, Georgia. (717)

HUMAN AIDS

I place the Ten Commandments, the Golden Rule, our Constitution, and the Bill of Rights as the best human navigational aids ever conceived by man. – CHARLES L. GOULD, Newspaperman. (718)

HUMAN BEINGS

The human being does not stand still – either he slips backward or he strides forward. – ELMER G. LETERMAN, *The Sale Begins When the Customer Says "No"* (Macfadden-Bartell). (719)

HUMAN BEINGS – Progress

Human beings tend to be both dynamic and inert. They desire the abundance that progress makes possible, but they resist paying the price of progress – change – especially changes which interfere with their habitual way of doing things; which entail inconvenience and discipline and some measure of hardship; which create an element of uncertainty about the future. – RICHARD J. ANTON, Manager, Business Education Service, General Electric Company.
(720)

HUMAN BRAIN

A man is not paid for having brains but for using them. – ELMER G. LETERMAN, *Gold Book,* New York Life Insurance Company. (721)

HUMANITIES

The humanities are furnishing a language, not only to enable scientists and non-scientists to talk to each other, but they are also providing a common language for today's many different specialists. In technical communities nowadays, there are men and women working on rocket fuels or the metallurgy of nickel, whose fields of activity are as different as those of an FBI agent and a sailor. – J. PAUL AUSTIN, President, The Coca-Cola Company. (722)

HUMAN MIND

The struggle for world domination that now engages our attention is being fought in many places and with many weapons. But the ultimate weapon is now as it has been always . . . the human mind. — JOHN ALSOP, President, The Mutual Insurance Company, Hartford, Connecticut. (723)

Through the years, proponents of physical fitness have offered us a multitude of activities to tone up the muscles of the body — everything from the simpler techniques, like running-in-place and isometric exercises, to the more elaborate programs like those offered at health resorts. But little has been provided to help us tone up our mental muscles, even though we are told the mind may be the least developed part of the body in terms of our using it to full capacity. — M. J. WARNOCK, President, Armstrong Cork Company. (724)

HUMAN ORGANIZATION

The first human organization was a very simple one: one man and one woman: one Adam and one Eve. The organization was simple. But they managed to get one another into an extraordinary amount of trouble. — F.J. BORCH, President and Chief Executive Officer, General Electric Company. (725)

HUMAN RELATIONS

The greatest problem of business — and of the world — is the problem of human relations . . . of the dignity of man . . . and of the sacredness of human rights. — HARVEY C. JACOBS, Under Secretary, Rotary International, Evanston, Illinois. (726)

It (human relations) is an art and not a science. Too often we see really brilliant people fail because they do not understand and practice the Art of Human Relations. They don't know how to work with people. In practicing the Art of Human Relations, things are not always clear-cut. It isn't all "black and white" — there is a lot of "grey." — LEE S. BICKMORE, President, National Biscuit Company. (727)

People live together because they can't exist separately. And while it is true that they sometimes can't endure one another, that they constantly make trouble for one another, and that they make of human relations an almost impossible problem — nevertheless people live together in a society because they need one another. — RALPH M. BESSE, President, The Cleveland Electric Illuminating Company. (728)

135

HUMILITY

We must somehow face the problems of our time with humility rather than cynicism. — ROBERT ALAN CHARPIE, BS, MS, D.Sc, Director of Technology, Union Carbide Corporation, New York.

(729)

HUNGER

If we agree that we are going to attack hunger world-wide, we are taking on an obligation of tremendous enormity. Even the thought of overcoming human misery on such a scale tends to numb our capacity to comprehend it. Nor should we forget that hunger is merely one visible part of a mass of related complex problems. Hunger sticks out like the tip of an iceberg we see above water. Looming under the surface are such involvements as economics, culture, ideology, education, agriculture, administration, industrialization, and politics on every level from the international down to the smallest rural hamlet. — A.N. McFARLANE, Chairman, Corn Products Company.

(730)

I think we all know that the stork has outpaced the plough. . . . The sight of a ragged child bloated with hunger and racked by malnutrition must fill us with compassion, and the grim knowledge that there are millions of such children must compel us to action. — LOUIS B. LUNDBORG, Chairman, Bank of America N.T. and S.A.

(731)

HUNGER — Automation

To me, the great promise of the thing we call automation is that it may help us solve one overriding global problem. Today, nearly one third of the world is hungry. Men still face the age-old problem of scarcity — of a grinding poverty which more and more splits the top half of the globe from the bottom half. — THOMAS J. WATSON, Jr., Chairman of the Board, IBM Company.

(732)

I

IDEALS

Ideals live only as long as they are upheld by the conscientious and consistent efforts of men. — JAMES M. ROCHE, President, General Motors. (733)

IDEAS

Ideas are dynamic forces which take form in action and mold practical affairs. They are not pale and insubstantial shadows. They are not pretty baubles with which the mind plays games. Every practical "thing" began as an idea. — ELMER G. LETERMAN, *Commissions Don't Fall from Heaven* (MacFadden-Bartell). (734)

The most important things in life are ideas. Ideas make money, win or lose wars, create new industries, sell products and generally make life worth living. — GLENN TALBOTT, President, Dairymen's League, *Dairymen's League News.* (735)

The seeming suddenness with which a brilliant idea bursts on us is the boiling point of thoughts long on fire. It is neither accident nor inspiration. — ELMER G. LETERMAN. (736)

In searching for big ideas most of us are overlooking dozens of little ideas. The little ideas are perfectly good; often they are better than the new and so-called big ideas. — WILLIAM FEATHER, William Feather Company, *William Feather Magazine,* (737)

When an idea comes to you, call up various ways in which you can express it. Everyone has the power to do this in some degree. — ELMER G. LETERMAN, *Nylic Review,* New York Life Insurance Company. (738)

Victor Hugo said there is one thing mightier than the tread of marching armies and that is the power of an idea whose hour has come. It may be your idea, or it may be the idea of someone else, but this is the way crises are solved, and progress is achieved. The tool which is used may be government or it may be something else, but it will be the idea which will make the whole thing possible. — LAMMOT DU PONT COPELAND, President, E.I. Du Pont de Nemours & Company, *Quote.* (739)

In these changing times, ideas are the life blood which will keep us moving forward. These ideas may come to us from unexpected places — and we must be open-minded enough to welcome them. — MARTIN J. CASERIO, General Manager, Delco Radio Division, General Motors Corporation, Kokomo, Indiana.   (740)

IDEAS — Conformity
   Strangely, the expounders of many of the great new ideas of history frequently were considered on the lunatic fringe for some or all of their lives. If you stand up and are counted, from time to time you may get yourself knocked down. But remember this: A man flattened by an opponent can get up again. A man flattened by conformity stays down for good. — THOMAS J. WATSON, Jr., Chairman of the Board, IBM Corporation.   (741)

IDEAS — Response
   People respond to an idea in which they see real benefits for themselves. — E.M. CLARK, President, Southwestern Bell Telephone Company, St. Louis, Missouri.   (742)

IMAGE
   Today ... thousands of normal people have become concerned about their "image," and a new concept has come into popular use. Nearly all of us are image-conscious. — HARVEY C. JACOBS, Under Secretary, Rotary International, Evanston, Illinois.   (743)

INDIFFERENCE
   Too many times when men get a big position, they start to rest on their laurels. They climb a little way, put in effect new and oftentimes much needed reforms or changes. Then they level off. They feel so comfortable on the new plateau, they just settle back and say, "here we go — I will slide along." At this point, the three "I" sins usually show up: Indifference, Ignorance and Indecision. Sometimes people settle down so hard, they flatten out. — LEE S. BICKMORE, President, National Biscuit Company.   (744)

INDIVIDUALITY
   In a mass production economy the individual is so highly specialized that he loses sight of his end product and its place in the world. This is true of the manager and worker in big business, and of the citizen and civil servant in big government. Work is fragmented; it is too easy to view life from a fragmented perspective. Keeping alive the reality of individualism in the larger society of the twentieth century is a great challenge for us all. — GABRIEL HAUGE, Vice

Chairman of the Board, Manufacturers Hanover Trust Company, New York. (745)

INDIVIDUAL LIBERTY
On no other matter is the U.S. watched more closely by the rest of the world than on the matter of individual liberty. If America cannot guarantee individual freedom to every citizen of the United States, how can we expect to exert leadership in a world where the majority of the population is non-white? — CHARLES H. PERCY, President, Bell & Howell Company, Chicago, Illinois. (746)

Certainly every fair-minded person is in favor of doing everything possible to extend individual liberties. It is these liberties that have made this nation the great nation that it is. However, we must maintain a constant vigil lest in our zeal to extend democracy, we end up destroying the very institutions that have made democracy possible. I say constant vigil because virtually every time we seek to extend one man's liberties we risk limiting another's. — STANFORD SMITH, General Manager, American Newspaper Publishers Association. (747)

INDIVIDUALS — Assistance
The sooner we, in this country, understand that we are dealing with people and not statistics and begin giving individuals genuine help and encouragement in advancing toward their personal aspirations, the nearer we will be to solving our national problems. We must see to it that all of our people have access to education, training and opportunity for meaningful work — rather than reducing millions of them to accepting life-long "handouts" from the Federal Government. — GEORGE CHAMPION, Chairman of the Board, The Chase Manhattan Bank. (748)

INDIVIDUALS — Dignity
Our Creator sublimely designed men and women to be free and their faces and bodies to be beautiful, and their freedom of expression, creativity, and action to be a part of that beauty. But today we have denied this dignity of the individual in much of our American life — and the dignity of the individual person, in much of the world beyond our shores, has been destroyed by political, economic, and spiritual slavery. — BAY E. ESTES, Jr., Vice President, Marketing, United States Steel Corporation. (749)

139

INDIVIDUALS – Identity.

We live in a world where the individual is losing his identity. We are numbers to our banker, to the tax collector, to the social security department. Those nostalgic telephone exchange names, full of associations, are gradually disappearing and we are getting all-number dialing and without the voice of the operator, except occasionally on unresponsive tape. We live in zip code areas and are identified by credit card numbers. – JACK I. STRAUS, Chairman, R.H. Macy & Company, Inc. (750)

INDIVIDUALS – Power

Individual excellence and enterprise are America's greatest strengths. Too often, in this day of centralization, uniformity and conformity, the power of the individual has been over looked. – ROBERT R. SPITZER, Businessman. (751)

INDIVIDUALS – Recognition

Every great society in history – from the Greek city state to the true American democracy, was founded on recognition and respect for the individual. These societies grew and prospered as the dynamic contribution of the individual was encouraged to flower. These same societies decayed as individuals were restricted and oppressed. How often we forget this lesson of history. – ROBERT G. WINGERTER, President, Rockwell-Standard Corporation Automotive Divisions.

(752)

INDIVIDUALS – Support

Anyone who has come to believe that he has a right to be supported from the cradle to the grave, regardless of his personal contribution, has not only become of very little value to society – but he has become of very little value to himself. All the fun has gone out of his life. – JACK I. STRAUS, Chairman, R.H. Macy & Co., Inc. (753)

INDUSTRIAL PLANTS – Future

The typical plant of the future may be characterized by the separation of men and machines. Plant designers will plan one facility to house a process and another facility to house the people who either run that process or handle the management and clerical jobs connected with a modern day corporation. – FRANK L. WHITNEY, President, Walter Kidde Constructors, Inc., New York. (754)

INDUSTRY

Industry is not a bottomless well of money for either employees or the tax collector. If industry is not allowed to be prosperous and to produce at its potential capacity, we are all the losers. — EDWIN M. CLARK, President, Southwestern Bell Telephone Company, St. Louis, Missouri. (755)

Our immediate concern must be to be competitive with other countries. The long range concern is that we must not fall so far behind any country that it will be able to dominate this country. — MARTIN J. CASERIO, General Manager, Delco Radio Division, General Motors Corporation, Kokomo, Indiana. (756)

Industry in this country, as the seat of responsibility for most of our productivity, is the central source of power for good or for evil, and as such is instrumental in effecting the changes which take place in our society. We cannot give lip service to social progress; we must believe in it, we must work for it, and we must achieve it. — JOSEPH C. WILSON, President, Xerox Corporation, *Quote.* (757)

A company needs to be constantly rejuvenated by the infusion of young blood. It needs smart young men with the imagination and the guts to turn everything upside down if they can. It also needs old fogies to keep them from turning upside down those things that ought to be right side up. Above all, it needs young rebels and old conservatives who can work together, challenge each other's views, yield or hold fast with equal grace, and continue after each hard-fought battle to respect each other as men and as colleagues. — HENRY FORD II, *Quote.* (758)

INDUSTRY — Craftsmanship

There is, today, in industry an appalling lack of craftsmanship and pride in craftsmanship. — E.F. SCOUTTEN, Vice-President, Personnel, The Maytag Company. (759)

INDUSTRY — Managers

It is my belief that the role of manager in industry is the same today as it was yesterday. And I suspect it will be the same tomorrow. The tools are changing — and a good manager will have the ability to adapt to the changes. But the role is the same — performance. — WILLIAM T. INGRAM, Vice President, Executive Sales, Reynolds Metals Company. (760)

INDUSTRY — Men

The men most sought today (in industry) are those who have the qualities of self-reliance, courage, resourcefulness and the independence of judgment that all through history have distinguished superior men from their inferiors. — Dr. GEORGE L. HALLER, Vice President, General Electric Company. (761)

INDUSTRY — Science
Our job in industry is to assimilate the scientific revolution in such a way that practical values will flow to the public, to society at large, in the most orderly and economical way. — FREDERICK R. KAPPEL, Chairman of the Board, American Telephone and Telegraph Company. (762)

INFLATION
Creeping inflation at the rate of 1% to 2% a year is not much of a problem, over comparatively short periods of time, for the wage earner whose income continues to rise. But it is an entirely different situation for retired people and widows who may have to think in terms of 20 years or longer. Over two decades even a slow rate of inflation will raise havoc with income. Persons who 20 or 30 years ago thought that they had an adequate income from bond interest or annuities now find themselves destitute at today's cost of living. — HEINZ H. BIEL, *Forbes.* (763)

We must set an example in controlling inflation. Once inflation gets rolling in the United States, the impact cannot be resisted even in the strongest countries. — GEORGE CHAMPION, Chairman of the Board, The Chase Manhattan Bank. (764)

The systematic erosion of the dollar's purchasing power has sent us on a kind of inflationary joyride . . . and has hurt each and every one of us, young and old. — LOGAN T. JOHNSTON, President, Armco Steel Corporation, Middletown, Ohio. (765)

INFLATION — Poverty
Inflation is creating new classes of poor faster than any poverty program can help them. — WENDELL WYATT, *Public Utilities Fortnightly.* (766)

INFLATION — Wage Increases
The depression and wartime deficit spending fed the fires of inflation. This led to the bad habit of annual rounds of wage lifting. Let's stop inflation and abandon the automatic annual wage increases. — ARTHUR H. MOTLEY, President, Chamber of Commerce of the United States. (767)

142

INITIATIVE

In all the wailing we hear about the loss of various vague freedoms, we are in danger of losing our most important freedom — namely, the freedom to take a risk, rely on ourselves, and stand or fall by the results. One of our inalienable rights is the right to do our own job in our own way, and abide by the consequences — in other words, the right to lose our shirt trying, if that's what we want to do. — ROGER HULL, President, Mutual of New York, *Quote*.   (768)

INNOVATION

As a society, we must learn to manage the impact of innovation as well as to promote the introduction of innovation. — ROBERT ALAN CHARPIE, BS, MS., D.Sc., Director of Technology, Union Carbide Corporation, New York.   (769)

Our position of world leadership ... will not be maintained unless we purge ourselves of attitudes which place a diminishing value on innovation. — DAUSE L. BIBBY, President, Remington Rand Division, Sperry Rand Corporation.   (770)

INSECURITY — Security

The feeling of being insecure starts early in life. For the baby in its crib, security is a warm blanket. For a nation, security may appear to be represented by tons of missiles and the industrial strength necessary to produce them. Security for most of us is a home, a job, our friends and neighbors, our religion, and many, many other things too numerous to catalog. It is the feeling that we possess the resources — material, physical, mental and spiritual — to meet the foreseeable hazards of life as they arise. — ROGER M. BLOUGH, Chairman of the Board, United States Steel Corporation.   (771)

INSURANCE

The level of security provided by government is not going to be sufficient for most of our people, whose incomes will permit them to supplement what the government provides. Private enterprise insurance must be prepared to build on the foundation that government lays, taking up where government leaves off and filling in the crevices and the unprotected areas. America's affluent society — and it must be remembered that this affluence reaches down to the level of the factory worker who usually has a considerable amount of income to expend at his own discretion — will demand more than government will provide, and it is up to private enterprise insurance to meet this need if it expects to minimize the further expansion of government programs. — J. CARROLL BATEMAN, President, The Insurance Information Institute. (772)

INTERNAL SECURITY
Internal security is not bequeathed to us; nor can it be acquired in one complete bundle with a lifetime guarantee. It is something which we build for ourselves, block by block, as we develop and mature. — ROGER M. BLOUGH, Chairman of the Board, United States Steel Corporation. (773)

INTERNATIONAL BUSINESS
The investor of today must expect to inherit a portion of the ill will incurred by the builders of some of the business empires of long ago, whose view of their duty to society was sometimes a long way from what you and I would espouse today. The pity is that this heritage of anti-foreignism, justified or not, should still haunt us like a ghost from the past in an age when international business has such a vital contribution to make in the developing nations. — DAVID A. SHEPARD, Director and Executive Vice President, Standard Oil Company (New Jersey). (774)

INTERNATIONAL FINANCE
It is fashionable in some quarters to look upon business and finance as being so preoccupied with production and profit that they have little concern for human nature. No better refutation of this belief could be found than international finance. More than any other aspect of the business system, it lives by the saying that "a man's word is as good as his bond." — GEORGE CHAMPION, Chairman of the Board, The Chase Manhattan Bank. (775)

INTERNATIONAL MANAGERS
In whatever place you work, you have an opportunity to be pioneers of the more abundant life to which humanity aspires. Your success or failure, as reported in your company balance sheets, will affect not just your personal prosperity and that of your investors, but the welfare of whole nations and regions. — DAVID A. SHEPARD, Director and Executive Vice President, Standard Oil Company (New Jersey). (776)

INTERNATIONAL MONETARY SYSTEM

Unless a nation has the basic character to put its own financial house in order, it will be in trouble regardless of what is done to reform the international monetary system. — GEORGE CHAMPION, Chairman of the Board, The Chase Manhattan Bank.   (777)

INTERNATIONAL RELATIONS

The one area of human relations where we are still comparatively closest to the jungle and most greatly in need of more civilized patterns of expectation is that of international relations. However, in view of the revolutionary reorientation within the social sciences that is in the making, I think there is good reason to hope that here too, during the next generation, we shall succeed in abandoning what has been referred to as the delicate balance of terror in favor of a more civilized pattern of behavior within the society of nations. — OLAF HELMER, Senior Mathematician, The Rand Corporation.   (778)

INVENTION

Invention is a combination of brains and material. The more brains you use, the less material you need. — CHARLES F. KETTERING.   (779)

INVENTION — Failure

A study made a number of years ago said the more education a man has, the less likely he is to be an inventor. Now the reason for that is quite simple. From the time the boy, or girl, starts in school he is examined three or four times a year, and, of course, it is a very disastrous thing if he fails. An inventor fails all the time and it is a triumph if he succeeds once. Consequently, if education is an inhibition to invention, it is due entirely to the form by which we rate things and not because of any intellectual differential. — CHARLES F. KETTERING.   (780)

ISOLATIONISM

Die-hard isolationism is passing out of the picture — and it has even less of a following in the once notoriously isolationist Middle West than in the country as a whole. — ELMO ROPER, Public Opinion Analyst.   (781)

J

JOB INTEREST

There are very few jobs that can hold a man's interest more than five years. After that time he isn't innovating; he's minding the store. — LESTER J. WEIGLE, Humble Oil & Refining Company, *Personnel Administration*. (782)

JOBS — Downgraded

The social status symbol of "college" has actually cast a stigma on many needed, important, and worthwhile occupations. If you have tried to have a lawn mowed, or a car washed, or a wood lot cleaned up, or a TV or radio set properly serviced, or a leak in the roof patched, or someone in to help clean the house, or a homemaker to whom you really felt comfortable in delegating the responsibility for the care of your house and your children while the wife was away, you know what I mean. Thousands of needed, honest, paying jobs go unfilled. Countless thousands more go slackly, slovenly, disgracefully, poorly done because we have downgraded them in our own and in everyone's estimation. — Dr. VAN W. BEARINGER, Vice President and General Manager, Systems and Research Division, Honeywell Inc. (783)

JOHNSON, LYNDON B.

No President in history has known the travail, the monumental significance of decision, the potential of danger that has befallen Lyndon Johnson. He is a harried, beleaguered man — and just a mere man. He is not sainted, he has no mystic power to brush away awesome predicaments and problems. . . . He is only a man, a troubled man who throughout his life has sought the rewards of political life and now he has reached a zenith of achievement — only to find the terrible responsibility that is part of the trappings. — FELIX R. McKNIGHT, Executive Vice President and Editor, *The Dallas Times Herald*. (784)

President Lyndon Johnson is the direct spiritual heir of a number of the great American Presidents. The first is President Jefferson. President Johnson has done something more than merely adopt President Jefferson's theory of government. He has elaborated it into

146

the most effective method of party responsibility in the history of our country. — Hon. JAMES A. FARLEY, Chairman of the Board, Coca-Cola Export Corporation. (785)

JOURNALISM SCHOOLS
We are willing to pour millions into medical schools to produce people who try to cure our bodily and mental ills — and that's important — or into producing lawyers who seem to be primarily interested in protecting property rights, or in turning out engineers and scientists on a mass-production basis, but we spend precious little in producing people who have the instrument, and sometimes the will, to protect the only thing that really means anything in the missile-hydrogen world — our civilization, imperfect as it is, at home and abroad. — MARK ETHRIDGE, Chairman of the Board, *The Louisville Courier-Journal* and *The Louisville Times*. (786)

JOURNALISTS — The Press
The journalist has never been so critical of himself, and the public never so critical of the press, as in the last few years. — ARVILLE SCHALEBEN, Executive Editor, *The Milwaukee Journal,* (787)

JUDGMENT
Goethe once said that "Art is long, life short and judgment difficult." He was right. Judgment is difficult, extremely difficult. And for this reason, it is an indispensable characteristic of the successful executive. A man may be an encyclopedia of business knowledge, but unless he is able to demonstrate sound judgment in his decisions, then he can never reach the top positions. — DON H. MILLER, President, Skelly Oil Company. (788)

JUVENILE DELINQUENCY
I strongly suspect that children today are much the same as children have always been. But the world they live in is radically different — increasingly so. What was considered perfectly normal and even delightful conduct for a couple of boys in Hannibal, Missouri, during Mark Twain's day, would be regarded as serious delinquency by the citizens of Hannibal in 1962. — LEROY COLLINS, President, National Association of Broadcasters. (789)

JUVENILES — Crime
The most terrible indictment of contemporary society lies in the

147

stark fact that the crimes of violence committed on our city's streets are increasingly committed by juveniles. Listen, human beings are not born bad; they are made bad by bad environment, by bad homes, by inadequate schools, by slum living, by being allowed to grow up hopelessly unfit for any useful employment in the community. — ALAN BARTH, Editorial Board, *Washington Post.*   (790)

K

KNOW-HOW

There is very little in which we pride ourselves more in this country than know-how. And there is very little with which we are more generous in industry than know-how. We are not only sure we have it in abundance, we are also sure that if there is any more of it we need, we can get it. — Colonel BARNEY OLDFIELD, U.S.A.F. (Ret.) of Litton Industries, Inc.   (791)

KNOWLEDGE

Most men can learn anything, but it's a clever man who knows what to learn. The basis for everything we hope to achieve in life depends upon our ability to consume, digest, and employ knowledge. — A.J. BARRAN, President, General Telephone Company of Indiana, *Public Utilities Fortnightly.*   (792)

Now, much has been said about various types of explosions, from population to atomic. But overlooked, it seems to me, is the greatest explosion of all — the explosion of knowledge. This is a chain reaction, because the greatest advances in knowledge are the developments and discoveries by which still more knowledge is being acquired. — JAMES A. FARLEY, Chairman of the Board, Coca-Cola Export Corporation.   (793)

We hear a lot about the population explosion in the world. But we are in the midst of a much more important explosion — a knowledge explosion. — L.F. McCOLLUM, Chairman, Continental Oil Company.   (794)

KNOWLEDGE — Action

A man can know all there is to know about farming, and in addition be chairman of his board of deacons, president of his civic club, and head of the school board; but he will never grow a cabbage or harvest a boll of cotton until he does something about farming. — ED LIPSCOMB, National Cotton Council, Memphis, Tennessee.   (795)

KNOWLEDGE — Automation

I believe in the infinite expansion of human knowledge. In this expansion, automation is a powerful asset — possibly the greatest concept since movable type. — THOMAS J. WATSON, Jr., Chairman of the Board, IBM Company. (796)

KNOWLEDGE — Obsolescence

Knowledge grows and declines in usefulness so rapidly that we are hard put just to keep up, much less to move ahead, in our professions. It has been said, and I think truly so, that a technical man's knowledge goes out of date so fast that if he did not keep up with new developments, he would be obsolete in ten years. In fact, one educator has suggested that diplomas awarded to technical graduates be made of paper that would disintegrate in ten years. — CHARLES F. JONES, President, Humble Oil & Refining Company, *Journal of Marketing,* American Marketing Association.

(797)

KNOWLEDGE — Security

In a sense, knowledge is the set of tools which we carry around in our heads or in our hands; and as they become inadequate in number — or as they become rusty and obsolete — so does our security diminish. Conversely, as we add to this kit of tools — as we modernize them, increase their precision, and develop new skills in their use — our security is multiplied accordingly. — ROGER M. BLOUGH, Chairman of the Board, United States Steel Corporation.

(798)

KNOWLEDGE — Wisdom

The old proverb that knowledge comes but wisdom lingers certainly never had more meaning than it does today. If our need is great for knowledge, it is greater far still for wisdom. — RICHARD H. AMBERG, Publisher, *The St. Louis Globe-Democrat.* (799)

L

LABOR

We have reached a state in our national development where we are waiting on a lagging member of our economic family to catch up. Labor is a part of our team, but it's behind the times. Capital has grown wiser, management more efficient, the customer more discriminating, but labor clings to its old-time privileges like an insecure child hanging onto a familiar toy. — ALLAN SHIVERS, President, Chamber of Commerce of the United States.   (800)

I am disturbed that year after year, nothing is done to moderate the excessive powers of labor unions under the law. Irresponsible unions indulge in senseless strikes that do great harm to the public, in order to enforce demands that limit productivity, increase inflationary pressure and reduce employment. — HENRY FORD, II.   (801)

LABOR — Capital

The true objectives of labor and capital are in a very real sense the same, although sometimes it doesn't look that way. — HENRY T. BODMAN, Chairman of the Board, National Bank of Detroit. (802)

LABOR — Collective Bargaining

Since there is no effective alternative to collective bargaining in a democratic society, why don't we concentrate more on trying to make it work better than to seek always to replace it. — THEODORE W. KHEEL, Arbitrator to the National Industrial Conference Board, *Machinist.*   (803)

LABOR — Farm Workers

The farm worker is a forgotten man in this country. The yellow-dog contract (an employment contract in which the employee agrees not to join a union) and the black list is to you a dirty page in the history of labor. To us it is as modern as a supersonic plane. — CESAR CHAVEZ, President, National Farm Workers Association, *Quote.*   (804)

LABOR — Management

U.S. labor and management works harder, more efficiently, and

151

more intelligently than in any country I have visited or that I am aware of. This is fundamentally the reason for the superior standard of living we enjoy in the U.S. — ROBERT G. WINGERTER, President, Libbey-Owens-Ford Glass Company. (805)

The free world is torn by class divisions — owners and managers on the one hand and workers on the other. There is conflict between them as to how they shall share the products of the machines. The workers think the owners don't give them enough and they turn to giant labor unions and to Government to give them a larger share. Our freedom will not be secure until that basic conflict is resolved. It can be resolved by making the interests of owner-managers and workers identical. — EDWARD J. MEEHAN, Editor, *Memphis Press-Scimitar*. (806)

LABOR — Strikes

The right to strike, the freedom to leave work in protest over wages, hours, and working conditions is part of the price we pay for democracy. But the right to strike like nearly all rights recognized by a democratic society is not an absolute one. It is limited by the obligation to respect the rights of others. This is the duty those who have the fight to strike must bear. — PETER J. PESTILLO, Labor Relations Manager of the Chamber of Commerce of the United States. (807)

Willingness on the part of the public, government and management to accept a strike, if necessary, is part of the price we must pay for the preservation of free and responsible collective bargaining. — HENRY FORD, II, *Quote*. (808)

It is my belief . . . that wage disputes are less frequently the cause of strikes and work stoppages than other questions. — IRVING STERN, Director of Organization of the Amalgamated Meat Cutters and Retail Food Store Employees Union of Greater New York. (809)

The strike originally was developed as an economic weapon with which unions could pressure the enterprise for which management is accountable, so as to achieve better wages, hours, or working conditions for employees. The main source of public agitation now. . . is basically this: that the strike has now become a weapon, used by unions still, but which injures the public almost more than management or the enterprise at time. — VIRGIL B. DAY, Vice President, Personnel and Industrial Relations Service, G.E. Company. (810)

LABOR UNIONS

I believe that unions, where needed and when properly operated, have much to offer our progressive economic society. — MAURICE R. FRANKS, President, National Labor-Management Foundation, Chicago, Illinois and Editor of *Partners Magazine.*   (811)

I believe that unions should be what they orginally started out to be — namely, purely voluntary organizations. There should be no place in America for the closed shop, the union shop or any other kind of shop which makes payment of union dues the price of a job.)— JOHN DAVENPORT, Board of Editors, *Fortune Magazine.*   (812)

I am disturbed that year after year, nothing is done to moderate the excessive powers of labor unions under the law. Irresponsible unions indulge in senseless strikes that do great harm to the public, in order to enforce demands that limit productivity, increase inflationary pressures and reduce employment. It seems to me that we could find ways to correct the abuses committed by some unions without impairing the ability of unions to carry out their important, legitimate functions in our economy. — HENRY FORD, II, Chairman of the Board, Ford Motor Company.   (813)

LABOR UNIONS — Management

Unions, after all, are political organizations, in the sense that they are elected by employees, but it is up to management to help to make the climate in which it can be "good politics" for unions to follow policies which assist rather than harm the interests of the enterprise of which the employees are a part. Only in this way can unions and management combine in making possible the fullest employment of American industry in the service of the nation and the security of its people. — R. HEATH LARRY, Administrative Vice President, Labor Relations, United States Steel Corporation.   (814)

LANGUAGE — English

We need to know English and its flexible uses if we are to live successfully in a day when communication — clear, persuasive, effective communication — is a vital necessity. — ARTHUR P. LIEN, Research and Development Department, American Oil Company, Whiting, Indiana.   (815)

LANGUAGE — Foreign

We need to know foreign languages in order to survive without catastrophe in a world gone small as a man's fist. — ARTHUR P.

LIEN, Research and Development Department, American Oil Company, Whiting, Indiana. (816)

LANGUAGE – Teenagers

Those of us who are required to establish some form of communication with teen-agers had better stick to our own particular idiom of American English, or risk making damn fools of ourselves. It won't work for parents – and it might be disastrous for advertisers – to try to get chummy with teen-agers by telling them that their products are "boss, tough, out of sight, fab or dyno." Even though "bad" means "good" in teen, it could prove confusing and downright embarrassing for a client to say his product is bad. – PAUL C. HARPER, Jr., President, Needham, Harper & Stears, Inc. (817)

LATIN AMERICA

United States businesses operating in Latin American supply one-tenth of Latin America's production, pay one-fifth of all taxes and account for a third of all export earnings. An estimated 1,500,000 Latin Americans are employed by United States businesses, in many cases at higher wages than they would earn in other, local industries. United States citizens, on the other hand, account for only two percent of all employees of United States firms in Latin America. The United States investment in Latin America has fortunately been moderately successful on balance, but it can hardly be called "exploitative." – DAVID ROCKEFELLER, *Foreign Affairs*. (818)

There is no such thing as Latin America, and when we drop into the habit of using that word we automatically begin to misunderstand our neighbors. – JOSHUA B. POWERS, President, Joshua B. Powers Inc., New York City. (819)

I believe . . . that Latin America is of prime importance to the security and economic well-being of the United States. . . . I believe . . . that Latin America should be given top priority in our foreign relations and foreign aid. – J. PETER GRACE, President, W.R. Grace & Company, New York City. (820)

This, then, is Latin America. Youthful, growing, idealistic, nationalistic, producer of much that we consume, purchaser of much that we produce, friend and ally who is gravely troubled by social, economic and political pressure and problems. An area of great opportunity for businessmen willing to assume responsibilities. – JOHN F. GALLAGHER, Vice President for foreign administration,

Sears, Roebuck & Company, Chicago, Illinois. (821)

Cuba has become the Red beachhead in Latin America which was sought for forty years. And the Communists are mounting a military and propaganda bastion there aimed at all of Latin America. — CHARLES NUTTER, Managing Director, International House, New Orleans, Louisiana. (822)

LATIN AMERICA — Agriculture

Over one-half of the labor force of Latin America is engaged in agriculture and yet less than one-fourth of the gross national product comes from this industry, indicating its backwardness. Less than 5 per cent of the landowners own 70 per cent of the land, and less than 5 per cent of the land is cultivated, compared with 18 per cent in the United States. In some countries such as Bolivia, Colombia, Peru and Venezuela less than 3 per cent of the land can be cultivated. — HERBERT V. PROCHNOW, President, First National Bank of Chicago, Illinois. (823)

LAUGHTER

Laughter today is stored in Hollywood in cans, just as the gold was once stored at Fort Knox. It is taken out as needed and pasted onto TV films. And the laugh track tips us off to when things are funny. — CHARLES H. BROWER, President, Batten, Barton, Durstine & Osborn, Inc., New York. (824)

LAW

Unless, and until, laws can be made applicable to all, democracy itself is a farce. — RAYMOND W. MILLER, President, Public Realtions Research Associates, Inc., Washington, D.C. (825)

Law is as necessary to a community as its daily bread. — Hon. JAMES A. FARLEY, Chairman of the Board, The Coca-Cola Corporation. (826)

It is observance of the law that enables communities, cities, states and the nation itself to function. It is the law which assures men and women that they may in confidence purchase homes, own life insurance and buy an automobile. It is the law which assures us that we may protect our rights in pensions and in the ownership of hard-earned savings. It is the law which protects us in a thousand simple commitments in life. It is the law which assures the equality of men and makes life a vital experience. Respect for the law is essential to the survival of freedom. — HERBERT V. PROCHNOW, President, First National Bank of Chicago. (827)

LAW — Enforcement

It is rather easy, as you know, to devise rules and laws. The difficulty is to make them effective. — ARVILLE SCHALEBEN, Executive Editor, *The Milwaukee Journal.* (828)

LAW — Justice

In spite of turmoils and tensions pressing from all parts of the globe, one of the most significant developments of our times is the determined effort to establish law and justice as the essential and decisive substitutes for force. — ANDREW R. CECIL, Executive Vice President, The Southwestern Legal Foundation. (829)

The law gives an American security in his rights, and the courts give him confidence that justice dwells among peers. Law and justice protect the individual, the family, enterprises and groups, and our country. — ARVILLE SCHALEBEN, Executive Editor, *The Milwaukee Journal.* (830)

LAW — Riots

No matter how serious our problems of poverty and prejudice might be, there can be no excuse for rioting. Law and order is not an academic platitude to be respected only when convenient. It is a fundamental basis of the American Way of Life. — RICHARD G. CAPEN, Jr., Director of Public Affairs, Copley Newspapers, La Jolla, California. (831)

LAW — Violation

In a democratic society, we cannot condone law violation even for ends recognized as laudable. Society cannot condone an end run around the field of representative government. It cannot condone the circumvention of democracy. Encouragement to such actions is an invitation to anarchy, and the permissive arbitrariness of anarchy is hardly less tolerable than the repressive arbitrariness of tyranny. Indeed, too often the license of liberty is followed by the loss of liberty, because into the desert of anarchy steps the Hitler or the Mussolini on horseback. — JAMES C. HUMES, Executive Director, Philadelphia Bar Association. (832)

LEADERS

Plenty of people would like to be successful, would like to be president of their company, would like to be a leader, but not enough of them are willing to make the sacrifices necessary to attain that important position. They won't prepare; they won't qualify themselves. They won't become completely involved. A successful man is a leader. A leader stands out in front. He is a director; he is a coordinator; he is a dreamer; he is a planner. — LEE S. BICKMORE, President, National Biscuit Company. (833)

LEADERS — Followers
Somewhere there is somebody who looks to each of us for leadership in some field. At the same time, however, leaders are also followers. Followers, in fact, are the backbone of every organization. They are the backbone of the nation itself. — E.M. CLARK, President, South Western Bell Telephone Company, *Quote*. (834)

LEADERS — Future
Our business and industrial leaders of tomorrow will have to be men and women able to communicate with one another and with other people in other places; people who will know how to transmit and stimulate ideas; who will recognize that things human and humane are even more important than the computer, the test tube or the slide rule; who will understand that "know-why" is as important as "know-how"; who will try to see our problems as part of total human experience; and who will be able to understand something of what yesterday teaches us about today. In short, we will need young people who will be able to dream dreams and who will be unafraid to try to make them come true. — SOL M. LINOWITZ, Chairman of the Board, Xerox Corporation. (835)

LEADERS — Leadership
Leadership in our society is widely diversified. We have business leaders, government leaders, union leaders, education leaders, as well as leaders in agriculture, the arts, sports, etc. Taken collectively, they greatly influence public opinion and ultimately determine our course as a nation. — GENE C. BREWER, President, United States Plywood Corporation. (836)

To lead others, you must first win their acceptance and confidence. — HERMAN C. KRANNERT, Chairman of the Board, Inland Container Corporation. (837)

LEADERSHIP
I think we must all agree that the manager is important to the company he works for. Any business today owes its corporate identity to the personality of its first line of management men. Morale, good or bad, always trickles down through the enterprise

from the executive leadership. Good leadership has the ability — indeed, it may be measured by its capacity — to get things done through people, and to inspire people to their best efforts. — FREDERICK J. CLOSE, Chairman of the Board, Aluminum Company of America. (838)

The price you pay for leadership is not comfort. The glory of life is that it is worth the struggle. There are no bargains or markdowns at the "leadership" counter, but the effort to achieve represents the finest genius given to man. — LEE S. BICKMORE, President, National Biscuit Company. (839)

We need bright people in industry, as in every other walk of life. But being bright is not enough. The person who aspires to leadership must be both imaginative and *patient*. He must deal with human beings. *They* are his raw material. — HERMAN C. KRANNERT, Chairman of the Board, Inland Container Corporation. (840)

One of the main objects of leadership in a business, it seems to me, is to do what you can to arrange things so that people can grow. — FREDERICK R. KAPPEL, Chairman of the Board, American Telephone and Telegraph Company. (841)

We are supposed to have a democracy of opportunity in this country, and that is as it should be. We would not be realistic, however, if we did not also recognize that we have an aristocracy of achievement, for human progress is never automatic. It is necessary for someone to do something about something to have progress. The few who can be expected to do something are people who have minds receptive to ideas and ideals, who have imagination, and who have the courage to act. They are also the people who accept personal responsibility to see that what is worthwhile gets done. — LAMMOT DU PONT COPELAND, President, Du Pont de Nemours & Company, *Quote.* (842)

LEADERSHIP — Communication

Successful leaders of all ages from Saint Paul at Corinth to Winston Churchill during the Battle of Britain have found that effective leadership came about largely through effective communication. This is as basic and valid today as when Paul took the road to Corinth. The only difference is that in our time the importance of communication has grown very greatly. — HAROLD BRAYMAN, Director, Public Relations Department, E.I. du Pont de Nemours & Company. (843)

158

LEARNING

You can *never* stop learning if you expect to be a success. – L.F. McCOLLUM, Chairman, Continental Oil Company.　　　(844)

I say the classroom is an archaic device whose main purpose was to convene a group of students in one place with light and heat – and a teacher. Aren't we ready to admit that learning can take place wherever a student can read a book, watch a picture, hear a voice, ask a question. – RALF BRENT, President, Radio New York Worldwide (WRUL).　　　(845)

LECTURERS – Lectures

Lectures can make an audience feel dumb on one end and numb on the other, but they also can reveal the lecturer as both completely dumb and numb. – ARVILLE SCHALEBEN, Executive Editor, *The Milwaukee Journal.*　　　(846)

LEGISLATORS – Mail

A legislator reads his mail. He is guided by it. Not by pressure of sheer weights of numbers. Rather, by the thought-provoking letters from constituents who know what they're talking about. It is *important* that you write. It's *more* important that you know *what* you're writing about. Remember, he wants to know what *you* think. – WILLARD M. WILSON, Secretary, American Petroleum Institute.　　　(847)

LEISURE

I believe wise use of leisure time is of extreme importance to the American people as individuals and as a nation. For leisure is more than a by-product of work. It is an asset produced by work. At our time in history we cannot afford to waste it as too many of us are doing. – LAURANCE S. ROCKEFELLER, Chairman, Outdoor Recreation Resources Review Commission.　　　(848)

In our swiftly changing business environment, no one can foresee precisely what problems will have to be resolved in the future. But whatever they are, they will call for intelligence, imagination, resourcefulness and judgment – for these qualities never become obsolete. So we should use our periods of leisure to develop the whole man. – DAVID ROCKEFELLER, President, Chase Manhattan Bank.　　　(849)

I believe in the enlargement of constructive leisure. I do not agree with the prediction that the American people can conquer any enemy and overwhelm every challenge except spare time. –

THOMAS J. WATSON, Jr., Chairman of the Board, IBM Company. (850)

LEISURE — Culture
Mainly through the impetus provided by our business corporations, we have achieved in the United States a material abundance and a growing leisure unprecedented in history. It is sadly evident, though, that our cultural attainments have not kept pace with improvements in other fields. As people's incomes have risen, a proportionate share has not been devoted to artistic and intellectual pursuits. As leisure has increased, so has the amount of time given to unproductive and often aimless activities. — DAVID ROCKEFELLER, President, Chase Manhattan Bank. (851)

LETTER WRITING
Every letter writer's fairy godmother should provide him not only with a pen but also with a blue pencil — a good writer is one who knows also what not to write. Too many letters and reports, talks and conferences are long simply from lack of patience; it would have taken too long to have made them short. — LAWRENCE A. DYSART, Richfield Oil Corporation. (852)

LIBERTY
I believe nothing is more precious to our people than that inviolable individual liberty which recognizes the right and the dignity and the independence of every man and woman. — WARD L. QUAAL, Executive Vice President and General Manager, WGN, Inc., Chicago, Illinois. (853)

Our big threat is not some foreign military force in a far-off place. The real threat comes from what has been described as — "Revolution by Nibbling" — from the gradual erosion of liberty by well-intentioned men and women of zeal, encouraged by complacent citizens willing to let those who know more about government take care of such things. The preservation of liberty is a contest, but it is not a spectator sport. We cannot remain on the sidelines while professionals play the game for us. — WILLARD M. WILSON, Secretary, American Petroleum Institute. (854)

History has proved that individual liberty reaches its fullest expression in a free market economy where responsible men may and do seek work and reward according to their aspirations and talents. — WARD L. QUAAL, Executive Vice President and General Manager, WGN, Inc., Chicago, Illinois. (855)

160

LIBRARIES

The great contribution of the free public library is its untrammeled dedication to the individual and his own reading and learning needs as he sees them. It serves individual initiative and respects the dignity and privacy of each reader. In these terms the public library is a bastion of American society. — ROBERT VOSPER, President, American Library Association. (856)

LIFE

Of all the lessons I have learned, I think the most important of all is that life is a game and if played right can be a tremendous amount of fun. — GORDON SMITH, Vice President, Remington Rand Division, Sperry Rand Corporation. (857)

LIFE — Business, Personal

No one can separate the business life from the personal life of an individual. The two are interwoven together; they are the various threads of the same cloth; and they add up to one personality, one total life. — ELMER G. LETERMAN, *The Sale Begins When the Customer Says "No"* (MacFadden-Bartell). (858)

LIFE — Limitations

Life does not limit us as much as we limit ourselves. — L.F. McCOLLUM, Chairman, Continental Oil Company. (859)

LIFE — Living

It is a mistake to let life become complicated. Life is really very simple, and only by thinking of it in simple terms can it be mastered. — WILLIAM FEATHER, William Feather Company, *William Feather Magazine*. (860)

LIFE — Meaning

A person can never discover the meaning of life who does not know his own meaning, but if one does summon the courage to assign some meaning to himself, he will have, by the same insight, assigned a meaning to life. — JAMES O. DOBBS, Jr., Industrial Relations Consultant and Lecturer, Austin, Texas. (861)

LIFE — Religion

The key to man's greatest adventure — life — is religion. — ANDREW R. CECIL, Executive Vice President and Educational Director, The Southwestern Legal Foundation, Dallas, Texas. (862)

LIFE – Success

To succeed in life, we must have faith in others as well as in ourselves. We must be willing to tolerate a great deal, if we too are to be tolerated. For it's through genuine cooperation that the greatest personal and social good can be realized. – T.F. PATTON, President, Republic Steel Corporation, Cleveland, Ohio.   (863)

LISTENERS

A respectful listener not only makes a good impression – he stands a chance of learning something. – ELMER G. LETERMAN.
(864)

LISTENING

Develop the art of listening. Willingness to listen is a rewarding state of mind. You will never learn much if you insist upon being the only talker. – ROSCOE DRUMMOND, Editor and Columnist. (865)

LITERACY

We continually hear that nearly 8% of our adult population are college graduates, but no one mentions that nearly 9% of the same adult population are so illiterate they have difficulty reading a newspaper. Or that eleven and one half million adults have less than a sixth grade education; that twenty-three million never completed grade school; and 2.7 million have never been in school at all. – ERNEST JONES, President, McMannus, John & Adams Advertising Agency.   (866)

LITTER

A few years ago a Russian leader threatened to bury us, but there is the ever-present danger we will bury ourselves. – SMITH L. RAIRDON, President, Keep America Beautiful, *Quote*.   (867)

LIVING

In today's world, more than at any previous time, the business of living calls for broader and deeper understanding of the business of making a living. – CHARLES G. MORTIMER, Chairman of General Foods Corporation.   (868)

LIVING STANDARD

It is good for the country – not bad – to have ever higher standards of living. This is the only thing that makes sense in an economy of plenty like ours. It is more participation in the market-place — by more people — that builds the wider and stronger foundation that is necessary to our country's total strength. — M.C. PATTERSON, Vice President, Chrysler Corporation.   (869)

The great mass of the American people enjoy the highest level of living of any nation in all history. — ARCH N. BOOTH, Executive Vice President, Chamber of Commerce of the United States.   (870)

If we want to maintain and increase our high standard of living — both in the material and cultural sense — it is essential that the importance of the profit incentive be reaffirmed and encouraged by all sectors of the economy — by individuals as well as by the government. — JOHN D. HARPER, President, Aluminum Company of America, New York City.   (871)

The real test of the economic effectiveness of a country is the standard of living it attains for its people. — AMYAS AMES, President, Investment Bankers Association of America.   (872)

The American people have been given the highest standard of living in history. — HERBERT V. PROCHNOW, President, First National Bank of Chicago.   (873)

Our economic system has yielded the highest standard of living in the world, and even the impoverished among us are more fortunate than a majority of the people in a majority of the nations around the globe. — L.W. MOORE, President, American Oil Company.   (874)

LOS ANGELES — Freeway

I'm constantly amazed at the progress you're making in Los Angeles — especially in your Freeway system. I understand that during the morning rush hour, a man can now get from the San Fernando Valley to City Hall in twenty-five minutes — whether he wants to or not. — ROBERT W. SARNOFF, President, Radio Corporation of America.   (875)

LOVE

The most precious of human potentialities, love, is the law which will provide common values and aspirations to the community of free nations. This law is world-wide in character, but it has never been tried. We have thrown up our hands in despair over the wickedness of the world, leaving Christ standing outside the arena of life. Perhaps nothing less than faith and the law of love can save the world. — ANDREW R. CECIL, Executive Vice President, The Southwestern Legal Foundation.   (876)

163

LOVE – Hatred

People have to live for something. If they will not live for the love of something, they will live for the hatred of something. – HAROLD R. McKINNON, Attorney, Bronson, Bronson & McKinnon, San Francisco, California. (877)

LUCK

Ten minutes of good luck will make you forget all the bad luck you ever had. – WILLIAM FEATHER, William Feather Company, *William Feather Magazine.* (878)

LUCK – Opportunity

Luck is preparation meeting opportunity. – ELMER G. LETERMAN. (879)

M

MACHINE AGE

In the years ahead a steadily shrinking part of our population will be needed to produce all the goods and services even the most affluent society can absorb. It will simply not be economical to use people for the performance of machine-like jobs, and the range of what machines can do will become increasingly sophisticated, right up into the upper levels of management. – A.H. RASKIN, Assistant Editor, *New York Times* Editorial Page. (880)

MACHINES

The machine is diabolical if it overworks and enslaves man; if it produces more goods than he knows how to use and makes him poor in the midst of plenty. . . . The machine is heavenly if it is operated by man expressing his divine nature, which is intelligence and love. Then the machine blesses mankind. It then becomes a miracle for which we should praise God who has given such power unto men. – EDWARD J. MEEMAN, Editor, *Memphis Press-Scimitar.*
(881)

MACHINES – Man

A machine could never conceive even the rude elements of the Magna Carta or the Constitution of the United States of America. A machine will never learn to contemplate a sunset, respond as live men and women and even children have responded to *Hamlet* or a Beethoven symphony, or the promise of a better life. To do these things, you have to be human. – THOMAS J. WATSON, Jr., Chairman of the Board, IBM Company. (882)

MAGAZINES – Readers

The habits of the American reader are one of the most powerful and underrated forces in this country. When you hear that a famous magazine has died, remove your hat for a moment of silence – and then look about for the magazine that has crowded it out. It is the readers who force these changes, and what they want is something that is fresher and that comes closer to their interests. – EDWARD WEEKS, Editor, *Atlantic Magazine.* (883)

MAN

There is no real conflict between man and man, no real divergence of interests. If anything is not good for all men, it is not good for any man. There is seeming conflict, but it is only in the erring human mind and human emotions. — EDWARD J. MEEMAN, Editor Emeritus *The Memphis Press-Scimitar* and Conservation Editor of the Scripps-Howard Newspapers.   (884)

MAN — Growth

Every man grows into the image of that which he believes in his heart is the Good, the True and the Desirable. — ELMER G. LETERMAN, *Nylic Review,* New York Life Insurance Company.

(885)

MAN — Machines

No instrument, however versatile, and no system, however universal, can substitute for man's own will for truth and understanding. It can only provide the means. — ROBERT W. SARNOFF, President, Radio Corporation of America.   (886)

I have faith in two things: One is the beneficence of machines. The other is the perfectibility of human beings. — THOMAS J. WATSON, Jr., Chairman of the Board, IBM Company.   (887)

MAN — Nature

The challenge to us is to build and operate what we need in such a way that man can live in harmony with nature. — LAWRANCE S. ROCKEFELLER.   (888)

MAN — Potential

Even the best of us may never live up to our full potential because of lack of ambition, courage, or inner direction. — T.F. PATTON, President, Republic Steel Corporation, Cleveland, Ohio.

(889)

There are vast riches of human personality, intelligence and energy in our society which are only partially used. When I contrast what people are thinking, saying and doing with what they are capable of thinking, saying and doing, it seems to me that mankind is a race of sleep-walkers, only half alive. . . . Man needs to awaken his tremendous potentiality, now only half realized. — EDWARD J. MEEMAN, Editor Emeritus, *The Memphis Press Scimitar* and Conservation Editor of the Scripps-Howard Newspapers.   (890)

MAN — Underdeveloped

One problem facing our world today is the underdeveloped nation. But the underdeveloped man is a greater danger. — GUILFORD DUDLEY, Jr., President, Life and Casualty Insurance Company of Tennessee. (891)

MAN — World

It seems to me that the people who note that high speed transportation and instant communication are shrinking the size of the world miss the point. It is not the world which is shrinking, but the mind and soul of man which is expanding. — JAMES A. FARLEY, Chairman of the Board, Coca-Cola Export Corporation. (892)

Man today has the ability to reshape his world according to his desires. However, if his desires continue to violate the inherent requirements of his nature or destroy the world's capacity to support him, the human race itself will be destroyed. — ROBERT THEOBALD, Economist. (893)

MANAGEMENT

In an industrial and social society such as the one we have in the United States, the need for qualified managers is one of prime concern. Many are the organizations that have become statistics among those who "failed" because of inadequate or incompetent management. — LEONARD NADLER, President, Leadership Resources Inc., *Personnel Journal.* (894)

Good management consists of showing the average people how to do the work of superior people. — JOHN D. ROCKEFELLER, *Personnel Administration.* (895)

Management is an art, not a science. — WILLIAM T. INGRAM, Vice President, Executive Sales, Reynolds Metals Company. (896)

Management is one of the most commonplace activities in our lives. It is also one of the most complex. And like any activity in our civilized society, it is subject to constant change. But management is more than bookkeeping and warehousing, more than organized charts and chains of command. The supervision of men and resources is basic in its function. But the fundamental purpose of management is to bring cohesion and vitality to the human effort within its control — to change ideas and materials into units of greater value, to add value. — R.S. REYNOLDS, Jr., *Quote.* (897)

167

MANAGEMENT – Experience

In management, thirty years of experience does not count for much if it merely means ten times three of the same kind of experience. It is exposure to a variety of greatly differing situations that makes experience a treasurehouse. – NEIL J. McKINNON, Chairman, Canadian Imperial Bank of Commerce, *Public Utilities Fortnightly.* (898)

MANAGEMENT – Labor

The interest of the public is generally best served when management and labor can sit down to bargain with neither side having an undue advantage. Even the remotest possibility that the National Administration will make an eleventh hour appearance makes the bargaining little more than a frustrating charade. – WILLIAM VERITY, President, Armco Steel. (899)

MANAGEMENT – Methods

The most underdeveloped phase of most businesses today is management methods . . . and management is going to have to substantially upgrade its tool kit and application techniques. If we could just recapture the rudimentary element of individual industry that enables small business to compete and inject it into our management techniques, we would be making giant strides in the right direction. A corporate life can only be sustained by forcing a growth program – growth through intensified product research and diversification to strengthen the corporate posture. Young talent with the courage and stamina required to carry the greater responsibility will only be attracted by a business still on the make, offering new challenges and potential gain. – CHARLES C. GATES, Jr., President, Gates Rubber Company, *Gates Industrial News.* (900)

MANAGERS

There was a time when a man became a manager because he knew how to do a particular job better than others in his department. His success was being able to show newcomers how to do this particular thing. This day is past, or rapidly passing, because the traditional skill itself has often been superseded. Today the manager depends upon an ability to mold people. – Dr. ROSS M. TRUMP, *Manage.* (901)

MANPOWER – Trained

Trained manpower is indispensible for the development and use of all other resources. – WILLIAM H. CHISHOLM, President, Oxford Paper Company. (902)

MARKETING

The aim of marketing under our system, which has brought us a steadily rising economy, is to supply the whole range of products and services to serve consumers' very human cravings of the mind and spirit, as well as of the body. I submit that this is a *social right*. For it is not society as a whole, but the *social individual* who establishes the social value of any product — by his or her purchases. — C.W. COOK, Chairman, General Foods Corporation.   (903)

When United Airlines changed from piston engines to jets, their senior pilots received seven weeks of special training. The changes in marketing techniques produced by the marketing revolution are much more extensive than the changes in flight techniques from piston engines to jets. Ninety-five per cent of the marketing people have not been given adequate training to perform the tasks they are now expected to discharge successfully. — EDWARD J. GREEN, Vice President, Westinghouse Air Brake Company, *Manage.*   (904)

MASS COMMUNICATIONS

As our society has become more and more complex with swiftly growing numbers of events and ideas, more and more it has become dependent upon mass communications. — LEROY COLLINS, President, National Association of Broadcasters.   (905)

MASS MEDIA — Truth

Truth . . . is harder to get at these days. But an even more important contributing factor to the widening of the "understanding gap," has been the way in which the mass media have been going after the truth. Or — to put it more accurately — not going after the truth. . . . The search for the truth has been seriously hindered because we of the mass media have become so fascinated with our technical revolution in communications that we have mistaken the means for the ends. — ARTHUR R. MURPHY, Jr., President and Chief Operating Officer, McCall Corporation.   (906)

MASS PRODUCTION — Detroit

I regard Detroit as the home and citadel of what is probably the single most important feature of American private enterprise capitalism — mass production. —G. Keith Funston, President, New York Stock Exchange.   (907)

MATERIAL GAIN

Our emphasis on material gain has become an idol at whose feet most of us worship. — J.K. STERN, President, American Institute of Cooperation, Washington, D.C.   (908)

MATURITY

Society is providing teen-agers with many new devices to make them look mature sooner, but basically each one of them has to bumble and fumble his way to adulthood according to his schedule, which applies to him alone and which even he only dimly senses. You can't buy emotional maturity; you can't teach it; and you certainly can't bottle it. — PAUL C. HARPER, Jr., President, Needham, Harper & Steers, Inc.

(909)

MEDIOCRITY — Complacency

The forces of mediocrity and complacency are strong today and are growing stronger. Too many people are still *sitting* it out instead of *sweating* it out. — GUILFORD DUDLEY, Jr., President, Life and Casualty Insurance Company.   (910)

MEGALOPOLIS

Megalopolis is here to stay. Call it what you will — urban sprawl, slums of tomorrow, ticky-tack houses. It is here and it will be expanded. — FRANK L. WHITNEY, President, Walter Kidde Constructors, Inc., Engineers and Builders.   (911)

MEN — Evil, Good

The evil that men do, ably reported, sells newspapers, the good is good only in autobiographies. — EDWIN P. NEILAN, President, Chamber of Commerce of the United States.   (912)

MEN — Society

One of the great fears as a nation is that as the structure and scope of our endeavors become more complex, the individual is going to be submerged and defeated. I do not believe this. Whether we are looking out at next year, or 1984, or the turn of a new century, I cannot see how an improved society is going to come from any source but improved men. — GERALD L. PHILLIPPE, Chairman of the Board, General Motors Co., *Personnel Administration.*   (913)

170

MICROPHONES — Women

I am . . . sensitive about microphones, because a microphone is somewhat like a woman. She always wants you to come slightly closer — a little bit nearer . . . but if you do, she squeals! — Prof. Dr. ANTHONY EDWARD RUPERT, Chairman and Managing Director, Rembrandt Group of Companies. (914)

MIND

The frontier today has changed, but there are still frontiers to be conquered. They may not be geographical frontiers, but rather, frontiers of the mind and spirit, and pioneers are needed as never before. The frontiers of the human mind are just beginning to open up. — ROGER HULL, President, Mutual of New York, *Quote.* (915)

MISTAKES — Overcoming

Nobody ever gets any place or accomplishes anything who hasn't somewhere along the path fallen down and gotten a bloody nose. The point is, that when you do stumble and fall down, you pick yourself up right there where you were and you go on. You haven't lost — and in one sense, you've gained, because you learn from your mistakes and when you get right down to it you only progress by experience. — L.F. McCOLLUM, Chairman, Continental Oil Company. (916)

MODERN AGE

It has become the age of the easy way out, the evaded responsibility. — RALPH M. BESSE, President, The Cleveland Electric Illuminating Company. (917)

If I were forced to characterize in a single word the age in which we live, I believe I would choose the word "Compression." At no other time in mankind's history have events moved with the speed with which they are moving today. At no other period in the human odyssey has there been such a compression as that which is now collapsing time, space and values. — ALBERT J. NEVINS, M.M., Editor. (918)

It is the age when Americans as a whole have shrugged off much of the burden of freedom — because it is getting heavy, and because they feel Washington can carry it better. — RALPH M. BESSE, President, The Cleveland Electric Illuminating Company. (919)

MODERN GENERATION

This generation is physically impressive. They're taller — heavier — stronger — and healthier than any similar group before

171

them. And when you add the fact that they're better informed, better educated, and generally more intelligent, you've described a generation which indeed has potential for greatness. — W.O. ROBERTSON, Vice President, Armco Steel Corporation.　　(920)

MONEY

Money is a resource which at first should be invested only in basic necessities and in one's future. People who sink it into pursuits which have no objective other than transitory pleasure are spend-thrifts. As I travel around the country I see young men pouring every cent they earn into chromium-plated sports cars, sleek boats, flashy ski ensembles, and flashier blondes, brunettes and redheads. These people are going about the pursuit of happiness the wrong way. — ELMER G. LETERMAN, *How Showmanship Sells* (Harper & Row).　　(921)

Money is a medium of exchange. It facilitates the trading that fosters the specialized division of labor and mass production. Money is thus the greatest tool for the multiplication of human satisfaction. It is also the catalyst of the golden rule. It permits us to help others as we help ourselves. — PERCY L. GREAVES, Jr., Economist, Dobbs Ferry, New York.　　(922)

Put in its proper place, money is not man's enemy, not his undoing, not his master. It is his servant, and it must be made to serve him well. — HENRY C. ALEXANDER, Chairman of the Board, Morgan Guaranty Trust Company of New York.　　(923)

If you've money to burn, someone is always willing to lend you a match. — ELMER G. LETERMAN.　　(924)

Money . . . has no value in and of itself. It is, by classical definition, a medium of exchange. For money to have value, somebody, initially, has got to work to put value into it. Work, production, is what validates money — not a printing press or an arbitrary decision. — T. COLEMAN ANDREWS, Chairman of the Board and President, American Fidelity & Casualty Company. (925)

MONEY — Devaluation of Pound

The fate of the British pound should be a clear warning that no nation, no matter how rich or powerful, can go on year after year living beyond its means. — RICHARD G. CAPEN, Jr., Director of Public Affairs, Copley Newspapers, La Jolla, California.　　(926)

MONEY — Easy

The heyday of easy money is over. — PIERRE A. RINFRET,

Chairman of the Board of Directors and Head of the Economics Division, Lionel D. Edie & Company, Inc.. (927)

MONEY — Happiness

The greatest humbug in the world is the idea that money can make a man happy. I never had any satisfaction with mine until I began to do good with it. — CHARLES PRATT, *Forbes*. (928)

MONEY — Responsibility

You may hesitate to believe this, but I really don't think I have ever done anything in my life because of the money I was going to get from it. Don't bargain too hard for money. Bargain for the chance to carry real responsibility, and the money will follow automatically. — HERMAN C. KRANNERT, Chairman of the Board, Inland Container Corporation. (929)

MONEY — Shortage

Today, and looking into the future, we can see a worldwide shortage of money as a chronic condition. This means that from now until as far into the future as any of us here can see, finance will be the critical element in every form of economic activity. — LOUIS B. LUNDBORG, Chairman of the Board, Bank of America National Trust and Savings Association. (930)

MORALITY

Ours is the era of frenzied nonsense; of cries to "legalize pot," of "topless waitresses," of "intellectualism by mob rule." We may accept these phenomena, we may ignore them, we may dismiss them as unimportant, but by no stretch of the imagination can we claim that they contribute to high standards of morality. — AUSTIN S. MURPHY, Managing Director, Savings Banks Association of New York State. (931)

The fact is that, in every area of human existence, the wheel turns. It always has; it still does; and it always will. What's "up" today is "down" tomorrow. What was "in" yesterday is "out" today. In our current affairs, we have seen it happen with the ups and downs and ups again of publications, movies, radio, records, railroads and, most currently, rapid transit. And, in morals, it has been the same way throughout the ages. — WILLIAM I. NICHOLS, Publisher and Editorial Director, *This Week Magazine*. (932)

Our example to the world must be, above all, an example of morality. — GEORGE CHAMPION, Chairman of the Board, The Chase Manhattan Bank.

Morality is not just a set of numbered points chipped out on a stone tablet. Morality is not just precepts and platitudes wrapped up in a book. Morality is not just a switch on the woodshed wall. Morality is something that is inside you. Its other name is Freedom of Choice. And it consists of knowing the difference between right and wrong, and which to choose, and when and why. — WILLIAM I. NICHOLS, Editor and Publisher, *This Week Magazine.* (934)

Although man's inventions are getting bigger and faster, it does not necessarily follow that man himself is getting better. While we have become a nation of technological giants, we are also rapidly becoming a nation of spiritual midgets. Morality is determined by self interest. "What's in it for me?" has become almost a national motto. Short weight scales, rigged quiz programs, disc jockey payola, basketball scandals are but symptoms of our moral bad health. — ALBERT J. NEVINS, M.M., Editor. (935)

MOTIVATION — Self

Only self-motivated people bring to a job initiative as well as intellect, heart as well as head. — NORMAN G. SHIDLE, Consulting Editor, *Society of Automotive Engineers Journal.* (936)

MOTTOES

The communist has a motto: Bury the world. We have a motto: it is found on our coinage: In God We Trust. — HAROLD R. McKINNON, Attorney, Bronson, Bronson & McKinnon, San Francisco, California. (937)

N

NATIONAL CHARACTER

Our national character was tempered in a climate of explosive expansion, continent-wide. This expansion was in part a by-product of and in part an inducement to certain traits of national character — ingenuity, hard work, and the willingness to venture. It would have been stifled by conformity, the exaltation of leisure, half-hearted work, over-indulgence in concern for security. — GABRIEL HAUGE, Vice Chairman of the Board, Manufacturers Hanover Trust Company, New York. (938)

NATIONAL DEBT

Modern medicine is doing so much to increase our life expectancy that we had better demand control of the size of our spending and our national debt. We might end up having to pay it all ourselves instead of passing it along to our children. — EDWIN P. NEILAN, President, Chamber of Commerce of the United States. (939)

NATIONS — Business

Nations build themselves, unquestionably. Yet nation building is what business does best. — ROY L. ASH, President, Litton Industries, Inc. (940)

NATIONS — Defeated

I do not fear Russia. I do not fear China. I do not fear any external enemy, because the history of the world is clear. No nation has ever been defeated from the outside. A nation has only been defeated because it has become rotten and vulgar and cheap. It became a pushover as the barbarians marched into the Roman Empire and took it over. — GEORGE SOKOLSKY, Columnist. (941)

NATIONS — Developed, Underdeveloped

Today the world is, in fact, a Siamese twin, made of a union between the sophisticated, industrialized nations and the unsophisticated, poverty-ridden, underdeveloped nations. The analogy can be carried further. If one twin of a Siamese set becomes ill, so does the other. — J. PAUL AUSTIN, President and Chief Executive Officer, The Coca-Cola Company. (942)

NATIONS — Developing

In our relationship with the rest of the world, no problem is more pressing, no challenge more exciting than the emergence of the developing nations. As new nations come into being and as old nations seek new economic, social and political achievements for their people, America and the free world have a deep obligation to provide leadership, to offer assistance, to give guidance from our experience and to be constantly on guard to be absolutely certain that the foundling nations do not mire in a chaos of unrealistic aspirations and fall in with the easy delusion that individual freedom can be realized in a captive nation. — CHARLES H. PERCY, President, Bell & Howell Company, Chicago, Illinois.   (943)

The greatest service that can be extended to a developing country is to adapt products and processes realistically to the economic stage that country has reached. In countries where labor is plentiful, for example, automation may not be the right first step on the road to progress. — LYNN A. TOWNSEND, President, Chrysler Corporation.   (944)

I believe greater attention to education may be the single most important contribution these (developing) nations can make to their own economic development in general and agricultural development in particular. Modern farm technology needs farmers whose dedication to the soil will bring forth a more bountiful harvest because they can study manuals, read instructions and apply mathematical formulas. — DAVID ROCKEFELLER, President, Chase Manhattan Bank.   (945)

NATIONS — Economic Development

The world is divided on many questions, but there seems to be one over-riding aspiration common to all people in this age. From the most advanced industrial nations to the most primitive societies, there seems to be a universal, irresistible determination to achieve new and higher levels of economic development. — RALPH J. CORDINER, Chairman of the Board, General Electric Company, New York.   (946)

NATIONS — Economic Progress

Economic progress is stimulated by the ambition of nations to be better off than they are, and those that have assumed risks have progressed, and those that merely stayed with the hand that had been dealt them either regressed or perished. — H. BRAINARD FANCHER, General Manager, General Electric Apollo Support Department. (947)

NATIONS — Education
There is absolutely no question that the nation which does the best and most thorough job of educating its citizens today will lead the world tomorrow. — RALF BRENT, President, Radio New York Worldwide (WRUL). (948)

NATIONS — Great
No nation has ever remained strong, or responded to new challenges, without the quality of a state of mind that accepts growth, change, and progress as a way of life. This dynamism, meaning the readiness of the individual to court and assist all the processes of healthful change, is as essential to national greatness as liberty, humanity, and reason. The spirit and verve of people is as important as their competence and skill. — FRED J. BORCH, President and Chief Executive Officer, General Electric Company. (949)

A country need not be large in numbers to be great. Since the time of the Greeks, no country has achieved more, in such a relatively small territory, than the English. And this includes every sphere of human endeavor — from Shakespeare to Stephenson — from steam engines to jets. — Prof. Dr. ANTHONY EDWARD RUPERT, Chairman and Managing Director, Rembrandt Group of Companies. (950)

NATIONS — Individuals
A nation is no stronger than its component parts — the individual, the family, the community, the state. It all must start with the individual. — RICHARD H. AMBERG, Publisher, *The St. Louis Globe-Democrat*. (951)

NATIONS — Industrialized
If Russia and China are criteria of the pace with which a nation can become industrialized, then by the year 2000 all the nations of Asia and Africa will be industrialized and possess a tremendous power. — CONRAD N. HILTON, President, Hilton Hotels Corporation. (952)

We will find, I think, that just as capitalism could never have flowered in national environments where its fruits were not widely shared, so the industrialized democracies will not be safe in a world environment which permits the poor nations to get poorer while the rich nations get richer. — ROSCOE DRUMMOND, Editor and Columnist. (953)

NATIONS — Inflation
Nations which shield themselves from inflation by artificially high interest rates and controlled shortages of credit not only will inevitably depress their own economies and upset international monetary equilibrium but by their actions take the first steps on the high road to economic isolationism, exchange controls, rising tariffs and trade war. — R.A. PETERSON, President, Bank of America, N.T. & S.A. (954)

NATIONS — Law
It is a reasonable idea that since peace and order within nations came through the rule of law, peace and order among nations may be achieved by the same system. — CHARLES S. RHYNE, Past President, American Bar Association. (955)

NATIONS — People
It is a country's total productivity — including that in agriculture — that truly determines its level of economic well being. In fact, the most valuable "capital" any country can have is the know-how of its people. Even gold and oil take second place. — ROY L. ASH, President, Litton Industries Inc. (956)

NATIONS — Propserous, Poor.
The greater the disparity between prosperous and poor nations becomes, the higher world tensions will mount. — HENRY FORD, II, Chairman of the Board, Ford Motor Company. (957)

NATIONS — Security
A nation is most secure and its future brightest when its citizens are trained in self-discipline, self-reliance, and resolution. — CHARLES H. PERCY, President, Bell & Howell Company, Chicago, Illinois. (958)

NATIONS — Underdeveloped
Too often, in past centuries, the more advanced countries considered it to their advantage to keep the less developed countries in their place — playing the role of raw-material suppliers. What we

have begun to realize in our time is the enormous gain coming to the developed and to the less developed countries through the mutually beneficial and self-regenerating investment of private capital. — LYNN A. TOWNSEND, President, Chrysler Corporation. (959)

It has been truly said that every country, rich and poor, is to some extent underdeveloped; every country has problems of economic progress, whether it be keeping up with population growth, coping with the confusion of rapidly growing cities, satisfying the rising aspirations of consumers, or reducing areas of poverty and unequal opportunity. — DAVID A. SHEPARD, Director and Executive Vice President, Standard Oil Company (New Jersey). (960)

NATURAL RESOURCES

As a nation, we are not unlike a beautiful woman approaching the age of forty. She's apt to spend an increasing amount of time before her mirror each day fretting over what time is doing to a pretty face and realizing all the while that she shall never again be twenty. — MILLARD E. STONE, Vice President, Sinclair Oil Corporation, (961)

Our renewable natural resources, our soil, water and air must be passed along unravaged to future generations. This concept of stewardship is not only good citizenship, but in the long run it is good business. — LAURANCE S. ROCKEFELLER. (962)

The question of conserving natural resources can never be totally divorced from the question of costs — to industry, to government, and ultimately to the people as consumers and taxpayers. — MILLARD E. STONE, Vice President, Sinclair Oil Corporation, (963)

NEED

Need is not a new thing. It is human and therefore as old as the human race. The ability to satisfy need, however, is not only new, it is uniquely American. — LEO CHERNE, Executive Director, Research Institute of America. (964)

NEGROES

It is up to the business and industrial leadership of the country, of the state, of the community to take the lead in changing the economic status of American Negroes and adjusting the scales of economic and social imbalance. — JAMES P. MITCHELL, Senior Vice President, Crown Zellerbach Corporation. (965)

Today, America needs to use every available resource it has in its tremendous struggle against worldwide communism. Yet we're neglecting the Negro. We're failing to qualify one-tenth of our total population to join fully in this competitive effort, even to support himself. And this is waste: waste of people we definitely need. All of us are very prone to speak of what we're doing "for the Negro." We've reached a point now where we'd better start thinking: "What can the Negro do for us?" — RALPH M. BESSE, President, The Cleveland Electric Illuminating Company. (966)

NEGROES — Demonstrations
Where demonstrations of civil disobedience slop over into actions that cause the necessity of mass arrests and arouse widespread public resentment, the progress of Negro rights is harmed and retarded. — JAMES P. MITCHELL, Senior Vice President, Crown Zellerbach Corporation. (967)

NEGROES — Hometown
In America, a Negro's hometown is the place from where he migrated or got chased from to go somewhere else to find work and take care of the family. — SIMON BOOKER, Author and Head of Washington Bureau of the Johnson Publishing Company. (968)

NEWS MEDIA
It is the job of seasoned producers and editors to decide what news goes in news broadcasts and to make certain that the doctrine of Fairness and Balance enunciated by the Federal Communications Commission is strictly observed. I am convinced that we have succeeded in doing this. — ELMER W. LOWER, President, ABC News. (969)

NEWSMEN — Viet Nam
Besides its baffling intrinsic nature, the Viet Nam war has also been a baffling one for our newsmen, our reporters, and our cameramen. Operating on their own in a war of no fixed positions, they have had to use ingenuity, persistence, and sheer guts to bring the harsh reality of this agonizing war home to us here in the United States. They have to provide for themselves and work in isolation from their colleagues. For their pains — and I use the word literally — they have been attacked more often than they have been praised. — FRANK STANTON, President, C.B.S., *Quill*. (970)

NEWSPAPERMEN — Communism

Just as I believe that newspapermen will be and are the first victims of the Communistic conquest of any country, I also believe it the newspapermen's duty to lead the fight against Communism throughout the free world. — CHARLES NUTTER, Managing Director, International House, New Orleans, Louisiana.   (971)

NEWSPAPERS

Newspapers, I believe, must never forget they serve man — not a state — but man and his Western civilization and the moral ethics of it — those papers which are interested enough will survive. — RALPH McGILL, Publisher, *The Atlanta Constitution*.   (972)

In addition to reporting the current happenings of events in general, fashions and sports and providing funny papers, newspapers have, I believe, a responsibility in common with the rest of us — indeed above the rest of us in the light of the millions of people they daily reach, many of whom look to them not only for information but for guidance — to aid in the defense of our Country, and to inform the people of impending dangers — not to alarm them, but to alert them. — W.L. GRUBBS, Vice President-Law of Louisville and Nashville Railroad.   (973)

A newspaper, I firmly believe, must make its news and, equally, its editorials, a part of the tangible issues of the daily lives of its readers. It may thereby make some angry. It may lose some circulation. But even those who are made angry will know that what they read touched their lives. — RALPH McGILL, Publisher, *The Atlanta Constitution*.   (974)

Outside forces can't be wholly blamed for the economic squeeze in which too many newspapers find themselves. The bald truth is that newspapers are at least a generation behind in the sort of research that would make production more efficient. There has been no generally accepted major improvement in the process of printing newspapers in the past sixty years. Publishers have done precious little to help themselves. — MARK ETHRIDGE, Chairman of the Board, *The Louisville Courier-Journal* and *The Louisville Times*.   (975)

America isn't built by electronics; America was not built by machines; our fourth estate may be on the verge of sensational mechanical improvements, but great papers, whether small or large in circulation, weren't built by machines — they are the creation of dedicated men and women. There is not — and never will be — any substitute for a human mind, a human heart, a human soul. — ALAN C. McINTOSH, Editor and Publisher, *Rock County Star Herald*, Luverne, Minnesota.   (976)

We have spent too much time promoting the newspaper as an advertising medium . . . and far too little time promoting it for its primary reason for being . . . as the source of news of all kinds . . . as the total information medium. – JOHN H. MURPHY, Executive Director, Texas Daily Newspaper Association, *Quote.*   (977)

NEWSPAPERS – Britain

As dreadful as a great many British papers are, there are still a good many things we can learn from them, such as light writing and the sort of profiles and light essays which make the annual edition of *The Bedside Guardian* a pure delight and an exemplar of good writing. – MARK ETHRIDGE, Chairman of the Board, *The Louisville Courier-Journal* and *The Louisville Times.*   (978)

NEWSPAPERS – Communist News

Everything the Communists do or say is propaganda, and I believe they have lost all right to fair and impartial press coverage; every word of Communist news is manipulated and twisted; it should be presented not as fact but as propaganda, and we should no longer donate the headlines of our papers to this enemy which needs to be exposed instead. This can be done by an understanding press. – CHARLES NUTTER, Managing Director, International House, New Orleans, Louisiana.   (979)

NEWSPAPERS – Editorial

A newspaper without an editorial page is a sterile thing – not a newspaper – it means that the editor either had no opinions or is too timid to voice them. – ALAN C. McINTOSH, Editor and ˉ ıblisher, *Rock County Star Herald,* Luverne, Minnesota.   (980)

NEWSPAPERS – Smalltown

Never, never underestimate the power of the smalltown newspapers. – ALAN C. McINTOSH, Editor and Publisher, *Rock County Star Herald,* Luverne, Minnesota.   (981)

NEWSPAPERS – Television, Radio

I believe strongly that newspapers are indispensable to the full enlightenment of the American people. . . . Television is capable of excellent documentaries . . . but neither television nor radio will ever adequately cover spot news except through the wire services which newspapers created. – MARK ETHRIDGE, Chairman of the Board, *The Louisville Courier-Journal* and *The Louisville Times.*   (982)

NEWSPAPERS – World News

If newspapers are to fulfill their function of enabling and equipping a people to be self-governing, they must tell the people about what is going on in the world in a way that will make the world's developments understandable and real. – ALAN BARTH, Editorial Writer, *The Washington* (D.C.) *Post.* (983)

NEW-YORK

New York has absolutely everything except a past. – LOUIS AUCHINCLOSS, President, Museum of the City of New York, (984)

NON-INVOLVEMENT

Only in the past quarter century, it seems to me, has non-involvement become an accepted way of life. For when we were poor, we had to sweat it out. We couldn't afford detachment from the life and fate of our country. And one of the great dangers of affluence is that it permits such detachment. – CHARLES H. BROWER, President, Batten, Barton, Durstine & Osborn, Inc., New York. (985)

O

OBSOLESCENCE
In everything from power tools to breakfast cereals, a new product is hardly on the shelves before it is made obsolete by something newer, and better. — E. HORNSBY WASSON, President, Pacific Telephone and Telegraph Company.   (986)

OCEANS — Beneath
Man has propelled himself more than a hundred miles above the earth yet he has only a vague notion of what his own planet looks like seven or even five miles beneath the surface of the oceans. — CHARLES F. JONES, President, Humble Oil & Refining Company.   (987)

OCEANS — Resources
Although it has been speculated by science fiction writers that our outer space rocketry may provide a means for man to transfer some of the earth's population to other planets, the facts of life are that man will have to provide food and shelter for billions more people right here on earth during the next decades. The most practical way to do this is to tap and manage the vast but infinite resources of the world's oceans. — Dr THEODOR F. HUETER, General Manager, West Coast Operations Ordnance Division, Honeywell, Inc.   (988)

OIL COMPANIES
In all the history of commerce, there has never been another type of endeavor like the international oil business. It is unique in its international scope, in its capital requirements, in the vital nature of its service, and in the complexity of the environment in which it performs that service. — ALBERT L. NICKERSON, Chairman of the Board, Socony Mobil Oil Co. Inc., New York City.   (989)

OIL INDUSTRY
Of all the amazing changes of the past generation, I can think of none more complete than that in the oil industry. . . . When I — and some of you — landed our first oil company jobs, the symbol of our

trade was the grimy rough-neck waving from a rig. Today It's a white coated scientist bent over a test tube, or a dude in an ascot tie peddling petrochemical fibers to a fashion house in Paris. — ALLAN SHIVERS, President, Chamber of Commerce of the United States.

(990)

OIL — Offshore
' Today, we have arrived at a point where roughly a sixth of the world's proven oil reserves lie offshore. — CHARLES F. JONES, President, Humble Oil and Refining Company. (991)

OPPORTUNITY
Many fail to recognize opportunity because its favorite disguise is hard work. — ELMER G. LETERMAN, *Personal Power Through Creative Selling* (Harper & Row). (992)

Your generation is on the threshold of a world which will offer the greatest opportunities ever presented to the individual who has the fortitude and character to use them. — JAMES A. FARLEY, Chairman of the Board, Coca-Cola Export Corporation. (993)

OPPORTUNITY — Equality
We can't all be equal, but we can have equal opportunity and I feel it is a fundamental duty of education, business and government to make this a reality. — GENE C. BREWER, President, United States Plywood Corporation. (994)

We say in our Declaration of Independence that all men are created equal, but it is an equality of opportunity rather than a fixed equality of strength and position. Each uses his strength at the moment to get the best for himself, which certainly is not considered unduly detrimental to the rights of his fellow men. — RICHARD M. JACKSON, President, Seaboard World Airlines, Inc. (995)

OPPORTUNITY — Risk
Great opportunities are invariably accompanied by great risks. — GERALD J. LYNCH, President and Chairman of the Board, Menasco Manufacturing Company. (996)

OPPORTUNITY — Security
Opportunity involves change and growth. Security does not. A man who seeks only security will not achieve, he will not move forward. Like a vegetable he will take root in the place where he stands and inevitably, like all vegetables that remain in the ground,

185

he will rot. — GUILFORD DUDLEY, Jr., President, Life and Casualty Insurance Company. (997)

OPTIMISM — Pessimism
The optimist sees opportunity in every calamity — the pessimist sees calamity in every opportunity. — RAY R. EPPERT, President, Burroughs Corporation. (998)

OUTDOORS
The outdoors . . . is more than a place to acquire a suntan. Along with physical activity, which is an important element, the outdoor experience should be a re-creative experience. It should recharge our emotional and spiritual batteries. Otherwise it is providing nothing more than an escape. — LAURANCE S. ROCKEFELLER, Chairman, Outdoor Recreation Resources Review Commission. (999)

P

PARENTS – Children

The happiest and best parents in the world are those who have real enthusiasm for rearing their children . . . to help them realize the very best potential that is in them, and to help them become the kind of men and women all of us want our children to be. – EDWIN M. CLARK, President, Southwestern Bell Telephone Company, St. Louis, Missouri. (1000)

Parents are forever saying, "How can I convince my children of the right way?" It's easy. They have only to live the right way themselves. They have only to set the right example and demonstrate to their children the wisdom of what they are saying. But this is usually too big a job. It is much easier to wallow in a well-dug rut and pass out gratuitous advice. – EARL NIGHTINGALE, Chairman of the Board, Nightingale-Conant Corporation. (1001)

PARTY POLITICS

There's nothing disreputable about party politics. There can be, and sometimes are disreputable men in politics. But the system of parties itself has been the operating basis of our government for most of our history as a nation. Party politics is a fact of life in our society today. – JAMES M. PATTERSON, Director of Public Relations, American Oil Company. (1002)

PAST

As we look back today it is clear that the 1920's were as tranquil as a cup of tea; we shall never know such national tranquility again. – EDWARD WEEKS, Editor, *Atlantic Magazine*. (1003)

PAST – Future, Present

Yesterday is but a cancelled check, and tomorrow is a promissory note. But today is cash. – RAYMOND W. MILLER, President, Public Relations Research Associates, Inc., Washington, DC. (1004)

PAST – Present

In the past, the most basic drive of Western man was to provide himself with the certainty of food, clothing and shelter. To achieve these necessities, he felt justified in constraining almost all the members of the society to toil. Today, we have the technological potential to provide all human beings with their fundamental physical needs: the scarcities we now perceive as being most acute are in terms of time to do what we wish, space in which to do it, and the imagination to solve our problems. — ROBERT THEOBALD, Economist. (1005)

PAST — Present, Future
Forget the past and live for today and the future. The only thing you really want from the past is to benefit from the experiences that can give you the guidelines necessary to solve today's and tomorrow's problems. — A. CLARK DAUGHERTY, President, Rockwell Manufacturing Company. (1006)

PATIENCE
Patience can degenerate into complacency, but demonstrated wisely, it is indeed a virtue. — DON H. MILLER, President, Skelly Oil Company. (1007)

PATRIOTISM
Patriotism is a fine and positive force if it inspires you to win by being better. But it can be negative, vicious and destructive if it makes us smug, lazy, arrogant or complacent. — WILLIAM I. NICHOLS, Editor, *This Week*. (1008)

PEACE — Aggression
The insignia of peace belongs to those willing to join in resisting aggression at its start — not to those, however sincere, who turn their heads and hope a little aggression will satisfy the aggressor. — ROSCOE DRUMMOND, Editor and Columnist. (1009)

PEACE CORPS
I think it's fair to say that few programs ever proposed have been so skeptically considered by the older generation, or so beautifully made to work by the younger. — LYNN A. TOWNSEND, President, Chrysler Corporation. (1010)

PEOPLE
Books are important, learning is important, teaching is important (indeed I would put it near the top in my hierarchy of vocations); scholarship is important. But people matter most! — KENNETH

IRVING BROWN, Executive Director, Danforth Foundation, St. Louis, Missouri. (1011)

PEOPLE — Energy, Ingenuity
The energy and ingenuity of its people ever remain a nation's most important resource. — DAVID ROCKEFELLER, President, Chase Manhattan Bank. (1012)

PEOPLE — Good, Bad
We would all like to believe that people are always honest and decent, hard working and loyal. The fact is that people are a mixture of good and bad. In some situations they're heroic and gallant and in others they're petty and disappointing. — HERMAN C. KRANNERT, Chairman of the Board, Inland Container Corporation. (1013)

PEOPLE — Ordinary
Most people are ordinary because they have never taken the trouble to convince themselves that they can be more. — ELMER G. LETERMAN, *Commissions Don't Fall From Heaven* (MacFadden-Bartell). (1014)

PEOPLE — Primitive, Educated
Paradoxically, we need education and educated people more than ever before . . . yet it is the educated and technically competent people who can cause world disaster. Primitive peoples are not a global menace. — JOSEPH H. McCONNELL, President, Reynolds Metals Company. (1015)

PERSONAL CONTACT
One of the greatest of our resources — one we are likely to overlook or take for granted — is the resource of friendship, acquaintance, and personal contacts. All of us are aware of the fact that we can benefit personally by exposure to great people. But not every one is aware that we can learn something from every person we meet. And sometimes the lesson we need most can best be learned from one of low and humble estate. — ERWIN L. McDONALD, Editor, *Arkansas Baptist Newsmagazine*. (1016)

PERSONAL LIBERTY
After an unnaturally long period governed — on the surface at least — by the "Puritan ethic," we have entered a new phase of

personal liberty. What concerns us is the fear that — if it proceeds too far and too fast, and without the necessary controls — then liberty can become license and libertinism; and our society can die of inner moral decay, just as others have before us. — WILLIAM I. NICHOLS, Publisher and Editorial Director, *This Week Magazine.*
(1017)

PHILOSOPHY — Communicating
From my travels in much of the world — and as a result of conversations with literally thousands of people — I have become convinced that we in the United States have failed to master the art of communicating to others our basic philosophy of life. — RAYMOND W. MILLER, President, Public Relations Research Associates, Inc., Washington, D.C. (1018)

POLITICAL PARTIES
Party conventions resemble tribal rituals. Almost everything about them is phony. The spectacular campaigns and "give 'em hell" speeches reduce office-seeking to the intellectual level of professional wrestling. — GEORGE GALLUP, Director, American Institute of Public Opinion, *Quote.* (1019)
Our nation always needs a strong opposition party, but this does not mean that the parties must be diametrically opposed on major issues. On the contrary, it means that both parties must be sufficiently within the mainstream of public opinion to have a real chance at the polls, and therefore a real opportunity to influence policy. — HENRY FORD, II, Chairman of the Board, Ford Motor Company. (1020)
To Americans who both understand and love their country, the appeals of right and left are petitions in bankruptcy. We are a nation of middle roaders — Republicans a bit right of middle, Democrats a bit left of middle — whose major *two* party system has provided us over most of our history of choice, with change, and with stability. — ROBERT H. HINCKLEY, Former President of the American Broadcasting Company. (1021)

POLITICAL PARTIES — Contributions
Businessmen ought to take the lead in contributing to political candidates and political parties — and they ought to encourage their employees to do the same. — JAMES M. PATTERSON, Director of Public Relations, American Oil Company. (1022)

POLITICAL PARTIES – Platforms

Once a political party in this country could stand for election on a platform merely of a full dinner pail. Then it advanced to a chicken in every pot. Then a car in every garage. Now President Johnson has abandoned this material approach. He stands on a platform of an education for every child and the necessary books and schools and scholarships to develop its talents. – Hon JAMES A. FARLEY, Chairman of the Board, Coca-Cola Export Corporation.   (1023)

POLITICIANS

The politician is interested first, last and always in one thing – votes. – ARTHUR H. MOTLEY, President, Chamber of Commerce of the United States.   (1024)

POLITICIANS – Elections

We condemn the politician, but we do not actively participate in his election. We are losing by apathy in the elective process the very things to which we give allegiance. – PRIME F. OSBORN, III, Vice President and General Counsel, Atlantic Coast Line Railroad Company.   (1025)

POLITICS

The United States has been unique because its people accepted political responsibility and guided their own lives and destinies right from the beginning. We will remain great and become greater only insofar as we refuse to deviate from the fundamental principles upon which the political edifice was reared. – JOHN E. SWEARINGEN, President, Standard Oil Company (Indiana).   (1026)

Anyone who thinks he can get away from frustration, confusion, and compromise in politics and diplomacy should make arrangements to get himself reborn into a different world than this one. Or if that is beyond his powers, he should move to some country where there are no newspapers to read. – WALTER LIPPMANN, Columnist.   (1027)

Ours is a political system. It is incumbent upon each of us to participate in the party of our choice at the local level and at the national level, and to give to politics, as citizens, a portion of our time and talents and money. Furthermore, we must serve in government when the specialized skills we possess are needed. – JOHN E. SWEARINGEN, President, Standard Oil Company (Indiana).   (1028)

The machinery of American politics functions with an almost

monumental imprecision. It is so untidy, in fact, that it repels many types of excellent men who are appalled when they try to come to grips with it. The realities of political life, the lack of precision and neatness, is often a shocking discovery to the man of business and industry suddenly projected into the political limelight. — JAMES P. MITCHELL, Vice President, Crown Zellerbach Corporation, San Francisco, California.   (1029)

Being active in politics can mean two things: contributing money and giving your personal time and effort. Both are important. — JAMES M. PATTERSON, Director of Public Relations, American Oil Company.   (1030)

POLITICS — Politicians

We cannot all be experts in the profession of politics, any more than we can all be doctors, scientists or the managers of large industrial organizations. But we can exercise intelligence in the choice of men and women who enter it. We can adjust our educational system to train people for it, at least more effectively and pointedly than we do today. — JAMES P. MITCHELL, Vice President, Crown Zellerbach Corporation, San Francisco, California.

(1031)

POLLUTION — Air, Water

While industrialization raised man's standard of living, it lowered the quality of his most vital resources — air and water. — M.A. WRIGHT, President, Chamber of Commerce of the United States.

(1032)

The best solution to the problem of restoring and maintaining the quality of our air and water lies in a well-coordinated, community-wide effort. No single segment of society is capable of accomplishing the job that lies ahead. — M.A. WRIGHT, President, Chamber of Commerce of the United States.   (1033)

POPULATION — Growth

The roots of the population growth problem are social and ethical and cultural — not technical. . . . We must find a way to achieve the social understanding of the necessity for stabilizing populations around the world. It is not enough that some parts of the world can accomplish stability. The problem is not solved until the world-wide population, as a whole, is stabilized — for any small remnant which continues to grow explosively will soon outstrip in numbers the whole rest of the "controlled" world. — ROBERT

ALAN CHARPIE, BS, MS, D.Sc, Director of Technology, Union Carbide Corporation, New York. (1034)

POPULATION — Stabilization

Population stabilization is not a brake upon human development, but rather a release that, by assuring greater opportunity to each person, frees man to attain his individual dignity and to reach his full potential. — JOHN D. ROCKEFELLER, III, *Quote*. (1035)

POVERTY

We must live with the present and we must fight for the future. For — despite the herculean expenditures of the Federal Government, pockets of poverty still maintain in our Great Society. — CHARLES L. GOULD, Publisher, *San Francisco Examiner*. (1036)

I am deeply convinced that if we are to make significant strides in the war on poverty, we must gear our efforts to realize the great potential of the individual. We must concentrate on the development of his fullest capabilities as an independent being, rather than a ward of the Federal government. Above all, we must emphasize private participation, as opposed to total government participation, with private entities such as the business community shouldering the major burden of helping individuals to help themselves. — GEORGE CHAMPION, Chairman of the Board, The Chase Manhattan Bank.

(1037)

Poverty can be abolished. . . . But it will be abolished more by Peace Corps projects abroad than by campus protests at home. — JAMES C. HUMES, Executive Director, Philadelphia Bar Association. (1038)

I believe that the solution of the economic ills of a substantial segment of our population will be achieved only through the combined efforts of business and industry, government, social welfare organizations, churches, schools, and the responsible leadership in the Negro community itself. I also believe, however, that without the conscientious involvement of business and industry the activities that are undertaken are rather apt to be palliatives instead of cures. — L.W. MOORE, President, American Oil Company. (1039)

POVERTY — Elimination

The barriers to the elimination of poverty are not economic: the funds which will be released at the end of the Vietnam war would suffice to allow the introduction of the guaranteed income. The barriers are moral and social. The United States is not willing to

193

apply its vast productive potential to the elimination of poverty and hides its unwillingness with statements about the need for motivation and incentives. – ROBERT THEOBALD, Economist. (1040)

Eliminating poverty temporarily by handouts can actually perpetuate the cause. Filling a man's belly and emptying his heart can destroy the greatest weapon for eliminating poverty – enterprise. – ROBERT R. SPITZER, Businessman. (1041)

POVERTY – Free Enterprise

Free enterprise is our greatest weapon in the war on poverty. – ROBERT C. TYSON, Chairman, Finance Committee, United States Steel Corporation. (1042)

POVERTY – Incomes

We must be concerned not only with raising the income of our poor, but also with finding the most efficient and effective means of achieving this aim. We must in fact – as we pursue this commendable goal – be constantly alert to what is in the best longterm interest of our country and our people. – M.A. WRIGHT, Chairman of the Board, Humble Oil and Refining Company. (1043)

POVERTY – Prejudice

It is my personal opinion that much of today's unrest can be attributed to the frustrations of those who have expected immediate results from the promises of others. As a result, many have come to believe – in fact, to expect – that poverty and prejudice can be conquered overnight. They believe that Congress can recognize a problem, pass a law, fund a program, and all our problems will fade away. – RICHARD G. CAPEN, Jr., Director of Public Affairs, Copley Newspapers, La Jolla, California. (1044)

POVERTY – The Poor

As compassionate individuals, we look upon poverty as a blight which deprives fellowmen of life's enjoyment. As responsible citizens, we also see the poor as a drain on society who should be made into contributors to society. As businessmen, we add a third view – the poor simply are not very good customers for our products, even the most basic necessities. – HENRY FORD, II, Chairman of the Board, Ford Motor Company. (1045)

POVERTY – World

The combination of world wide poverty and rising expectations

194

is as volatile and threatening in its own way as is the total nuclear arsenal of the world, and certainly not to be put out of mind in any view of the world ahead — even for the short run. — ROY L. ASH, President, Litton Industries Inc. (1046)

PREJUDICE
We must not allow prejudice to become a barrier to the full and effective use of our greatest national resources — the talents of our people. The Creator does not discriminate in bestowing talent. Whether as employers or associations of employes, we must live up to the spirit as well as the letter of the law assuring equal opportunity to all, regardless of age, race, color, sex, creed or national origin. — JAMES M. ROCHE, President, General Motors.
(1047)
We human beings love to coddle our own prejudices, and a lot of what passes for thought, as we all know, is a mere rearrangement of our prejudices. — LYNN A. TOWNSEND, President, Chrysler Corporation. (1048)

PRESENT — Future
It is all too easy for us to become so enmeshed in administration of the present that we feel we have no time to take a long look into the future. — RICHARD J. ANTON, Manager, Business Education Service, General Electric Company. (1049)

PRESENT — Past
The present builds on the past. Each person must construct his own meaning upon the wisdom and the folly of preceding human experience. — JAMES O. DOBBS, Jr., Industrial Relations Consultant and Lecturer, Austin, Texas. (1050)
Anybody who is satisfied to live in the present will quickly find he is living in the past. — L.F. McCOLLUM, Chairman, Continental Oil Company. (1051)

PRESS, The
The American press needs to start prizing its readers more and its headlines less. This does not mean less leg work — it means more. It does not mean less contact with the government — but more. But it also means visits to universities, better use of libraries, more control of foreign languages and a refusal to think of all reality only in its relationship to the lead (opening paragraph of a news story.) — McGEORGE BUNDY, President, Ford Foundation. (1052)

The press has a unique function. It is the meeting ground of all the elements of our society — agriculture, labor, business, the professions, the church, schools and colleges, the theater, radio and television, civic organizations, philanthropic organizations, political organizations, politicians and statesmen, foundations, government in all its branches, local, state and federal. The press is the forum even of the nations. Here all these elements come, to report themselves and be reported, to criticize and be criticized, to seek that understanding and support from others which all human beings crave. — EDWARD J. MEEMAN, Editor Emeritus *The Memphis Press-Scimitar* and Conservation Editor of the Scripps-Howard Newspapers. (1053)

Journalism has its seamy characters, and some of them are very big. There are chinks in its virtue and kinks in its practices. While its saints go marching by, its stinkers snicker in the newsroom. We readily grant all that, for the press is of the fabric of America, sharing the virtues and the faults of her citizens, her Constitutions, her legislators, executives and judges. — ARVILLE SCHALEBEN, Executive Editor, *The Milwaukee Journal.* (1054)

PRINCIPLES

We have always found that if our principles were right, the area over which they were applied did not matter. Size is only a matter of the multiplication tables. — HENRY FORD, *Quote.* (1055)

PRIVATE ENTERPRISE

Economic development is the special capability of business and industrial organizations. All of the economically advanced countries attest to that. In them industry has clearly demonstrated its unparalleled ability to create, produce and market a veritable cornucopia of products — to many, multi-faceted markets. Given the freedom to take risks, and to reap rewards if successful, private enterprise has achieved more good for more people than any other system in the history of the world. — ROY L. ASH, President, Litton Industries Inc. (1056)

PROBLEMS — Domestic, Global

I believe that both logic and duty require that we demonstrate an ability to start solving our most urgent domestic problems before attempting global solutions. — ROBERT W. SARNOFF, President, Radio Corporation of America. (1057)

PRODUCTIVITY

I cheer every increase in productivity — every report that American workers can turn out in an hour more shoes, more trucks, or more wheat than ever before. I believe we can and must increase the rate at which we produce — and export — because our ability to raise world living standards directly affects the advance or retreat of communism. If our system will not begin to alleviate poverty and hunger, the world will try a different approach. — THOMAS J. WATSON, Jr., Chairman of the Board, IBM Company.   (1058)

PROFESSIONALS

One sure mark of a professional in any field is his constant effort to extend his knowledge, and then to apply to his work the best of what he learns. — JOHN G. MAPES, Chairman, Executive Committee, Hill and Knowlton, Inc.   (1059)

PROFIT

Many otherwise intelligent people seem to think of the word "profits" as a synonym for "greed." In reality, profits are synonymous with economic and social health, for we could not have a healthy economy or a healthy society without the profits earned by business. — C.W. COOK, Chairman, General Foods Corporation.
                                                                (1060)

Despite the fact that profits are generally regarded as merely something left over after consumption has been taken care of by production, that's not the way our economy works. Profits are vital to investment, and we must invest before we can produce and we must produce before we can consume. — CHARLES G. MORTIMER, Chairman, General Foods Corporation.   (1061)

Profit is the most important word in our economic language. — AMYAS AMES, President, Investment Bankers Association of America.   (1062)

Profit is the weathervane of American business. — DONALD L. JORDAN, Chairman, The National Association of Manufacturers.
                                                                (1063)

The final goal of industry must be to make a profit. . . . We must make everyone realize that we must make a profit — or there will not be high wages, and all the other benefits. Unless we do make a profit, there just won't be those jobs. — MARTIN J. CASERIO, General Manager, Delco Radio Division, General Motors Corporation, Kokomo, Indiana.   (1064)

The unrelenting search for profit is a vital stimulant; it speeds

197

research and helps develop new products; it makes efficiency a by-word in plant and office; it helps lower prices. — DONALD L. JORDAN, Chairman, The National Association of Manufacturers.

(1065)

Profit is a frame of mind . . . a philosophy . . . a principal that must be ingrained throughout an organization . . . an object of pride for every man and woman in the company. — A.C. DAUGHERTY, President, Rockwell Manufacturing Company. (1066)

There are some people who would have you believe that profits, in and of themselves, are objectionable and that the individual or the business enterprise which earns a profit has somehow or other done so at the cost of the sweat, blood and tears of other human beings. Actually, profits are the lifeblood of our Free Enterprise system, which has given us the highest standard of living the world has ever known. — E.F. SCOUTTEN, Vice President, The Maytag Company.

(1067)

PROFIT — Loss

Young people today in particular seem to pride themselves on avoiding business risks. They want a "sure thing" to start with — and a good retirement program, too. They seem not to comprehend — or show any interest in — the fact that ours is a profit *and* loss system; that profit is the *earned* reward for successfully managing to avoid the ever-present possibility of loss; that profits must be adequate to make up for the probability that there will be some losses; and that without the successful risk-takers — and a business and political climate that encourages them — there is no real security for any of us. — JOHN D. HARPER, President, Aluminum Company of America, New York City. (1068)

PROFIT — Work

Men and women when given the direct, personal incentive of profit, work harder for themselves and for their communities. — AMYAS AMES, President, Investment Bankers Association of America. (1069)

PROGRESS

Progress comes from discontent, not from complacency. — HENRY FORD, II, Chairman of the Board, Ford Motor Company.

(1070)

You will never stub your toe standing still. The faster you go, the more chance there is of stubbing your toe, but the more chance you have of getting somewhere. — CHARLES F. KETTERING, *Management Review*. (1071)

Progress is a tide. If we stand still, we will surely be drowned. To stay on the crest, we have to keep moving. — HAROLD MAYFIELD, Director of Personnel Relations, Owens-Illinois, *Supervisory Management*. (1072)

Every advance of man has begun when he has questioned his world. Because he has questioned it, he has made it over. — ELMER G. LETERMAN, *Commissions Don't Fall From Heaven* (MacFadden-Bartell). (1073)

PROGRESS — Executive

I make progress by having people around me who are smarter than I am — and listening to them. And I assume that everyone is smarter about something than I am. — HENRY KAISER, *Personnel*. (1074)

PROPAGANDA

Our military can cope with the Communists in a clash of firearms but we are dropped pitifully in our tracks in any war of words. — ARTHUR E. MEYERHOFF, President, Arthur Meyerhoff Associates, Inc., Chicago, Illinois. (1075)

Propaganda has been defined as "lying in such a way as nearly to deceive your friends without ever deceiving your enemies." — RICHARD M. RALSTON, Director of Communications, Blue Cross Association. (1076)

PROPERTY — Owning

If we are to have a continuance of the property system, the vast majority should be property owners. Human dignity is best secured when the individual has the responsibility of owning property and has the freedom that comes from its use. When a man owns private property he can obtain his education where he pleases, work where he pleases, or quit a job, or move about as he pleases. He is not dependent on the resources and will of others. — EDWARD J. MEEMAN, Editor, *Memphis Press-Scimitar*. (1077)

PUBLIC OFFICE

Of all men in public life, the representative in a legislative body is the most available individual in American society. — JAMES P. MITCHELL, Vice President, Crown Zellerbach Corporation, San Francisco, California. (1078)

PUBLIC OFFICE — Businessmen

There is a generally held notion that public office is the preserve of politicians and lawyers. Many businessmen feel that because their backgrounds are business backgrounds, they would go down in defeat if they ran for office. It may surprise you to learn that this is not so. A businessman can be far more acceptable to voters as a candidate for public office than the professional politicians. I tested this recently and found it to be true. — ARNOLD MAREMONT, President, Maremont Corporation, Chicago, Illinois. (1079)

PUBLIC OPINION

More than ever before in our history, public opinion is king. — JOHN D. PAULUS, Director of Public Relations, Allegheny Ludlum Steel Corporation, Pittsburgh, Pennsylvania. (1080)

Public opinion cannot be directed, or pushed around, but it can be led. It responds to thoughtful teaching, to fuller information, and to englightened and light-giving comment. If we can lead public opinion toward the stimulation of individual incentives, instead of the blunting of them, toward creativeness and productivity so that there will be plenty for all, instead of just legalized thievery to divide what exists; toward equality of opportunity, rather than just plain equality, which would inevitably lead to poverty and ignorance for all; toward freedom and personal responsibility as the ideal goal, rather than supine prostration before an all-powerful state; then we will be both exercizing a constructive influence on government and our society, and also serving the best long-term interest of all the people. — HAROLD BRAYMAN, Director of Public Relations, Du Pont Company, (1081)

PUBLIC RELATIONS

Today's well-rounded public relations practitioner must know more than how to write and how to use the mechanics of communications. He must also be something of a seer into the future, a strategist, and have the knowledge to advise management on the possible public relations consequences of different courses of action. — JOHN G. MAPES, Chairman, Executive Committee, Hill and Knowlton, Inc. (1082)

The day any government body can determine which individuals, which companies, which industries, which institutions can or cannot use the techniques of public relations to present their case to the American people — that will be a dark and very dangerous day for America. — ROBERT VAN RIPER, Vice President and Director of

Public Relations, N.Y. Ayer & Son, Inc.　　　　　　(1083)

PUBLIC UNDERSTANDING
True public understanding is the necessary springboard to the accomplishment of great progress in any public endeavor. – LEROY COLLINS, President, National Association of Broadcasters.　(1084)

PURITAN ANCESTORS
It is fashionable these days to scoff at the so-called "Puritan ethic" as something hopelessly outmoded. But our Puritan ancestors were remarkable people. They wrested a living from rocky land, built our earliest colleges, started our literature, and fired our industrial revolution. – GEORGE CHAMPION, Chairman of the Board, The Chase Manhattan Bank.　　　　　　(1085)

PURPOSE
Great motives yield great deeds. Given a strong purpose, there is little we cannot do. Without purpose, life is dull, empty and meaningless. – BRENDAN BYRNE, American Heritage Foundation.
(1086)

Q

QUESTIONS

Men who don't question, don't remain. — WILLIAM F. MAY, Executive Vice President, American Can Company. (1087)

R

RAILROADS

History has been an albatross around the necks of the railroads. The industry has been so proud and so conscious of its history that it forgot it was a business. Most railroads were run like institutions. If someone brought them some freight, they'd look it up in the rate book. Now we go out after business and we sometimes show shippers what they ought to be doing. We're ready to challenge our traditional way of doing things anywhere, any time. — MYRON M. CHRISTY, President, Western Pacific Railroads, *Forbes*. (1088)

You can't have a great nation, or any great society for that matter, without great railroads. — DANIEL P. LOOMIS, President, Association of American Railroads, Washington, D.C. (1089)

RAILROADS — Government

People who have lived with government operation of railroads will tell you that political tampering with the working of an economic enterprise is much like pouring tar into a fine machine. It thoroughly gums up the works. — JAMES N. SITES, Assistant to the Vice President, Association of American Railroads, Washington,D.C. (1090)

RAILROADS — Transportation

Mass production and nationwide marketing of autos or any other product would be impossible without the railroads' mass transportation services. — DANIEL P. LOOMIS, President, Association of American Railroads. (1091)

RECESSIONS — Depressions

Businessmen tend in times of uncertainty to become more cautious and conservative in their investment and spending policies. Loss of confidence on the part of the public takes the form of postponement of purchases. I have said before, and I strongly believe, recessions and depressions in this country start and end in the minds of men. Confidence is a delicate thing — an illusive, mercurial state of mind — and a severe flight of confidence usually ushers in a recession. — CHARLES G. MORTIMER, Chairman, General Foods Corporation. (1092)

RELIGIONS

The great religions are founded on simple beliefs in the great goals of mankind. Dogma *follows* faith, it does not lead it. — W. HOWARD CHASE, Howard Chase Associates, Inc. (1093)

RESEARCH

Today, in this year of 1966, 15 billion dollars will be invested in research and development. I'll qualify that to this extent — about 5 billion is in Government. But 10 billion dollars of that investment is for American industry to bring out the exciting, the newer and the better product or service. In that connection, I have no validation for this, but I believe about 10,000 new products will have been introduced to the marketplace in 1966. . . . It takes an average of 405 ideas, channeled into research and development, before one successful product goes to the market place — 405 ideas to produce just one successful product. — FEN K. DOSCHER, Senior Vice President, Lily-Tulip Cup Corporation, *Quote.* (1094)

With the stepped-up pace of technological change in recent years, businessmen have come to recognize that spending for research is an investment no different in purpose and character from investment in buildings and machines. Applied research is the protection of tomorrow's profits against the coming obsolescence of today's products. — HENRY FORD, II, Chairman of the Board, Ford Motor Company. (1095)

When money is spent for a consumer product such as a car or refrigerator, that product is used and eventually discarded, at which time it has no value. When money is spent in the search for knowledge, however, this knowledge begets new knowledge and develops techniques for a better standard of living, and so on — and at lower total cost. In other words, money spent in the quest for new information keeps coming back to us again and again, whereas money spent directly for a product gives us something of value only once. — RICHARD W. DARROW, President, Hill and Knowlton, Inc. (1096)

RESEARCH — Government Financed

It must be understood that research, the constant, unceasing search for something better, is of the very essence of our competitive, industrial society. It has always seemed to me that one of the great dangers of our generation, in which massive government

204

efforts have been repeatedly utilized in war, in foreign aid, and in social benefits, is that we may go too far and eliminate the very atmosphere of freedom we seek to defend, help, or improve. Yet, we must go far enough. It is a delicate and a difficult balance that has to be struck and none more so than in the matter of government-financed research. — JOHN J. POWERS, Jr., President, Charles Pfizer & Co. Inc.   (1097)

RESEARCH — International Trade
Research is one of the few proven weapons we have in our international trade arsenal. — A.C. DAUGHERTY, President, Rockwell Manufacturing Company.   (1098)

RESEARCH — Progress
Research is the door that will open the way to progress. — JOHN W. QUEENAN, Managing Partner, Haskins & Sells.   (1099)

RESOURCES — Destruction
The growing destruction of our resources of air, water, land and silence through intentional and unintentional abuse threatens the stability of the world's ecology and, in particular, man's survival on this planet. — ROBERT THEOBALD, Economist.   (1100)

RESPONSIBILITY
As you move up the administrative ladder, you will find that you first deal primarily with things; then as you get more responsibility you deal with people and things; and finally you deal only with people. Accordingly, matters that involve human motivation, interpersonal relationships, human communications, become of greater and greater importance. — EDWARD J. HANLEY, President, Allegheny Ludlum Steel Corporation, *Personnel Journal.*   (1101)

Responsibility is the cement of a free society. As free citizens, each of us — individually — must supply that cement. We cannot get along without others. And we must contribute to the common good to the best of our ability. — JAMES M. ROCHE, President, General Motors.   (1102)

As the years pass, I find that my appraisal of people tends to become simpler, perhaps over-simplified. However that may be, I have finally concluded that, for most purposes, people may be divided into those who accept responsibility and those who do not. — CHARLES F. MOORE, Jr., Vice President, Public Relations, Ford Motor Company, Dearborn, Michigan.   (1103)

When man brings himself to believe that he has no responsibility to the ongoing generation, that his only responsibility is to himself alone and that his responsibility consists solely of making any and all concessions, no matter what, simply to preserve his own physical life a bit longer, no matter how abject his poverty of mind, spirit and body becomes, he has then reached a deplorable condition of mind, with a total absence of any philosophy of life. — KARL R. BENDETSEN, President, Champion Papers Inc., Hamilton, Ohio. (11 (1104)

The thing I've told everybody around here is not to accept responsibility but to fulfill it. There's one hell of a difference. — GORDON GRAND, President, Olin Mathiesen Chemical Corporation, *Quote*. (1105)

RESPONSIBILITY — Individual
This sense of individual responsibility is the key to healthy nationhood. Look around the world today. The nations that are prospering are the ones whose economic systems unleash the full measure of people's energy, ability, character and initiative, and provide them with the freedom they need to make the most of their opportunities. — GEORGE CHAMPION, Chairman of the Board, The Chase Manhattan Bank. (1106)

REWARD — Punishment
Expectation of reward and punishment may not make a moral man, but at least it makes man well-behaved. Where virtue is its sole reward, few are on their best behavior. — GABRIEL HAUGE, Vice Chairman of the Board, Manufacturers Hanover Trust Company, New York. (1107)

RIOTS
For the past few years, headlines have featured riots, civil disorders, human conflict resulting in destruction of lives and property as a demonstration of racial embitterment, hatred and frustrations. This is not happening in some remote jungle between semi-civilized tribes. This is back home. Certainly it is criminal to loot and burn. But long seething, underlying, unattended grievances are also deplorable — and also criminal. — HARRY R. HALL, President, Michigan State Chamber of Commerce. (1108)

An ironic and baffling aspect of the recent riots is that many of the cities hardest hit had the most active anti-poverty programs. They had received larger-than-average shares of the billions of dollars

206

dispensed each year by the Federal Government to aid the underprivileged. — GEORGE CHAMPION, Chairman of the Board, The Chase Manhattan Bank. (1109)

RISK-TAKING — Security.

The idea of security seems to have grown so rapidly in recent years that the spirit of risk-taking — historically the dominant mark of youth has become a little dulled. — GERALD J. LYNCH, President and Chairman of the Board, Menasco Manufacturing Company. (1110)

RUSSIA — America

As the Russians begin to achieve the position of affluence that they strive for, the Communist Party will probably become more a mediator between various divergent forces and groups within the country than a central dictator. This would be a salutary development, from which might emerge a more friendly and less lethal relationship between the Soviet Union and ourselves. — JOHN SCOTT, Special Correspondent, Assistant to the Publisher, *Time*.

(1111)

RUSSIA — Education

Russia boasts of its higher learning. But the facts in the case are that the percentage of young people in America who complete four years of college education, under freedom, is three times as great as the percentage of young people in Russia who complete four years of college education, under state control. Three times as great. — ARCH N. BOOTH, Executive Vice President, Chamber of Commerce of the United States. (1112)

RUSSIA — Women

Girl-watching is a good deal less rewarding in Russia than in most places. You do see some good-looking girls, of course, in their late teens and early twenties. But from the late twenties on, and sometimes earlier, the starch diet, the hard work, the monotony and deadly seriousness of living — these things take over, and you don't often see a pretty, smiling, well-dressed woman over 30 with a good figure. And the lack of foundation garments doesn't improve the scenery. — LEE HILLS, President, American Society of Newspaper Editors. (1113)

RUSSIANS

In dealing with the Soviets, we must be as difficult and mean as they are. We must obstruct them as much as possible and we must not concede anything. — G. KEITH FUNSTON, President, New York Stock Exchange, (1114)

S

SAFETY

Safety comes not only from the natural human fear of injury. Safety comes also from a general awareness that doing a thing in the right way means doing it in the safe way — whether we are on the highway, in the home, at school, or on the job. — L.L. COLBERT, Chairman of the Board, Chrysler Corporation, Detroit, Michigan.

(1115)

All the books on safety, the legislation, the scare headlines, and the pointing fingers have done nothing to change the fact that a major part of the safety problem depends on community action for its solution. — BYRON J. NICHOLS, Vice President, Marketing, Chrysler Corporation. (1116)

It's better to have unmarked police cars than to have well-marked graves. — DAVID W. CRAIG, Pittsburgh's Safety Director, *Quote*.

(1117)

SAFETY — Automotive

Many comments have been made that the auto industry is foot-dragging in safety innovations because "safety doesn't sell." This simply is not true. Safety does sell cars. It is, however, only one of several factors that sell. Safety is high on the list — along with good engineering, styling and quality construction — among car-buying influences. — HENRY FORD, II, Chairman of the Board, Ford Motor Company, *Trial*. (1118)

SALESMANSHIP

Salesmanship can function like a chain reaction. Every closed sale can lead to an open door. Start with the sales that have ended, and there's no end to the sales that can start. — ELMER G. LETERMAN, *The Sale Begins When the Customer Says "No"* (MacFadden-Bartell).

(1119)

The men who sizzle with success are the fellows who know what they want and refuse to give up until they reach their destination. Dream big dreams . . . fight big battles . . . want more than you have today. Darwin, who gave the world the concept of the "survival of the fittest", proved that it pays to struggle against big odds. If you

208

fight hard enough, you may win. If you sit back and accept the role life dishes out, you'll deserve everything you get. — ELMER WHEELER, Salesman, *Salesman's Opportunity*. (1120)

As an automobile man, I have always subscribed to the idea that the way you sell anything — whether it's cars or ideas — is to take a positive approach and stick to it. — L.L. COLBERT, Chairman of the Board, Chrysler Corporation, Detroit, Michigan. (1121)

Salesmanship is the key to our economy — to our way of life. — FEN K. DOSCHER, Senior Vice President, Lily-Tulip Cup Corporation. (1122)

The biggest problem in retaining bright young men in retail selling is the silent problem of relieving the boredom of a job where there is absolutely nothing to do over 50% of the time. — JAMES W. COBB, Marketing Services Director, *Time Magazine, Quote.* (1123)

The salesman cultivates all kinds of people to improve his knowledge of human nature in general. He then translates this skill by turning it into personal service sales. — ELMER G. LETERMAN. (1124)

America is a nation of salesmen. We are a race of salesmen. We have mastered the art of production — both in terms of quality and quantity. — S. JOHN INSALATA, Associate Legislative Counsel for the National Automatic Merchandising Association. (1125)

No one is more to be pitied than the salesman who does not understand the function he is playing in society — how completely dependent the world is upon him and those like him. — ELMER G. LETERMAN, *The Sale Begins When the Customer Says "No"* (MacFadden-Bartell). (1126)

There is no better salesman in the world than the American businessman once he gets going. — JOHN I. SNYDER, Jr., Chairman of the Board and President, U.S. Industries, Inc. (1127)

Every salesman has two sides, as it were. One consists of his personality, his powers of persuasion, his knowledge, and his integrity. The other consists of his reputation, his prestige, his renown. One is the ability that he actually has; the other is what the world thinks he has. — ELMER G. LETERMAN, *The Sale Begins When the Customer Says "No"*, (MacFadden-Bartell). (1128)

SALESMEN — Abroad

The day is past when the American salesman abroad could speak any language — so long as it was English! — E.J. HANLEY, President, Allegheny Ludlum Steel Corporation, Pittsburgh, Pennsylvania. (1129)

SALESMEN — Words

To marshal words, to add reserves to them constantly, to be able to call from among them those best suited to particular missions, and to have all under such control that none ever run loose — this is the way of a successful salesman with his words. His vocabulary is an army, regimented and equipped to march at his will. — ELMER G. LETERMAN, *Nylic Review*, New York Life Insurance Company.

(1130)

SATELLITES — Food

Satellites, with their capacity for instantaneous observation and reporting of potential and actual agricultural conditions, also offer part of the solution to the ominous shortage of food problem. Some agencies have estimated the future potential economic payoffs in crop planning, harvest scheduling, pest control, and water supply management can add several billion dollars' worth of food to the world economy. — JOHN R. MOORE, Vice President, North American Rockwell Corporation, President, Aerospace and Systems Group.

(1131)

SCHOOLS — Children

No school should proceed on the theory that any child is unreachable or unteachable, whatever the niggardliness of his background or the paucity of his own will to learn. — A.H. RASKIN, Assistant Editor, *New York Times* Editorial Page.   (1132)

SCHOOLS — Dropouts

It is quite plain that the dropout is going to be the shutout in tomorrow's economy. — A.H. RASKIN, Assistant Editor, *New York Times* Editorial Page.   (1133)

SCHOOLS — Students

The finest contributions that any school can make to a student are: to stimulate his thirst for knowledge; to teach the habits and systems of learning; to encourage the use of knowledge and ability; to implant a desire to help others to learn and to do; and finally, to teach a willingness and desire to excel. — BYRON J. NICHOLS, Dodge General Manager and Vice President, Chrysler Corporation, Detroit, Michigan.   (1134)

SCIENCE

The age of science is in. In its sturdy infancy it offers the greatest change man has yet had to express himself, to be truly personal. We can avoid over-planning and the mob assaults on hot issues of the fashionable science of our time by the wisdom of seeing that science is for people. – WILLIAM O. BAKER, Vice President for Research, Bell Telephone Laboratories, *Public. Utilities Fortnightly*.   (1135)

If we press too hard for more scientists, scientific quality will suffer or we will rob some other area of its creative people. Sooner or later our expenditures for research and development must be brought to some constant relationship to gross national product. We must have able men in government, able men in business, able men in the professions, our full share of creative output in literature and in the arts, no less than we need of these things in science. The society which creates scientists by diminishing the ranks of its philosophers may in the end have little need for either. – C.H. GREENEWALT, Chairman of the Board, E.I. duPont de Nemours & Co., *Quote*.
(1136)

SCIENCE – Liberal Arts

The scientist who knows all about monomolecular films and nothing about the work of a deMille or a Rank with another kind of films is a man skewed, awry, incomplete. The man with a Ph.D. who is exhaustively expert about the use of metaphor in Shakespeare's tragedies but knows nothing of metabolism is also a man skewed, awry, incomplete. The liberal arts can teach the scientist about values, purposes, and the deep unrationalities of the human condition. The sciences can teach the generalists in liberal arts about patient observation, the repeated verification of hypotheses, and the grave importance of open-minded skepticism. Each, I am convinced, must learn from the other. – ARTHUR P. LIEN, Research and Development Department, American Oil Company, Whiting, Indiana.
(1137)

SCIENCE – Politics

It takes no social historian to observe that if we ran our factories, conducted our communications, and nurtured our health at the same rate of scientific and technical advance as we conduct our political affairs, we would still be taking weeks to make a pair of shoes, delivering the mail by pony express, and treating pneumonia by bloodletting. – FRANK STANTON, President, Columbia Broadcasting System, Inc.   (1138)

211

SCIENCE — Religion

"A soul?" the scientist used to say. "God? I've never yet seen a soul or God, so how can you expect me to believe in them?" Today's scientist doesn't say it. He can't. He has never seen an atom or an electron or a proton either — but he knows they exist. And the more he studies their complexity — the more he deduces about their nature — the more he is filled with a growing, reverent sense of law and beauty. Perhaps he has even pointed the way to a deeper faith in God and the unseen wonders of his creation. — ARTHUR P. LIEN, Research Development Department, American Oil Company, Whiting, Indiana. (1139)

SCIENCE — Technology

Since 1900, there has been more scientific and technological progress than in all the previous centuries of recorded history. — DAVID SARNOFF, Chairman of the Board, Radio Corporation of America. (1140)

One of the paradoxes of our age is that advances in science and technology are far outstripping man's ability to manage his affairs. — DAUSE L. BIBBY, President, Remington Rand Division, Sperry Rand Corporation. (1141)

One of the essential tasks of the generations ahead, as well as our own, is to put to broad social uses the scientific discoveries and technical innovations that have proliferated so fast in our time that their uses lag far behind their capacities. — FRANK STANTON, President, Columbia Broadcasting System, Inc. (1142)

SCIENCES — Behavioral

Study of the behavioral sciences is something new for industry. We've been so wrapped up in the physical sciences, in the things we can feel, smell, measure, touch and calculate, that we've ignored the study of thought processes that permit man to create. — A.C. DAUGHERTY, President, Rockwell Manufacturing Company. (11
(1143)

SCIENCES — Humanities

It seems to me that there is wisdom in achieving in our institutions of higher learning a realistic balance between the sciences and the humanities. While no man can be all things to all people, it is becoming increasingly apparent that proficiency in a specialty — whether it be engineering, accounting, economics or teaching — is simply not enough. — CHARLES G. MORTIMER, Chairman, General Foods Corporation, White Plains, New York. (1144)

SEA

If we compare the pay-off of outer space ventures with the pay-off of inner space ventures, it is perhaps fair to say that going to the moon will mainly give us access to new dimensions of knowledge whereas going to the bottom of the ocean will give us access to new physical and vital resources. – Dr. THEODOR F. HUETER, General Manager, West Coast Operations Ordnance Division, Honeywell, Inc.

(1145)

SEA – Power

We are a fulcrum of history when we must consider our sea power not only as a military force but as a force for economic and social advances. Like land power and air power, sea power will then take on a larger stature not only as a deterrent to aggression but as a creative force for peace. – EDWARD WENK, Jr., Executive Secretary, National Council on Marine Resources and Engineering Development.

(1146)

SEA – Wealth

Whatever else the future holds, I feel our industry and our country must develop our sea wealth. Years ago Sir Walter Raleigh said, "Whoever commands the seas, commands the trade, whoever commands the trade . . . , commands the riches of the world. . . . " I believe these words from the past point a direction for the future. – CHARLES F. JONES, President, Humble Oil and Refining Company.

(1147)

SECURITY

It is my belief that it is difficult, if not impossible, to discover security. I believe that security must be attained – and when attained, that it must be maintained. I also believe that the probability of attaining security, when pursued as a life goal, is far less than if it is sought as a by-product of adventuresome and successful living. – GERALD J. LYNCH, President and Chairman of the Board, Menasco Manufacturing Company.

(1148)

SECURITY – Complacency

Security is a natural desire, but we must bear in mind that it is only a short step from security to complacency, and complacency is the most insecure footing of all. – RAY R. EPPERT, President, Burroughs Corporation.

(1149)

213

SECURITY – Opportunity

Today, too many young folks and older ones looking for a job are willing to trade security for opportunity. – J.K. STERN, President, American Institute of Cooperation, Washington, D.C.

(1150)

SELF-DETERMINATION

We are what we accept ourselves as being. We can be what we convince ourselves we can be. – ELMER G. LETERMAN.   (1151)

SELF-DISCIPLINE

The quality that is valuable above all others is self-discipline. Thus are great men, great families, and great nations made. The progress of the human race has been a measure of the individual's ability to gain control of himself. – WILLIAM FEATHER, William Feather Company, *William Feather Magazine.*   (1152)

SELF-ESTEEM

It may not seem of major importance the way your shoes are shined, the way you scatter ashes when you smoke, the way you sit or stand. However, many men make the mistake of indicating through such small things that they don't think too much of themselves, and you can't expect other people to think much of you unless you hold yourself in high regard. – HERMAN C. KRANNERT, Chairman of the Board, Inland Container Corporation.

(1153)

SELF-HELP

The best place to find a helping hand is on the end of your arm. – ELMER G. LETERMAN, *Quote.*   (1154)

SELF-IMPORTANCE

I don't think anybody is as important to you as you. – ARTHUR H. MOTLEY, President, Parade Publications.   (1155)

SELF-KNOWLEDGE

The surest of all ways to find yourself is to lose yourself in something bigger than yourself. – ELMER G. LETERMAN, *Personal Power Through Creative Selling* (Harper & Row).   (1156)

SELF-MANAGEMENT

Self-discipline is self-management. And you can literally bet your life on this. If you don't manage yourself, somebody else will manage you, and you will spend the rest of your life working for him and not for yourself. – ELMER G. LETERMAN, *Personal Power Through Creative Selling* (Harper & Row). (1157)

SELLING

Personal selling goes all the way back to the Yankee peddler. In fact, it can be traced back to Biblical days. Surely, among Adam, Eve, The Apple and the Snake, there was at least one salesman. – E. CABELL BRAND, President, Ortho-Vent Shoe Company, *Salesman's Opportunity*. (1158)

Selling is at the bottom of everything. It has made all sorts of things possible in our daily lives. It's been responsible for the mass production in the United States. It's been responsible for giving us an economy of free choice. It has been the miracle ingredient that stuffs pay envelopes and fills the grocery bag to help feed, clothe and educate our children – and a myriad of other things. – ARTHUR K. WATSON, President, IBM World Trade Corporation. (1159)

I subscribe to the adage that nothing happens in industry until somebody produces an order – that machinery and equipment, bricks and mortar and an industrial organization, have no life or vitality until something is sold. – ROBERT G. WINGERTER, President, Libbey-Owens-Ford Glass Company. (1160)

SERVICE

A large number of people are seeking happiness in the wrong places, by the wrong methods. There is only one way to find happiness, and that is in the pathway of service. Many a position attained can never result in happiness, except as they are used to benefit the condition of those outside our household. – J.C. PENNEY, *Christian Herald*. (1161)

You can assess the contribution a person is making to society by observing his environment. You can do much the same thing by looking at a place of business, a company of any sort or size. You can quickly see what the business is doing for the community by observing what the community is doing for the business. Our rewards in life will always be in direct ratio to our contribution, our service. – EARL NIGHTINGALE, Chairman of the Board, Nightingale-Conant Corporation. (1162)

SERVICE INDUSTRIES

The United States is becoming a service economy. It was

predominantly an agricultural and manufacturing economy, but today more than half the working population of the country is employed in service industries. – JACK I. STRAUS, Chairman, R.H. Macy & Co. Inc. (1163)

SERVICE TO OTHERS

There is no man in the world so big that you cannot do something for him that will please him, and make him remember you and your name favorably. – ELMER G. LETERMAN, *Sales Marketing Today*. (1164)

SEX

Wherever you go, you find people speaking of "The New Morality," "The New Freedom," "The Erotic Revolution," "The Libertine Age," "The Sex-Affirming Culture." And, whatever you call it, it all adds up to the same thing – a contagious spirit of permissiveness, of "anything goes," in all areas of social conduct, in manners, dress, and sexual relationship. It applies at all age levels, and to married and unmarried alike. All America seems to be engaged in one vast, all-pervading, all-permissive, Sexological Spree. – WILLIAM I. NICHOLS, Publisher and Editorial Director, *This Week Magazine*. (1165)

SEXES

I believe in two sexes – each distinguishable from the other by clothing and hairdo. – JO FOXWORTH, Vice President, Calkins & Holden. (1166)

SHOWMANSHIP

The practice of showmanship is not a chore. It does not make Jack a dull boy. On the contrary, it is a lark. I can honestly say that my life has been one long ride on a merry-go-round. I grabbed the brass ring when I was still in my teens, and I still find the ride as exciting as ever. If I had my life to live over again, I wouldn't change a thing. For this reason I can heartily recommend the practice of showmanship to anyone who wants to get the most out of his business career. – ELMER G. LETERMAN, *How Showmanship Sells* (Harper & Row). (1167)

Too many talented people settle for far less than their abilities entitle them to. What these people often lack is the knack of showmanship – the ability to make themselves stand out in a crowd. – ELMER G. LETERMAN, *How Showmanship Sells* (Harper & Row). (1168)

SILENCE

Modern man, whose destiny seems directed as much by technology as spirituality, has not lost the need for the tranquility of silence. . . . Silence has always been the essential condition of the creative life. Clamor and creativity do not mix. The disciplined writer, sculptor, painter, or musician insulated himself from the ceaseless importunities of his fellow man. Man may be a social animal, but the great man is a lonely man and he relies on solitude to establish the communication necessary to his condition, that is, communication with himself. — RICHARD M. RALSTON, Director of Communications, Blue Cross Association.   (1169)

SLUMS

The slums of our nation are the shame of our nation — urban and rural. Economically excluded fellow human beings have been dumped into stinking, rodent ridden, disease infested areas like cast off debris on mammoth rubbish heaps — the hidden poor — the prejudicially impaired, unwanted, unrecognized, neglected smoldering heaps of human frustrations that refuse to disappear no matter how hard we have tried to ignore them. — HARRY R. HALL, President, Michigan State Chamber of Commerce.   (1170)

SLUMS — Clearance

Just as long as the Government of the United States delays a nationwide slum clearance and low rent housing program of proper proportions, just so long does it threaten its cities with insolvency, retard the capital goods industry, delay re-employment in the building trades, and continue the manace of slums to real estate values. — CHARLES F. PALMER, President, Palmer, Inc., Atlanta, Georgia.   (1171)

SMALL BUSINESS

What all social engineers fail to see is that the very controls they propose, and the burdensome tax structure that finances them, make smallness in business a practical impossibility. Today a business must either expand or die. The little fellow with a great product or a unique system will sooner or later sell out to a giant to improve its product performance and its operating efficiency. — LAWRENCE H. ROGERS, II, President, Taft Broadcasting Company.   (1172)

SMALL BUSINESS – Government

Any involvement by government in the mechanics of our marketing and distribution system would make it even more difficult for the small firm to be competitive and thus to retain its share of the market. The impact of such interference unquestionably is greater on the small firm because it forces higher costs. – LLOYD E. SKINNER, President, Skinner Macaroni Company.   (1173)

SMILES

When you see a man without a smile – give him one. – ELMER G. LETERMAN.   (1174)

SOCIALISM

I am against Socialism because Socialism is the child of materialism and when Socialism walks in the front door, the record shows that religious faith goes out the back and with it goes individual rights and individual opportunities to achieve. – J. THOMAS GURNEY, Attorney.   (1175)

The Pied Piper of Socialism still plays his soothing and alluring melodies of wealth without work, security without sacrifice, results without responsibilities, rights without effort, and the naive children of the Socialist regime continue to follow him into the land of oblivion. – J. THOMAS GURNEY, Attorney.   (1176)

SOCIAL PROGRESS

What really counts, when we measure social progress, is not the ingenuity of technology or the growth of national product, but the quality of our society and our individual lives. The basic measures of social achievement are such things as human satisfaction and fulfillment and the growth of harmony, goodwill and respect among men. – HENRY FORD, II, Chairman of the Board, Ford Motor Company.   (1177)

SOCIAL SECURITY

People live partly by hopes and struggles for a better life. Social Security provides a footing on which they can work their way up from a bare existence to comforts and security. – ALLAN SHIVERS, President, Chamber of Commerce of the United States.   (1178)

SOCIETY

What we need is a society where people do a little more than the law requires and a little less than the law allows. — J. IRWIN MILLER, Chairman, Cummins Engine Company, *Quote*.   (1179)

SOCIETY — Healthy
A healthy, progressive society depends on people who recognize that disagreement is normal and healthy. They respect the other fellow and his right to be different. They know that the need to live in harmony and goodwill is as important as the need to be true to themselves. They fight for what they want within the bounds of civilized behavior and rational discourse. And they understand that compromise is the only realistic solution to most problems. — HENRY FORD, II, Chairman of the Board, Ford Motor Company.   (1180)

SOCIETY — Improvement
A high percentage of one hundred million youngsters seem bent on improving our society, on giving it greater spiritual values along with the unmatched material success. And like it or not, business cannot rest on the sidelines. We are in the game by definition. It is not for nothing that we are known and think of ourselves as an industrial civilization. — PETER W. ALLPORT, President, Association of National Advertisers.   (1181)

SOCIETY — Perfect
As a living tree is the result of molecular configurations and life forces which man is utterly incapable of designing or creating or arranging, so is the quality of a society the result or consequence of tiny, individualistic forces. Imperfect man cannot manipulate imperfect men into a perfect society. The perfection of any society can be approached only as imperfections are overcome by its members, a project of infinite proportions, for man is imperfect by nature; man can never do more than approximate perfection. The quality of a society cannot be superior to the quality of its leaders. Rock or bramble or barren soil cannot be organized to show forth as a garden of roses. — LEONARD E. READ, President, The foundation for Economic Education, Inc., Irvington, New York.   (1182)

SOLITUDE
The finest hours of life are not those spent among groups of people, but in good conversation with a few, in reading good books, in listening to great music, wandering in a forest of giant Sequoias, peering into a microscope, unravelling Nature's secrets in the

laboratory. The men who have the most to give their fellowmen are those who have enriched their minds and hearts in solitude. It is a poor education that does not fit a man to be alone with himself. — JOEL H. HILDEBRAND, Chemist, Berkeley, California, *Sunshine.* (1183)

So seldom does our mad way of life offer us the opportunity to be alone, with nothing before us but a chance to think, that there are those among us who have lost all capacity for formulating their own philosophy. Instead of seeking solitude for its own sake, they fear it, and those convictions which they hold are those which they have borrowed, ready-made, from others. — CLARENCE B. RANDALL, Retired Chairman, Inland Steel Company. (1184)

Solitude is such a dreadful prospect for most people that they can actually find companionship in transistor radios when friends are unavailable. — RICHARD M. RALSTON, Director of Communications, Blue Cross Association. (1185)

SPACE

Space actually is a technological tapestry upon which we may embroider the outline of a new dimension of social, economic and hopefully, political progress. — H. BRAINARD FANCHER, General Manager, General Electric Apollo Support Department. (1186)

SPACE AGE

It would be ironic if — at the moment we were successfully reaching out toward the stars — we were to perish through inability to manage our affairs on earth. — JOHN E. SWEARINGEN, Chairman of the Board, Standard Oil Company (Indiana). (1187)

Once the phrase "reaching for the moon" indicated all that was vain, unreal and impossible. Today we have men in training who will shortly go there. — ALBERT J. NEVINS, M.M., Editor. (1188)

If we in this country have the good sense to continue the pace we have started in reaching the moon and the planets beyond, I think the astronautics industry in ten years will be larger than the combined automobile industries of the world. — M.G. O'NEIL, General Tire and Rubber Company, *Quote.* (1189)

SPACE BUDGET

The annual space budget has never represented more than one per cent of the gross national product. Economists have estimated, because of the way it is spent, that our one per cent probably generates more employment and more production than do any other programs with the possible exception of the nation's education programs. — JOHN R. MOORE, Vice President, North American Rockwell Corporation, President, Aerospace and Systems Group.

(1190)

SPACE EXPLORATION

Our space programs are not stunts or gimmicks or voyages for gold or jewels or spices. Rather, they are catalysts in a formulative process which will join scientific research to the needs of modern man. — H. BRAINARD FANCHER, General Manager, General Electric Apollo Support Department. (1191)

The great opportunity which space exploration offers us is *not* the chance of going to the moon, *not* the possibility of finding life on Mars — it is the opportunity to gain a new perspective on *ourselves*. If we do not stand humbled by the findings in the Universe, how can we lay aside our petty quarrels and differences on this earth? — CHARLES H. PERCY, President, Bell & Howell Company, Chicago, Illinois. (1192)

The purpose of our space program should not be to see who can throw the biggest engines into the sky, or to get some-place first. Our purpose must be to enlarge the scientific resources and potential of the United States. — H. BRAINARD FANCHER, General Manager, General Electric Apollo Support Department. (1193)

SPACE TRAVEL

Science isn't going to put men on the moon. It's going to be the engineer. — CLIFFORD H. SHUMAKER, President, American Society of Mechanical Engineers, *Quote.* (1194)

SPEAKERS — Speaking

I do not like to think of speech as one man talking at a group of people, but rather as a conversation between the speaker and the group. — EDWARD J. MEEMAN, Editor, *Memphis Press-Scimitar.*

(1195)

SPEAKING

I have more respect for a man who is articulate on most things — and makes an occasional mistake — than for one who refuses to speak and then moans because things happen with which he disagrees. — L.C. MICHELON, Director of Public Affairs, Republic Steel Corporation. (1196)

SPECIALIZATION

The mounting demand for special skills and the growing complexity of industry is increasing the need for business specialists. But educator and employers alike are coming to recognize that specialization alone will not be at all adequate in a world that demands ever-increasing flexibility and versatility. — BYRON J. NICHOLS, Dodge General Manager and Vice President, Chrysler Corporation, Detroit, Michigan. (1197)

Because no man is a computer, capable of total information storage and recall, he is penned increasingly into areas of specialization — forced to make a choice of interests, condemned to know more and more about less and less. The result is that at a time when he should encompass an increasingly wide range of knowledge, his scope has narrowed. Specialization has bred parochialism and ignorance of other fields. — ROBERT W. SARNOFF, President, Radio Corporation of America. (1198)

SPEECH

A gift of gab is all right — if you wrap it up in time. — ELMER G. LETERMAN. (1199)

SPEECH — Introduction

Public speaking has always had certain terrors for me. So I have wondered from time to time why I do it, and I've asked myself that question. There is an answer. The answer, I find, is not that I am infatuated with the sound of my own voice. It's simpler than that. It's that I like to be introduced. You know, there is an unwritten law that provides that if a fellow stands up and inflicts himself in an unendurable monologue on an unoffensive public, he shall be preceeded by someone who recalls everything good that can be dredged up about him, and avoids all of the unpleasant of his past. — ALAN BARTH, Editorial Board, *Washington Post.* (1200)

After dinner speaking is the art of saying nothing briefly. — ARVILLE SCHALEBEN, Executive Editor, *The Milwaukee Journal.* (1201)

In my travels abroad, I am continually impressed by the fact that most other countries restrict mealtime oratory to the brevity of a toast, and follow the noonday meal with a siesta. Here at home, though, we cling to the quaint notion that speeches are somehow an aid to digestion — a kind or rhetorical bicarbonate of soda! — GEORGE CHAMPION, Chairman of the Board, Chase Manhattan Bank. (1202)

SPIRITUAL DEVELOPMENT

Some people say the spiritual values of our society have deteriorated. I am not sure that is true. But I *am* sure that our nation's development of the human spirit has not matched our tremendous material progress. — JOSEPH H. McCONNELL, President, Reynolds Metals Company. (1203)

STATES RIGHTS

States never have had rights in this country, not even during their heyday under the Articles of Confederation. It always has been the people who have had the rights, who have held the ultimate sovereignty. This always has been at the heart of our American form of government. — LEROY COLLINS, President, National Association of Broadcasters. (1204)

STATISM — Individualism

When Americans are confronted with the choice between statism and individualism as exemplified by Russia and the United States, they have no difficulty in making a decision. They are overwhelmingly in favor of individualism. But when the same people are confronted with the same choice within our own nation, the decisions for the last thirty years have been largely in favor of statism. Not by voice. Not by vote. But by default. — RALPH M. BESSE, President, The Cleveland Electric Illuminating Company. (1205)

STEEL INDUSTRY

Our problem in the United States is not one of becoming competitive in a world steel market which we have never seriously exploited, or attempted to exploit. Instead, ours is a problem of finding ways and means to step up the rate of growth in our own domestic economy. — OTIS BRUBAKER, Research Director, United Steelworkers of America, *Quote*. (1206)

STRENGTH

If we are to meet our commitments to ourselves and to the next generation, it seems to me that at least three kinds of strength are involved: (1) military strength; (2) economic strength, and (3) moral and spiritual strength. — FRED J. BORCH, President and Chief Executive Office, General Electric Company. (1207)

STRENGTH — Determination

I believe that in individual as well as international relations strength and a wise determination to use that strength generates unity in association with others. — ROBERT MURPHY, President, Corning Glass International. (1208)

STUDENTS

I am one of those who are all for seeing students govern themselves, but have some apprehension about their governing everything else. — FREDERICK R. KAPPEL, Chairman of the Board, American Telephone and Telegraph Company. (1209)

STUDENTS — Business

Right now, with both an expanding population and, hopefully, a continually expanding economy, business needs an ever-growing supply of the best young talent available. Yet, increasingly, we're having trouble getting all the good people we need. And part of the problem is the attitude today's students seem to have. — A.F. JACOBSON, President, Northwest Bell Telephone Company. (1210)

STUDENTS — Unrest

However spooky some of the manifestations of the present campus unrest may look, they are at least higher up the intellectual ladder than devouring uncooked goldfish and stealing unoccupied women's underwear — which had their day — and they bespeak a more thoughtful generation. — LAWRENCE A. KIMPTON, Vice President, Standard Oil Company (Indiana). (1211)

STUDENTS — Viet Nam

Part of the criticism of students for marching around carrying placards demanding that the U.S. get out of South Viet Nam strikes me as intemperate — so long as they don't presume to take matters illegally into their own hands by lying down in front of troop trains. If all they are doing is voicing an opinion this is surely their right, however little we may happen to think of that opinion. — LAWRENCE A. KIMPTON, Vice President, Standard Oil Company (Indiana). (1212)

SUBURBS

The suburbs are becoming less and less free of slums. They are more and more tending to turn themselves into hideous blights they once offered refuge from. . . . Instead of facing up to the chore of city slum clearance, we have been clearing out for the suburbs, leaving great areas of urban blight. In most cases, this is the blight similar to the one in which Americans stripped the soil of its fertility and then moved west to start the same wasteful pattern all over again. — CRAIG A. SMITH, President, Sullivan-Smith Realty Company, *Quote*. (1213)

SUBVERSION
We are about as subversion-proof as a great power can be, and it is tragic that we spend so much of our time and energy attacking and defending the patriotism of our leaders and thereby divert them, and ourselves, from the monumental problems we do face. If the ship of state founders, it will likely do so on the rock of irrelevance. — HARRY S. ASHMORE, Editor-in-Chief, Encyclopaedia Britannica. (1214)

SUCCESS
The traits that make for success are not inborn, like a gift of music or painting. They are developed through hard work and planning, by a willingness to learn, from a determination to bounce back after rebuffs. — ELMER G. LETERMAN, *How Showmanship Sells* (Harper & Row). (1215)

The man who will use his skill and constructive imagination to see how much he can give for a dollar, instead of how little he can give for a dollar, is bound to succeed. — HENRY FORD, *Quote*. (1216)

Success is a lady who confers no favors on a coward. — ELMER G. LETERMAN, *Personal Power Through Creative Selling* (Harper & Row). (1217)

You cannot rest on your success of today if you want to do better tomorrow. — L.F. McCOLLUM, Chairman, Continental Oil Company. (1218)

Success, real success in any endeavor, demands more from an individual than most people are willing to offer — not more than they are capable of offering. — JAMES M. ROCHE, President, General Motors Corporation, *Chicago Sun-Times*. (1219)

SUCCESS — Failure
We make our own success or failure. — ELMER G. LETERMAN, *Commissions Don't Fall From Heaven* (MacFadden-Bartell). (1220)

SUCCESS — Responsibility
Too many people want success today without making the

necessary obligation and accepting responsibility to achieve it. — J.K. STERN, President, American Institute of Cooperation, Washington, D.C. (1221)

SUPER-HIGHWAYS
We have made the cloverleaf our national flower. — STUART T. SAUNDERS, Chairman of the Board, Pennsylvania Railroad, *Quote.* (1222)

SUPERVISORS
It takes much longer to develop a skilled manager of men than it does to build a machine, yet we often approach the training of supervisors much more haphazardly. — STEPHEN M. JENKS, Executive Vice President, United States Steel Corporation, *Quote.* (1223)

SURVEYS — Statistics
There is nothing wrong and much that is good about surveys and statistics ... if they are used as tools, and not venerated as deities ... if they stimulate our thinking, and can't merely replace it or stultify it ... if they lead to a creative grasp of new situations, rather than petrify our old prejudices and make us passive in the face of change. — PETER G. PETERSON, President, Bell & Howell Company. (1224)

T

TALENT

Sheer raw talent is heady stuff to discover in yourself. It's a tremendous thrill to find out that you can paint a landscape or write verse or kick a football farther than anybody else on your block. Any father who has successfully put together a knocked-down gym set for his kids can't help but swagger a little in front of his wife. It takes talent to understand the directions. But talent carries its own set of dangers. It can very readily be confused with solid achievement. — CHARLES F. MOORE, Jr., Vice President, Public Relations, Ford Motor Company, Dearborn, Michigan.   (1225)

TAXES

Certainly people have always complained about taxes — but I think we have to recognize that the average citizen today carries a tax load that really hurts. In some places, where local problems have piled up after long neglect, the tax situation assumes the proportions of a crisis. — JAMES M. PATTERSON, Director of Public Relations, American Oil Company.   (1226)

TAXES — Reductions

Cutting taxes can invigorate an economy to further economic expansion. Experience shows that individuals and corporations can both be depended upon to spend most of the increase in their income resulting from tax reductions. The multiplier effects of such spending are very good for the economy — if the economy is at less than full employment, and if the size of the tax cut is appropriate to the needs of the times. — JAMES F. OATES, Jr., Chairman of the Board, The Equitable Life Assurance Society of the U.S.   (1227)

TEACHERS

The teacher's greatest obligations go beyond the routines of imparting knowledge. We assume that he has the tools of his trade — that he knows his subject. But we expect and demand much more from him. He should be an inspiration to his students — an intellectual and moral leader. He must fire their imaginations — expand their intellectual curiosity — and fill their reservoir of spiritual

227

values. I don't think I could define *how* he accomplishes all this, but I know that great teachers do it. — JOSEPH H. McCONNELL, President, Reynolds Metals Company. (1228)

TEACHING — Computers

We hope to find out more — because we must find out more — about what is specifically meant when we say that every school-child learns but in his own way at his own rate of speed. We — and other companies — are experimenting with high-speed computers as aids in teaching children. Possibilities growing out of the new electronic-curriculum mix are without number. Whether tomorrow's machines will be mechanical tutors, television sets, do-it-yourself kits, or simply words printed on file cards, or combinations of all these, we don't yet know. But we are deeply engaged, in collaboration with the Federal government and local schools, in finding out. — LYLE M. SPENCER, President, Science Research Associates, Inc. (1229)

TEACHING — Humanities

Because no man is a computer, capable of total information storage and recall, he is penned increasingly into areas of specialization — forced to make a choice of interests, condemned to know more about less and less. The result is that at a time when he should encompass an increasingly wide range of knowledge, his scope has narrowed. Specialization has bred parochialism and ignorance of other fields. Ignorance has led to indifference, and indifference has sometimes festered into hostility. Nowhere is the schism more evident and nowhere is it potentially more perilous to the progress of mankind than the one which exists between technology and the humanities. — ROBERT W. SARNOFF, President, Radio Corporation of America. (1230)

TECHNOLOGICAL PROGRESS

The real danger facing our economy today is not automation. Rather, it is the possibility that we might fail to take complete advantage of every opportunity for technological progress which is economically feasible. — RAY R. EPPERT, President, Burroughs Corporation. (1231)

TECHNOLOGY

Technology is not the toy of the prosperous; it is, potentially, the servant of all societies trying to engineer an escape from their poverty. — GEORGE D. WOODS, President, World Bank, (1232)

We are "packaging" our modern technology for export to the depressed and underdeveloped nations of the world. Stored in the minds of American businessmen and our inventory of equipment are the means by which the "have-not" nations of the world can jump from more or less primitive levels to modern economies — viable and self-sufficient in the broadest sense of the word. — Dr. PHILIP NEFF, Vice President, Planning Research Corporation.   (1233)

Advancing technology and all other causes are eliminating jobs at the rate of 2% a year — lowest rate in our history. At the same time, however, new technology is creating three new jobs for every two we eliminate. — THOMAS F. PATTON, Chairman, Republic Steel Corporation, *Quote*.   (1234)

TECHNOLOGY — Future

If technology can match our ambitions in the early 1970's, a passenger can go to his shopping center, for instance, and insert a plastic credit card, punch a button to see if there is a seat on tomorrow's flight to Chicago; get an affirmative answer; punch another button and have a ticket drop into his hand — confirmed, recorded and ready to use. — STUART G. TIPTON, President, Air Transport Association, *Public Utilities Fortnightly*.   (1235)

TECHNOLOGY — Human Welfare

In our eagerness to explore the new technology, we have been looking at the trees and failing to see the forest. In our adulation of the computer and other new devices and techniques, we have dwelt too much on the amazing technological capabilities of new electronic hardware and have done far too little to demonstrate its equally amazing potential for advancing human welfare. — ARJAY MILLER, President, Ford Motor Company.   (1236)

TEENAGERS

Teenagers are the most colorful and persistent faddists in our society, but a fad is a symptom, not a disease. They wear funny clothes, funny haircuts, say and do strange things. But the fads they adopt are not to be confused with the immutable law which rules every generation of teenagers. This law says, "Thou shalt be different, but for pretty much the same old reasons." No matter how odd their behavior, they are responding to the same age-old urge for independence. — PAUL C. HARPER, Jr., President, Needham, Harper & Steers, Inc.,   (1237)

These five subjects are actually an inventory of the problems, the "big deals," facing teenagers today, and for many reasons they're worth taking a look at. It's worth asking the questions, "What's happening Baby?" .... Money — Teenagers today have enough money to make them a real economic force. Sex — Teenagers are reaching physical maturity at a somewhat earlier age — and there are more sexual stimuli around than ever before. Mobility — Teenagers today have a new dimension of independence — the automobile. They can get around. They can get away. School — Teenagers today are under more pressure from the educational establishment than ever before. War — Teenagers long-term, like the rest of us, have the bomb hanging over their heads ... short-term they've got Vietnam. — PAUL C. HARPER, Jr., President, Needham, Harper & Steers, Inc. *Quote*. (1238)

TEENAGERS — Communication
The problem of communicating with the younger generation would be less complicated if parents knew a little more about what was going on over there under that male or female wig. One way to find out, I have discovered, is to act as chauffeur for a group of teenagers. Keep your mouth shut, and within minutes of starting out you will be forgotten and conversation will go on as though you were an automatic pilot. I don't know if this is considered an illegal form of bugging, but it is effective. — PAUL K. CUNEO, Editor, *America*.
(1239)

TEENAGERS — Purchasing Power
Would you believe that at the present time, the teenagers of this country have a purchasing power of approximately twelve billion dollars a year. . . . Do you remember how simple life used to be when all we had to worry about was keeping up with the Joneses? Well, now we have to try to keep up with their kids as well! — W.O. ROBERTSON, Vice President of Armco Steel Corporation. (1240)

TELEVISION
We can hope that with further experience, the day will come when television will be admitted, together with other media, not only to legislative but also to suitable judicial proceedings, for public justice. — ROBERT W. SARNOFF, Chairman of the Board, National Broadcasting Company, *Public Utilities Fortnightly*. (1241)
Television is the greatest instrument for growth in this economy.

Television has democratized selling. It's given everyone a chance to speak to the whole country at once about his product. — LEONARD H. LAVIN, President, Alberto-Culver Company, *Quote.* (1242)

Television . . . has exposed millions to experience in the arts that range from great drama and music to the painting of Michelangelo or Van Gogh and the sculpture of Moore or Giacometti. Through television, the mass audience also has become aware of the challenges of conservation, the problems of air pollution, and the progress of medical science. The viewer is as familiar with space exploration as he is with the travels of Bob Hope. — ROBERT W. SARNOFF, President, Radio Corporation of America. (1243)

Television has made available to people of even the most modest means and in remote places, a spectrum of information, entertainment and cultural experience which fifteen years ago was restricted to the most affluent residents of the largest metropolitan area. — LOUIS HAUSMAN, Director, Television Information Office, New York City. (1244)

In the fanciful world of mythology, the more difficult problems were solved by gods and giants. In our own time we have been aided by the fortuitous arrival of a communication giant — television — that cannot solve our problems for us but can assist an entire population in understanding them. — ROBERT W. SARNOFF, Chairman of the Board, National Broadcasting Company, Inc. (1245)

Never before has the agony of war been brought with such brutal and unremitting force into our own living rooms, intruding almost hourly into our lives. And never before has a social revolution — the civil rights revolution, intruded so insistently into our lives — visually, for all of us to see. No wonder that so many people are upset by what they see on television. — ELMER W. LOWER, President, ABC News. (1246)

Man will find his true universal language in television, which combines the incomparable eloquence of the moving image, instantly transmitted, with the flexibility of ready adaptation to all tongues. It speaks to all nations and, in a world where millions are still illiterate and semi-illiterate, it speaks clearly to all people. — ROBERT W. SARNOFF, Chairman, National Broadcasting Company, *Quote.*
(1247)

Television, like the psychiatrist, is alternately loved and hated by the patient. — ELMER W. LOWER, President, ABC News. (1248)

TELEVISION — Advertising
It's impossible to look at The Tube for any length of time

231

without developing a tremendous inferiority complex. It's obvious that the manufacturers of consumer products have scientifically determined that the American buying public is divided into only two groups — there's the Bi-Focal Set. With this it seems all manner of white things are flying past, in or around Mrs What's-her-name's kitchen . . . and then there's the Swinging Set — those handsome, healthy young people who are either frantically coming alive in the Pepsi Generation, or seriously moving to Sunoco. Personally, I regret being catalogued with the first group, and I'm frustrated because I can't keep up with the second. — W.D. ROBERTSON, Vice President, Armco Steel Corporation. (1249)

TELEVISION — Children

After years of exposure to radio and television news and to newspaper headlines and news magazine digest, we have become accustomed to skimming the "top of the news." While adults have developed these habits and attitudes, they have become part of the very psyche of our children. This is pointed up by the experience of a teacher in an experimental school in Florida who was having difficulty teaching a group of small boys how to read. Then she got the idea of projecting the stories on a screen, page by page. The children could read them easily. Because of their experience with television, they understood the words looking at a screen. — ARTHUR R. MURPHY, Jr., President and Chief Operating Officer, McCall Corporation. (1250)

TELEVISION — Culture

For all its shortcomings, television has brought the culture of the world to every corner of the country. — FRANK L. WHITNEY, President, Walter Kidde Constructors, Inc., Engineers and Builders. (1251)

TELEVISION — Journalism

The massive influence of television journalism is demonstrated by survey results showing that more than half the nation gets most of its news from television. — ROBERT W. SARNOFF, Chairman of the Board, National Broadcasting Company, Inc. (1252)

TELEVISION — Public Hearings

The doors to public proceedings should be opened to television whenever they are open to other elements of the press, so that television can use its special capacities to enable the people to

232

witness the conduct of the people's business. This calls for abandonment of existing discriminatory rules barring television from federal, state and local legislative chambers and the hearing rooms of legislative committees. — ROBERT W. SARNOFF, Chairman of the Board, National Broadcasting Company, Inc.   (1253)

TELEVISION — Subscription

I think television has done remarkably well in bringing entertainment, news and other features to the home; but there are certain obvious limitations to the existing economic support of advertiser-sponsored television which frustrate the maximum potential of the medium, and particularly the development of a viable and vigorous UHF system. We believe subscription TV can overcome these limitations, and can provide programs and revenue sources for many marginal television stations which are now struggling to stay on the air. — JOSEPH S. WRIGHT, President, Zenith Radio Corporation.

(1254)

Subscription TV is a highly efficient method of distributing great box office events. It brings the stage and the concert hall, the arena and the motion picture theatre to the home rather than transporting the audience to the event. It was conceived as a way of adding a new dimension to TV by making it possible for the subscriber's home to become part of the theatre, just as the motion picture brought the stage via the medium of film to thousands of local communities far from production and cultural centers. — JOSEPH S. WRIGHT, President, Zenith Radio Corporation.   (1255)

TELEVISION — Work

I have nothing against fun and leisure, yet I find it alarming to learn that the population of my country is putting in more hours per year in front of picture tubes than in productive work. — ED LIPSCOMB, National Cotton Council, Memphis, Tennessee.   (1256)

TEXAS — Texans

It is no exaggeration to say that I always find it refreshing to visit your fine state because Texans have such a positive view of any situation. You take the attitude that yours is the greatest state in the union and you don't care who knows it. As a nation, we'd be better off if everybody had this Texas brand of enthusiasm. — GEORGE CHAMPION, Chairman of the Board, the Chase Manhattan Bank.

(1257)

THINKING

The capacity to think is the most precious possession we have. Thinking is fun. Thinking is habit-forming and you couldn't have a better habit. — ROSCOE DRUMMOND, Editor and Columnist.

(1258)

THINKING — Leisure Time

One of the best ways to spend leisure time is in thinking. Of course, this does take a little effort but after one has had a little practice it comes rather easily — or so we are told. In any event it is not a harmful pastime. — HUBBARD COBB, *American Home.*

(1259)

THINKING — Manners

The manner of a man's thinking shapes his manners. — ELMER G. LETERMAN, *Commissions Don't Fall From Heaven* (MacFadden-Bartell).

(1260)

THINKING — Objective

Everyone possesses the capacity to think objectively. There is no special dispensation for the capacity to think. It is our God-given birthright. — ROSCOE DRUMMOND, Editor and Columnist. (1261)

THOUGHT

We live in a world of physical comfort which was undreamed of by our ancestors a century or two ago, yet from their way of life they drew values which have been lost to us, and which we seem unable to recapture. If I were to select the particular value which those sturdy pioneers possessed, and which I would most like to see become an attribute of our daily living, I would choose the hours which they were compelled to spend alone. They had time to think. — CLARENCE B. RANDALL, Retired Chairman, Inland Steel Company.

(1262)

THOUGHT — Action

Every act is first a thought. Too many of us jog through life without giving enough serious thought to reaching a definite goal. — B.C. FORBES, *Forbes.*

(1263)

THOUGHTS

Our personalities are not merely mirrors giving back reflections of our thoughts. We are shaped, molded, colored, and defined by our thoughts. They work within us to make us what we are as organically as the life impulse within an acorn determines the form and glory of the oak. – ELMER G. LETERMAN. (1264)

We are today where yesterday's thoughts have brought us, and we shall be tomorrow where today's thoughts carry us. – ELMER G. LETERMAN, *Nylic Review*, New York Life Insurance Company.

(1265)

TOOLS – Man

Machines are not creative or imaginative, nor even responsible. They are simply tools, and tools do not work and serve mankind untilskilled hands take them up. Because our tools are growing in complexity and in potential usefulness, we must grow in order to use them profitably and wisely. – HOWARD A. MOREEN, Senior Vice President and Secretary, Aetna Life & Casualty. (1266)

TRADITIONS

The traditions are important; we should not be too eager to overthrow them. They are necessary because every individual needs an integrated view of himself and of his relationship to others. He needs an historic reference in which to place himself in order that he may build upon it an explanation of his presence on earth and an understanding of his purpose in life. – JAMES O. DOBBS, Jr., Industrial Relations Consultant and Lecturer, Austin, Texas. (1267)

TRANSPORTATION

Equality of treatment by government of all transport competitors, a freer competitive environment, and the maximum encouragement to merge and reorganize the national transport structure – these provide the keys to the super-transportation service of the American future. – DANIEL P. LOOMIS, President, Association of American Railroads. (1268)

I believe that under private investment and management the United States has today the best over-all system of transportation in the world. – ERNEST S. MARSH, President, The Atchison, Topeka and Santa Fe Railway Company. (1269)

Even though the United States is the most mobile society the world has ever known, our national transportation system is not nearly as advanced as it ought to be. – STUART T. SAUNDERS, Chairman of the Board, The Pennsylvania Railroad Company. (1270)

Much more intensive use of ocean, Great Lakes and river highways for domestic commerce in combination with rail is, I believe, an idea whose time has come. – W.J. BARTA, President, Mississippi Valley Barge Line Company. (1271)

What the nation needs in transport policies is a legal format that will not only give equal justice to all contenders in the highly competitive contest for traffic but, more important, will allow each carrier to serve the public and develop on the basis of its natural abilities and not on the basis of those artificially created by favored government treatment. In this approach and in this approach only lies the common sense possibility of reshaping the U.S. transportation machine and getting it into the sound working condition needed to meet the great needs of our future. — DANIEL P. LOOMIS, President, Association of American Railroads, Washington, D.C.
(1272)

Transportation in the United States, aside from accounting for about one-fifth of the Gross National Product, is the one industry that makes the functioning of virtually all other industries possible. — STUART T. SAUNDERS, Chairman of the Board, The Pennsylvania Railroad Company. (1273)

In an economy in which rising costs of materials and wages are becoming a matter of increasing concern, intensive utilization of low cost water transportation provides a major opportunity to achieve substantial savings in production and distribution costs for both industry and agriculture. . . . The opening of new water-rail routes could save the economy millions of dollars in transport costs. — W.J. BARTA, President, Mississippi Valley Barge Line Company. (1274)

TRAVEL

Instead of restricting travel abroad and further straining our relations with other countries, the United States should vastly increase its own appeal for foreign visitors. — EDWIN A. LOCKE, Jr., President, American Paper Institute. (1275)

They say that travel is broadening and that by getting around you come to learn more about other lands and their people. Yet, it seems to me that, if you think as you go, travel can give you an even more important dimension than breadth. It can give you *depth* in the form of a new insight, a new perspective, a new and deeper understanding of the facts and events of the day. — JOHN I. SNYDER, Jr., Chairman of the Board and President U.S. Industries, Inc. (1276)

Vacations offer us another opportunity to shake loose from the rigid traditions that may begin to bind us. Travel really is broadening for most of us, and the reason is that we can observe with a fresh outlook things that would pass unnoticed at home. — M.J. WARNOCK, President, Armstrong Cork Company. (1277)

U

UNCOMMON MAN

While this may be the first century in which the common man has come into his own in terms of human dignity and opportunity, I believe that the future of the world rests upon the shoulders of what I prefer to call the *uncommon* man. If the free world as we know it, is to survive in the perilous years ahead, it is the uncommon man in the fields of education, business, science and government who will preserve it. – Dr. GEORGE L. HALLER, Vice President, General Electric Company. (1278)

UNDERSTANDING GAP

Despite our ability to send a picture in full color instantly across oceans and continents, or print thousands of copies of a newspaper or magazine in a matter of hours, or to obtain an untold number of facts from a computer within seconds, there is evidence that an "understanding gap" of serious dimensions exists in this country today. – ARTHUR R. MURPHY, Jr., President and Chief Operating Officer, McCall Corporation. (1279)

UNEMPLOYMENT

Our problem is not unemployment, but unemployables. Nearly one million Americans – one-third of all the nation's jobless – lack elementary job skills and, in some cases, cannot even read or write. Even greater numbers are condemned by lack of education or skill to a life of subemployment, unable to find full-time work or earn enough money to support their families. – ROBERT W. SARNOFF, President, Radio Corporation of America. (1280)

The only effective way to combat unemployment, is to create a business atmosphere where businessmen will want to expand and hire more people. The only way businesses can expand is to attract new investment and the only way to attract new investment is with profits. The formula is Profits = New investment = Employment. – AMYAS AMES, President, Investment Bankers Association of America. (1281)

237

UNEMPLOYMENT – Automation

Instead of making automation the scapegoat of our unemployment problems, we should seek, through a large scale and unified research effort, the real causes of the various types of unemployment. – RAY R. EPPERT, President, Burroughs Corporation. (1282)

UNEMPLOYMENT – Education

The principal problem of the unemployed is lack of education. Educated people do not have trouble getting jobs and this applies to all nations and all races. – W.B. MURPHY, President, Campbell Soup Company. (1283)

UNEMPLOYMENT INSURANCE

Unemployment insurance is a social need but it has bad as well as good effects. It does not stimulate the desire to serve, which is essential to an economy as well as an enterprise. – JACK I. STRAUS, Chairman, R.H. Macy & Co., Inc. (1284)

UNIVERSITY

Living with a university should be like spending four years in the company of a very great man, one who – like Aristotle in ancient Greece – embodies all the accumulated knowledge, wisdom and ethics of his time. – JOSEPH H. McCONNELL, President, Reynolds Metals Company. (1285)

UNIVERSITY – Alumni

The alumni are the university's end product. What they accomplish in life and how they accomplish it are, in the final analysis, the true measurement of the quality of the university. I do not necessarily mean material success, or personal fame. I mean the kind of people they become, the standards they set for themselves, their attitude and behavior as they advance or fail. – JOSEPH H. McCONNELL, President Reynolds Metals Company. (1286)

URBAN GHETTOES

The cost of maintaining a great mass of unproductive people is already enormous. Unless cures are found, particularly to the ills that exist in the urban ghettoes, these costs will be even greater tomorrow and will increase geometrically as long as widespread poverty, immorality, crime, and violence continue to exist. – L.W. MOORE, President, American Oil Company. (1287)

238

V

VACATIONS
Every man carrying heavy responsibilities should take a genuine vacation, throw off the cares of daily tasks at least once a year — better still, twice — and leave all business cares behind. The men at the top who enjoy life most are those who have remained boys at heart, who have cultivated a sense of humor, who have learned to like people and to get along harmoniously, pleasantly, with them. — B.C. FORBES, *Forbes*.   (1288)

Whether it's the Jungfrau or Westhampton Beach, isolation from the contemporary scene is good medicine. It's wonderful for clearing the cobwebs from the brain. And all those problems that pile up as each day's mail floods the "in" box, they all seem much less important. — ELMER W. LOWER, President, ABC News.   (1289)

VALUES
We shall be rich or poor only as we seek or reject those values which make us so. — ELMER G. LETERMAN, *Nylic Review*, New York Life Insurance Company.   (1290)

Were you told to go into a great storehouse and take what would give you health and happiness and ecstatic moments, you certainly would not be foolish enough to choose poisonous food and drinks. When making our choices in the great storehouse of the universe, we are only silly, aren't we, if we choose anger, hate, jealousy, and selfishness? — THOMAS BREIER, Advertising Specialist, *Quote*.
(1291)

VEHICLE INSPECTION
Money spent on vehicle inspection is an investment in human life. — BYRON J. NICHOLS, Vice President, Marketing, Chrysler Corporation.   (1292)

VIETNAM
We have expended for the peaceful development of the people of Viet Nam more in the last few years than all imperialistic nations spent on all of Asia in the last century — and without hope or desire — for return — of anything but peace. — JAMES A. FARLEY,

Chairman of the Board, Coca-Cola Export Corporation.   (1293)

To defeat the aggression in Vietnam does not mean merely that we will have helped preserve the independence of South Vietnam. It means that we will have helped set back the whole pattern of Communist "wars of liberation" to which both Red China and the Soviet Union remain committed. It will mean that further aggression will be more difficult and more uncertain and more uninviting for the aggressor. — ROSCOE DRUMMOND, Editor and Columnist.

(1294)

VIOLENCE — Children

We are drowning our youngsters in violence, cynicism and sadism piped into the living room and even the nursery. The grandchildren of the kids who used to weep because The Little Match Girl froze to death now feel cheated if she isn't slugged, raped and thrown into a Bessemer converter. — JENKIN LLOYD JONES, Editor, *The Tulsa Oklahoma Tribune.*   (1295)

VIOLENCE — Law

We cannot sanction terror in New York or in Mississippi. Retaliation is not justified by bitterness or past disillusionment. No individual or group at any time, for any reason, has a right to exact self-determined retribution. All too often, retaliation injures the innocent at random and provokes counter-retaliation against those equally innocent. Our imperfections do not justify tearing down the structures which have given us our progress. The only solution is the free and open law society. — MORRIS I. LEIBMAN, Chairman, ABA Standing Committee on Education Against Communism.   (1296)

VOCATIONAL EDUCATION

One of the huge problems of education which we are very late in solving is the introduction of a proper range of opportunities for vocational training. Our public school curriculum emphasis is predominantly oriented to the literacy and pre-professional type of training. The industrial and commercial requirements of today call for a vast expansion of vocational opportunities to permit a very large segment of the population to be self-supporting. — RALPH M. BESSE, President, The Cleveland Electric Illuminating Company.

(1297)

VOTERS — Communications Gap

The typical voter of today is farther away from his government — and therefore less able to vote intelligently — than he was 25 years ago, or even five years ago. This is not because the government is bigger. It is because the information on which national decisions are based is either secret or it is too complex for the voter to understand. This situation worries the hell out of me. I believe the greatest single challenge before all of us today is to help find the means to bridge this frightening communications gap. — ROBERT VAN RIPER, Vice President and Director of Public Relations, N.Y. Ayer & Son, Inc.   (1298)

VOTERS — Voting

From primitive registration procedures right down to the casting of the ballot, we make voting as difficult, vexatious and inconvenient for the citizen as we can. — FRANK STANTON, President, C.B.S., *Quote*.   (1299)

Too often we vote on a man's looks instead of his principles. — ROBERT R. SPITZER, Businessman.   (1300)

WAR

Every war scatters seeds from which a new war may emerge. — ANDREW R. CECIL, Executive Vice President, The Southwestern Legal Foundation. (1301)

In no sense do I defend war. It is evil, it is immoral. But the tragedy of it is that we live in an evil and immoral world. It is folly to think that you can shroud war in respectability. — FELIX R. McKNIGHT, Executive Vice President and Editor, *The Dallas Times Herald.* (1302)

WAR — Deterrent

I think it should be recognized by all our citizens that in this tinderbox period of the hydrogen bomb, the greatest deterrent to war is the enemy's knowledge that we have the capacity to retaliate against the first attack. — CHARLES L. GOULD, Publisher, *San Francisco Examiner.* (1303)

WAR — Peace

For as long a time as we can see into the future, we shall be living between war and peace, between a war that cannot be fought and a peace that cannot be achieved. — WALTER LIPPMANN, Columnist. (1304)

WATER — Pollution

Just as the world needed a nuclear test ban treaty to protect us from radioactive fallout, the world now needs similar binding agreements to safeguard against the pollution of our planet's water resources and against the extinction of marine life which is man's main future protein resource. — Dr. THEODOR F. HUETER, General Manager, West Coast Operations, Ordnance Division, Honeywell, Inc. (1305)

WEALTH

Our wealth is *not* a result of government planning, natural resources, or a host of other reasons and apologies advanced by ivory tower dreamers — it is *directly* and almost completely based upon.

the physical hard work contribution of labor, the dedication of long hours of intensive effort by the managers of our enterprises, and the aggressive attitudes of U.S. capital towards the commitment of its funds. Wealth is not created until somebody *physically* makes something having usefulness and value. – ROBERT G. WINGERTER, President, Libbey-Owens-Ford Glass Company.

(1306)

WELFARE

The riots this past summer underscored the fact that a reappraisal of national priorities is long overdue. Our Welfare State, based largely on the priorities of thirty years ago, is hopelessly obsolete. We need new imaginative, result-oriented approaches to welfare – approaches designed to take full advantage of the strengths of private business and to give every individual a stake in our society. – GEORGE CHAMPION, Chairman of the Board, The Chase Manhattan Bank.

(1307)

WESTERN EUROPE – Defense

If there is one area in the free world which is today able to provide for its own defense, it is Western Europe. – HERBERT V. PROCHNOW, President First National Bank of Chicago, Illinois.

(1308)

WIRETAPPING

Wiretapping, and that form of electronic eavesdropping so commonly and so aptly referred to as "bugging" are now rather widely used by the police in their efforts to catch criminals. It is true that the Supreme Court said that these methods of investigation do not violate the Fourth Amendment. But they undoubtedly violate privacy. They undoubtedly interfere with the freedom of communication among law-abiding citizens, which is, or ought to be, a characteristic of a free society. And wiretapping, at least, just as undoubtedly violates an act of Congress. – ALAN BARTH, Editorial Board, *Washington Post*. (1309)

WISDOM

Despite the tremendous progress of man in our lifetime the great need which remains is for wisdom. – ROBERT R. SPITZER, Businessman. (1310)

WOMEN

The women of America have talent and ability, intelligence and character — and ideals. — ARCH N. BOOTH, Executive Vice President, Chamber of Commerce of the United States. (1311)

We in North America have emancipated the woman from drudgery. We have given her the vote and an electric kitchen. We permit her to hold a job. But we have failed to recognize that the brains of women are equal to — if not superior to — the brains of man. — RAYMOND W. MILLER, President, Public Relations Research Associates, Inc., Washington, D.C. (1312)

We can no longer tolerate the distaff side of the house retiring to the suburbs to a lifetime of intellectual vegetation. The problems are too hard, and the time is too short, for our society to scrap 50 per cent of its intellectual resources. We must find new ways for our capable women to continue to contribute professionally to the solutions of the world's problems. — ROBERT ALAN CHARPIE, BS, MS, DSc, Director of Technology, Union Carbide Corporation, New York. (1313)

Women have moved ahead, and have blossomed out in all directions through the years — and that is the way it should be. The women of America . . . have won their place in business and industry, and in the professions — and have done so with grace and charm and humor — and with great ability — and, I must add, with terrific thoroughness. — ARCH N. BOOTH, Executive Vice President, Chamber of Commerce of the United States. (1314)

WORDS

Only those who truly know words can be sure of speaking simply. — ELMER G. LETERMAN, *Nylic Review*, New York Life Insurance Company. (1315)

A word is not something wrapped in cellophane with its content always undisturbed. Words are living things, full of association, changing meaning as they go from one mind to another. — W.R. KELLY, Lawyer of Greeley, Colorado, *Sunshine Magazine*. (1316)

Words are the lubrication of the mind because it cannot run any more smoothly within itself than its command of words allows. A man's thinking is exact only to the degree that he has words to make it so. We can think in nothing but words. When our words run out, we come to the end of our thinking; all we can do is to repeat ourselves. — ELMER G. LETERMAN, *Personal Power Through Creative Selling* (Harper & Row). (1317)

Words are like water, once spilled cannot be recovered. — ELMER G. LETERMAN. (1318)

Words met for the first time are like unopened letters — their value known only to those who get inside them. — ELMER G. LETERMAN, *Personal Power Through Creative Selling* (Harper & Row). (1319)

Words are the tools with which the mind shapes ideas, they are the wings on which ideas fly. — ELMER G. LETERMAN, *Nylic Review*, New York Life Insurance Company. (1320)

WORK

The man who knows how will always find a job, but the man who knows why will be the boss. — ELMER G. LETERMAN, *Personnel Journal*. (1321)

I have never known any man or woman to succeed in any business or any profession who was jealous of the hours he gave to his job. — ALDEN PALMER, *Fraternal Monitor*. (1322)

I have come to the conclusion that work is the chief source of happiness. We both lose and find ourselves in work. Hard workers have few annoying complexes. Their minds and bodies are creatively occupied. — WILLIAM FEATHER, William Feather Company, *William Feather Magazine*. (1323)

The man who wants to do the job for the sake of seeing it done right is the one who will make it big both in the bucks and in prestige. — A. CLARK DAUGHERTY, President, Rockwell Manufacturing Company. (1324)

If you want to do our Nation a service, teach the idea that you work for what you get, and you get what you work for. — R.L. SHETLER, General Manager, Defense Systems Department, General Electric Company, Syracuse, New York. (1325)

If a society of free men is to flourish, its members must respect work. Where idleness can become the way of life of the rich and the aim of the not-so-rich, where a species of loafing goes by the name of contemplation, where malingering is condoned, progress is destined to be slow. — GABRIEL HAUGE, Vice Chairman of the Board, Manufacturers Hanover Trust Company, New York. (1326)

Our children should know that the only way to have more is to produce more. That the good things life has to offer are won by work . . . hard work! — NICHOLAS A. GEORGE, Vice President of Brunswick Corporation, Chicago, Illinois. (1327)

Work gives dignity and meaning to our individual lives. We need to ponder the possibly damaging effects to character and initiative if work is relegated to a minor position in daily life. — LAURANCE S. ROCKEFELLER, Chairman, Outdoor Recreation Resources Review Commission. (1328)

WORK – Ability

The average human being in any line of work could double his productive capacity overnight if he began right now to do all the things he knows he should do and to stop doing all the things he knows he should not do. – ELMER G. LETERMAN, *Personal Power Through Creative Selling* (Harper & Row).   (1329)

WORK – Challenges

I feel sorry for the man who doesn't look forward to going to work in the morning. I feel sorry for the people who work only to make a living so they can eat and sleep and have an occasional evening at the theatre. These people are missing one of the best treats life offers by not looking for the challenges in their work. – EDWIN M. CLARK, President, Southwestern Bell Telephone Company, St. Louis, Missouri.   (1330)

WORK – Hours

If you work twelve hours a day, you finally get to be boss so you can put in sixteen to eighteen hours a day. – DONALD M. KENDALL, President, Pepsi-Cola, *Quote*.   (1331)

WORK – Idleness

If it were not for the demands made upon me by my business, I would provide living proof that a man can live quite happily for decades without ever doing any work. – JOHN PAUL GETTY, *Quote*.   (1332)

WORK – Leisure

Hard work too seldom appears on any modern list of virtues – leisure too often. – HENRY C. ALEXANDER, Chairman of the Board, Morgan Guaranty Trust Company of New York.   (1333)

WORK – Sleep

A man should work eight hours and sleep eight hours, but not the same eight hours. – ELMER G. LETERMAN, *Gold Book*, New York Life Insurance Company.   (1334)

WORK – Smarter

One of the great needs of business is not to get its key men to work harder (no one has ever called them lazy), but to get them to work smarter. This often means to work less hard. — HAROLD MAYFIELD, *Supervisory Management*. (1335)

WORK — Training
I say, give a man a fish and he will soon be hungry again, but teach a man how to fish, and he can live for the rest of his life. — Rev. LEON H. SULLIVAN, Chairman and Founder, Opportunities Industrialization Center, Philadelphia. (1336)

WORK — Workers
The man who isn't capable of doing great things, but does the very best he can on the job he has, is worth more to himself than the potential genius who loafs his way through life just getting by. — EDWIN M. CLARK, President, Southwestern Bell Telephone Company, St. Louis, Missouri. (1337)

WORKERS
To meet the manpower challenge brought on by the changing demands of our economy, we must create an entirely new generation of workers — the well prepared, the well educated, the white collar worker, the white smock workers, the public administrator, the service worker, and the teacher. — T.F. PATTON, Chairman and President, Republic Steel Corporation. (1338)

WORKERS — Advancement
For workers and manager alike, the one who advances rapidly tomorrow will be the one who finds new tasks to set for the tools, new and diverse ways in which they may be directed, novel uses of material and more efficient methods of production. In the long term, it is he, not the assembly line, who will set the pace. — DAVID ROCKEFELLER, President, Chase Manhattan Bank. (1339)

WORKERS — Capabilities
It is my considered judgment that the limitation of our future success will not be lack of knowledge, or lack of material resources, nor even lack of professional and managerial talents to enable us, through instrumentation and the other elements of automation, to raise the level of our economy, of our education, our health, our arts, and our reference. What will limit us, possibly even stop us cold, will be a failure to engage and utilize to the fullest extent of his capability every responsible citizen of this great nation. — Dr. VAN W. BEARINGER, Vice President and General Manager, Systems and Research Division, Honeywell, Inc. (1340)

WORKERS – Handicapped

We've found that it really doesn't matter whether a company's workers have two legs, or one, or none. Insurance rates are not influenced. In fact, many insurance companies consider the handicapped a better risk than their able-bodied co-workers. – TOM GILLICK, Hughes Aircraft Company, *Quote*. (1341)

WORKERS – Unskilled

I think there is no question that the problem of unrest may be compounded, for the moment, because the rather significant progress that skilled and educated Negroes have made in recent years has increased the expectations of other unskilled and uneducated people beyond what they can reasonably hope to achieve in a short period of time. – L.W. Moore, President, American Oil Company. (1342)

WORKING CONDITIONS

Business and industry have lived with this concern about surroundings for a long time, and have long since learned that providing proper working conditions is not a liability but an advantage. Better conditions produce better workmen and better products and give the employer a wider choice in the hiring of employees. And in the end, better conditions produce more stability of employment as well as better public relations. – LAURANCE S. ROCKEFELLER. (1343)

WORKMEN – Tools

A good workman keeps his tools keen. As a craftsman, he knows that he will not be able to add the extra touch to his creation unless his steel has a fine cutting edge. – ELMER G. LETERMAN, *Nylic Review*, New York Life Insurance Company. (1344)

WORLD

If this is not exactly the kind of world you would like, it is nevertheless the kind of world we must operate in. It may not be "the best of all possible worlds," but it is the kind we have. It is the world to which we must adjust. – J. CARROLL BATEMAN, President, The Insurance Information Institute. (1345)

WORLD – Change

The world has changed more in the twenty or so years . . . since

World War II, than in all the previous millenia of recorded history. — ROBERT W. SARNOFF, President, Radio Corporation of America. (1346)

WORLD — Destiny
As we look back through the pages of history, we can see that the destiny of the world has been shaped largely by men whose leadership was born in the heat of crisis. From the time of Moses, whose leadership was born in the face of persecution of the Jews by the Pharoahs, to the present time, leadership has been born in pain of slavery and exploitation, as a reaction against poverty and misery. — ANDREW R. CECIL, Executive Vice President and Educational Director, The Southwestern Legal Foundation, Dallas, Texas. (1347)

WORLD — Economy
By far the greater part of the job of moving the world economy ahead will have to be done through the instrumentality of private business. — LYNN A. TOWNSEND, President, Chrysler Corporation. (1348)

WORLD — Future
The diaries, journals and letters of every age show that every generation of parents has despaired for the future of a world in the hands of its profligate sons, as, I am sure, will you in your time. And every generation of sons has feared that this same world, in the hands of their fathers, would not last that long, as I did in my time. — MARVIN C. WHATMORE, President, Cowles Communications Inc. (1349)

WORLD — Insecurity
Without doubt, the two great sources of insecurity in the world today are the underdeveloped nation and the underdeveloped person. — F.J. BORCH, President and Chief Executive Officer, General Electric Company. (1350)

WORLD — Leadership
To be capable of world leadership, we must have strong and able government. — NEIL McELROY, Chairman, Proctor & Gamble Company. (1351)
Whether we like it or not, we are a world leader and this places certain responsibilities upon us. — R.A. PETERSON, President, Bank of America. (1352)

The leadership of tomorrow's world will not be assumed by those who know a great deal about a very little, nor a very little about a great deal. It will be assumed by those whose horizons are wide enough to comprehend the world in which we live. — T.F. PATTON, President, Republic Steel Corporation, Cleveland, Ohio.   (1353)

WORLD — Living
We must recognize that the world does not owe us a living — in fact, that the world cannot afford to owe us a living even if it wanted to do so. Only we ourselves can provide that living. — ROGER M. BLOUGH, Chairman of the Board, United States Steel Corporation.

(1354)

WORLD — Man
The dreams of man finally shape the world, no matter his color or his home. — LOWELL SCHMIDT, Senior Vice President, Sertoma International.   (1355)

WORLD — Population
The great economic problem of the world today is over-population in areas and among people who are unable to provide themselves with good or even adequate standards of living. Making provision whereby these standards of living may be raised is humanitarian but it is not logical. As long as we offer economic aid in the manner in which we now extend it, we are doing nothing but holding a finger in the dike until the overwhelming floods of increasing population in those areas finally engulf us. Unless birth control is tied to our efforts to improve the conditions of poverty-stricken people in the world, we must ultimately stagger and fall under the weight of this undertaking. — J. THOMAS GURNEY, Attorney.   (1356)

WORLD — Strength
The greatest concentration of political, economic and military strength in the world today lies not in the Soviet Union, with or without its satellites and Communist China. It lies in the Atlantic Community, acting together and with other friendly powers around the world. — J.D. ZELLERBACH, Chairman, Crown-Zellerbach Corporation.   (1357)

WORLD — Understanding
We must acquire a better understanding of the language, history and culture of people of other lands. With present day mass-destruc-

tion weapons, this understanding is not just desirable — it's vital. — THOMAS J. WATSON, Jr., Chairman of the Board, International Business Machines Corporation. (1358)

WORLD LAW — Peace

The day on which a world rule of law prevails will be the day that any man can travel any place on the face of the earth, or in endless space, in freedom, in dignity, and in peace. — CHARLES S. RHYNE, Past President, American Bar Association. (1359)

Disarmament is a delusion. It cannot, should not come. War cannot be prevented either by armament or disarmament. Only world law, enforced, can give assured peace. — EDWARD J. MEEMAN, Editor, *Memphis Press-Scimitar*. (1360)

The ugly fact that man can now destroy the world lends great urgency as well as great opportunity to the effort to achieve and maintain world peace by burying war under an avalanche of law. — CHARLES S. RHYNE, Past President, American Bar Association. (1361)

WORLD TRADE

The United States has a long way to go to develop the attitudes toward world trade that exist in many other countries. And we have a long way to go to catch up with the performance of other nations in the international community, too. — B.K. WICKSTRUM, President, General Time. (1362)

The world today increasingly must be regarded as one market. Our private and public policies should foster exports and improve the climate for foreign investment anywhere in the free world. Business must recognize in government an effective ally and government for its part must facilitate the role business can play in developing a politically strong and economically viable free world. — KENNETH RUSH, Executive Vice President, Union Carbide Corporation, New York. (1363)

In its internal economy this country has the finest system of private enterprise freed from unfair restrictive or monopolistic practices, and substantially free from Government controls, and I would like it to lead the way to the adoption of the principles of this system in world trade and investment. The first need is to have a sufficiently strong budgetary policy so that the dollar's value is unquestioned and does not rely upon restrictive monetary measures which do not provide the long term solution of inflationary pressures and do so much harm internationally. — PAUL CHAMBERS, Chairman, Imperial Chemical Industries, Ltd. (1364)

The future success of American business in world markets may depend less and less on technological advantages, and more and more on human qualities — on the ability of Americans to establish friendly, honorable, and enduring relationships with fellow human beings in foreign lands. — CHRISTIAN A. HERTER, Jr., General Manager, Government Relations Department, Socony Mobil Oil Company, Inc. (1365)

I would like to see in this country the adoption of a policy which confines monetary measures to the purposes — mainly short-term — for which they, and they alone, can be effective, and to have a sufficiently sound budgetary policy so that all monetary measures designed to restrict overseas trade and investment in the short-term interest of the balance of payments, can be abandoned for good. — PAUL CHAMBERS, Chairman, Imperial Chemical Industries, Ltd. (1366)

It is our costs, versus those of our competitors, which dominantly affect the ability of our economy to compete against others in world markets. Only as we improve our ability to compete through relatively lower costs and better quality, can we increase our exports and eventually cover not only our imports as we do now, but also our military and economic aid and other payments. — LESLIE B. WORTHINGTON, President, United States Steel Corporation, Chicago, Illinois. (1367)

I am profoundly convinced that this is our national economic destiny; to engage in friendly and mutually beneficial commerce with the outer world; to help other countries toward their economic goals; to share in their progress, not as capitalist or colonial exploiters, but as working partners who respect and understand their needs. — HENRY FORD II, Chairman of the Board, Ford Motor Company, Dearborn, Michigan. (1368)

It is absolutely vital to the very act of living for us to be energetic participants in international trade. — ROSS D. SIRAGUSA, Chairman of the Board and President, Admiral Corporation. (1369)

I happen to believe that we are headed toward a period of greatly liberalized world trade in the next few decades . . . where business trips to Bangkok on a supersonic jet will be regarded as a "long commute" . . . and where trade with what we now call Red China will be no more difficult than trade with what we now call France. — B.K. WICKSTRUM, President, General Time. (1370)

We must face the hard and inescapable reality — that, despite the overwhelming strength of our economy, despite our position of leadership, despite our record and desire to do more than our share, and despite the essential soundness of our position as banker to the world, the United States alone cannot solve the problem of the world's trade and payment mechanism. — R.A. PETERSON, President, Bank of America N.T. & S.A. (1371)

WORLD WAR II

If all the nations that united to defeat our common enemy in 1941 had been equally united when aggression first started by Japan against Manchuria in 1931 and by Italy against Ethiopia in 1935, the subsequent German aggression might have been prevented and the war of 1939-1945 would not have taken place. — ANDREW R. CECIL, Executive Vice President, The Southwestern Legal Foundation. (1372)

Y

YOUTH

Young people are far and away our most valuable national resource. — M.C. PATTERSON, Vice President of Chrysler Corporation. (1373)

The youth of today remain as America's best hope for tomorrow. — NICHOLAS A. GEORGE, Vice President of Brunswick Corporation, Chicago, Illinois. (1374)

We expect our children and their generation to think like us, to behave like us, to react and interact like us, but the plain truth is that they are not like us. Nor can they be. Nor should we expect them to be. — L.W. MOORE, President, American Oil Company. (1375)

Our America of tomorrow will surely be judged by what becomes of the youth today. — DAVID ROCKEFELLER, President, Chase Manhattan Bank. (1376)

Today, the "Cult of Youth" is on the way to dominating our total society. On every side Youth is King. And whatever our actual age, we all seem to be engaged in a headlong, intoxicating race to see who can look, who can act and who can be the swingingest — who can live the youngest. — WILLIAM I. NICHOLS, Publisher, *This Week Magazine*. (1377)

Next to the words "new" and "now" there is no more powerful word in the advertising language than the word "young." — WILLIAM I. NICHOLS, Publisher, *This Week Magazine*. (1378)

The reward that comes from working with young people is not of benefit solely to the mature business manager. His youthful associates gain also. One of the main tasks that faces any society is passing on the accumulated knowledge and wisdom it has learned — helping its young people to understand the meaning of past victories they have not had to win in order that they may be ready to fight their own battles in the future. — M.J. WARNOCK, President, Armstrong Cork Company. (1379)

Our youngsters are no better and no worse than we were at the same age. Generally, they are wiser. But — they have more temptations than we had. They have more cars. They have more money. They have more opportunities for getting into trouble. — CHARLES L. GOULD, Publisher, *San Francisco Examiner*. (1380)

YOUTH — Adults

We must set aside this moralistic, holier-than-thou attitude of complacent superiority that we adults so often assume in front of our youngsters, and be willing instead to take a closer look at what it is the adolescent needs for his tasks of growth as he moves from childhood to adulthood, and what it is that we as the guardians of society are or are not providing to him to make that possible. — ROY W. MENNINGER, MD., President, Menninger Foundation. (1381)

YOUTH — Age

There is really only one thing wrong with the younger generation . . . some of us do not belong to it anymore. — L.F. McCOLLUM, Chairman, Continental Oil Company. (1382)

YOUTH — Business

Whether we like it or not, the youth of America simply does not believe that the larger portion of American business and industry has yet come to grips with what they regard as the dominant, motivating force of today. In a world in which the overriding concerns are social rather than material, they feel that the greatest challenge before us lies in the banishment of problems which have been plaguing the world for centuries. — SOL M. LINOWITZ, Chairman of the Board, Xerox Corporation. (1383)

If I could convey only one idea to the younger generation of graduates and undergraduates, it would be that business and industry have always offered young people the values of growth, progress, and human betterment. And, if anything, this is more true today than ever before. Business provides the machinery for building a better standard of living — and, with it, the means for improving our social and cultural level. Business *is* engaged in helping people. Business *is* challenging and personally rewarding. Business *does* seek new ideas, and prizes the man who has them. — FREDERICK J. CLOSE, Chairman of the Board, Aluminum Company of America. (1384)

YOUTH — Democracy

It is while our young people are growing up and being educated that we need to indoctrinate them with belief in democracy. We need to imbue them with the kind of faith which will alter cynical attitudes and dispel apathy and misunderstanding. It is with our budding citizens that we need to put across the points which are the very hope of our society for the future. We must make them realize that to build, rather than to tear down, is the measure of man's maturity, and that the progress of mankind is built upon faith and affirmative action. – CHARLES G. MORTIMER, Chairman of General Foods Corporation. (1385)

YOUTH – Dissent

Something serious must be wrong when so many young people who have every obvious advantage in life are so willing to reject the world they are about to enter. Between preparation for life and life itself, something is out of joint. Wherever the fault lies, it seems to me that our schools and colleges offer the best hope of teaching young people the difficult art of responsible dissent. – HENRY FORD II, Chairman of the Board, Ford Motor Company. (1386)

YOUTH – Idealists

Today's young people are idealists, but it's a new brand of idealism. It is what President Kennedy called "idealism without illusions." – LYNN A. TOWNSEND, President, Chrysler Corporation. (1387)

YOUTH – Modern

I would hate to have to be in again and compete with them (college graduates). They are terrific. Their only fault is their impatience with red tape and old-fogie practices. They make things happen – fast. They learn more in six months than my contemporaries learned in three years. Basically, the so-called "turned-down" generation is no different from the young "roughnecks" and "wildcatters" out West forty years ago. Today those people who were not satisfied as teen-agers, then, are now the leaders of the oil industry. – ALTON B. SLAYBAUGH, General Manager for Personnel, Continental Oil Company, *Public Utilities Fortnightly*. (1388)

AUTHORS' INDEX

260

261

1139;
LINKLETTER, ARTHUR G. (ART) – 135;
LINOWITZ, SOL M. – 204; 212; 484; 527; 668; 835; 1383;
LIPPMANN, WALTER – 1027; 1304;
LIPSCOMB, ED – 795; 1256;
LOCKE, EDWIN A. Jr. – 127; 438; 606; 1275;
LOOMIS, DANIEL P. – 1089; 1091; 1268; 1272;
LOWER, ELMER W. – 424; 969; 1246; 1248; 1289;
LUNDBORG, LOUIS B. – 131; 310; 731; 930;
LYNCH, GERALD J. – 996; 1110; 1148;

M

McCOLLUM, L.F. – 1; 31; 531; 715; 794; 844; 859; 916; 1051; 1218; 1382;
McCONNELL, JOSEPH H. – 612; 1015; 1203; 1228; 1285; 1286;
McDONALD, ERWIN L. – 1016;
McELROY, NEIL H. – 72; 156; 185; 238; 666; 669; 685; 687; 1351;
McFARLANE, A.N. – 730;
McGILL, RALPH – 583; 972; 974;
McINTOSH, ALAN C. – 976; 980; 981;
McKINNON, HAROLD R. – 333; 877; 937;
McKINNON, NEIL J. – 898;
McKNIGHT, FELIX R. – 433; 784; 1302;
McLAUGHLIN, DONALD H. – 411;
MacPEEK, WALTER – 430;
MacRAE, ROBERT H. – 264;
MAHER, EDWARD – 515;
MANN, GUY E. – 120;
MAPES, JOHN G. – 1059; 1082;
MAREMONT, ARNOLD – 232; 1079;
MARGULIES, WALTER P. – 15;
MARQUIS, WILLIAM C. – 203;
MARSH, ERNEST S. – 1269;
MAY, WILLIAM F. – 1087;
MAYFIELD, HAROLD – 4; 1072; 1335;
MEEMAN, EDWARD J. – 245; 339; 490; 542; 645; 806; 881; 884; 890; 1053; 1077; 1195; 1360;
MENNINGER, ROY W. – 11; 1381;
METZENBAUM, HORWARD M. – 196;

MEYER, PAUL J. – 101;
MEYERHOFF, ARTHUR E. – 26; 81; 348; 1075;
MICHELON, L.C. – 59; 260; 437; 467; 470; 565; 593; 1196;
MILLER, ARJAY – 36; 363; 711; 1236;
MILLER, DON H. – 98; 100; 165; 168; 522; 529; 788; 1007;
MILLER, J. IRWIN – 562; 1179;
MILLER, RAYMOND W. – 199; 242; 244; 334; 386; 423; 825; 1004; 1018; 1312;
MILLS, LEE – 335;
MITCHELL, JAMES P. – 183; 375; 654; 690; 965; 967; 1029; 1031; 1078;
MITCHELL, MERRILL M. – 66;
MOORE, CHARLES F. Jr. – 394; 400; 1103; 1225;
MOORE, GEORGE S. – 647;
MOORE, JOHN R. – 1131; 1190;
MOORE, L.W. – 190; 874; 1039; 1287; 1342; 1375;
MOREEN, HOWARD A. – 255; 480; 1266;
MORLEY, FELIX – 670;
MORTIMER, CHARLES G. – 243; 412; 414; 420; 421; 442; 450; 456; 461; 465; 481; 578; 579; 868; 1061; 1092; 1144; 1385;
MOTLEY, ARTHUR H. – 563; 608; 610; 698; 767; 1024; 1155;
MOTT, WILLIAM C. – 309;
MURPHY, ARTHUR R. Jr. – 321; 324; 906; 1250; 1279;
MURPHY, AUSTIN S. – 32; 931;
MURPHY, JOHN H. – 977;
MURPHY, ROBERT – 1208;
MURPHY, W.B. – 341; 541; 1283;

N

NADLER, LEONARD – 894;
NEFF, PHILIP – 1233;
NEILAN, EDWIN P. – 372; 912; 939;
NEVINS, ALBERT J. – 88; 270; 918; 935; 1188;
NEWMAN, J. WILSON – 154; 193;
NEWTON, GEORGE A. – 76;
NICHOLS, BYRON J. – 123; 125; 176; 222; 223; 468; 503; 1116; 1134; 1197; 1292;
NICHOLS, WILLIAM I. – 566; 932; 934; 1008; 1017; 1165; 1377; 1378;

WYATT, WENDELL — 766;

Z

ZELLERBACH, J.D. — 1357;

ACKNOWLEDGEMENTS

ADMINISTRATIVE MANAGEMENT, for permission to use a quotation by Susan J. Herman, for permission to use a quotation by Elmer Frank Andrews.

AMERICA, for permission to use a quotation by Paul K. Cuneo, for permission to use a quotation by A.N. McFarlane.

AMERICAN FURRIER, for permission to use a quotation by Merrill M. Mitchell.

AMERICAN SALESMAN, for permission to use a quotation by Dr. Napoleon Hill.

ARIZONA ARCHITECT, for permission to use a quotation by James M. Hunter.

ARKANSAS BAPTIST, for permission to use a quotation by Erwin L. McDonald.

ARKANSAS METHODIST, for permission to use a quotation by Robert H. MacRae.

BANKING, Journal of The American Bankers Association, for permission to use a quotation by Robert C. Liebenow.

B P SINGER FEATURES, for permission to use a quotation by Arthur G. (Art) Linkletter.

CAROLINA ISRAELITE, for permission to use a quotation by Harry Golden.

CHICAGO SUN-TIMES, for permission to use a quotation by James M. Roche.

CHRISTIAN HERALD, for permission to use quotations by J.C. Penney.

COMMERCE, for permission to use a quotation by Ethel Kaplan.

COMPUTERS AND AUTOMATION published by Berkeley Enterprises, Inc., for permission to use a quotation by Robert Silleck.

DAIRYMEN'S LEAGUE NEWS, for permission to use a quotation by Glenn Talbott.

DUN'S REVIEW, for permission to use a quotation by Robert F. Draper, for permission to use a quotation by W.F. Rockwell, Jr.

FORBES, for permission to use quotations by B.C. Forbes, for permission to use a quotation by Malcolm S. Forbes, for permission to use a quotation by James J. Shapiro, for permission to use quotations by Myron M. Christy, for permission to use a quotation by Pierre Rinfret, for permission to use a quotation by Charles Pratt, for permission to use a quotation by Heinz H. Biel.

FOREIGN AFFAIRS, for permission to use a quotation by David Rockefeller.

FRATERNAL MONITOR, for permission to use a quotation by Alden Palmer.

GATES INDUSTRIAL NEWS, for permission to use a quotation by Charles C. Gates, Jr.

GENERAL ELECTRIC FORUM, for permission to use a quotation by R.A. Peterson.

HARPER & ROW, for permission to use quotations from *How Showmanship Sells* by Elmer G. Leterman, for permission to use quotations from *Personal Power Through Creative Selling* by Elmer G. Leterman.

JOURNALISM QUARTERLY for permission to use a quotation by Pedro G. Beltran.

JOURNAL OF INSURANCE INFORMATION, for permission to use a quotation by Dudley Dowell, for permission to use a quotation by Guilford Dudley, Jr.

JOURNAL OF MARKETING, Published by American Marketing Association, for permission to use a quotation by Charles F. Jones.

MACHINIST, for permission to use a quotation by Theodore W. Kheel.

MANAGE, for permission to use a quotation by Dr. Ross M. Trump, for permission to use a quotation by Edward J. Green.

MANAGEMENT REVIEW, American Management Association, Inc., for permission to use quotations by Charles F. Kettering.

MICHIGAN BUSINESS REVIEW, for permission to use quotation by Frederick R. Kappel.

NATION'S BUSINESS, for permission to use a quotation by Howard Johnson, for permission to use a quotation by David Sarnoff, for permission to use a quotation by E. Robert Feroli, for permission to use a quotation by Allan Shivers; for permission to use a quotation by Lammot Du Pont Copeland.

NEWSWEEK, for permission to use a quotation by Vance Greenslit.

NYLIC REVIEW, New York Life Insurance Company, for permission to use quotations by Elmer G. Leterman.

PARKS AND RECREATION, for permission to use a quotation by Laurance S. Rockefeller.

PERSONNEL, American Management Association, Inc., for permission to use a quotation by Ralph S. Novak, for permission to use a quotation by Henry Kaiser.

267

PERSONNEL ADMINISTRATION, for permission to use a quotation by Lester J. Weigle, for permission to use a quotation by John D. Rockefeller, for permission to use a quotation by Gerald L. Phillippe, for permission to use a quotation by Peter Drucker, for permission to use a quotation by Cecil B. De Mille.

PERSONNEL JOURNAL, for permission to use a quotation by Elmer G. Leterman, for permission to use a quotation by Leonard Nadler, for permission to use a quotation by Edward J. Hanley.

PHI DELTA KAPPAN, for permission to use a quotation by Launor Carter.

PRINTERS' INK, for permission to use a quotation by Herbert Strauss.

PUBLIC RELATIONS JOURNAL, for permission to use a quotation by Theodore C. Sorenson, for permission to use a quotation by George C. Whipple.

PUBLIC UTILITIES FORTNIGHTLY, for permission to use a quotation by Stuart G. Tipton, for permission to use a quotation by William O. Baker, for permission to use a quotation by Alton B. Slaybaugh, for permission to use a quotation by Wendell Wyatt, for permission to use a quotation by Henry Ford II, for permission to use a quotation by Thomas J. Watson, Jr., for permission to use a quotation by J. Wilson Newman, for permission to use a quotation by Austin N. Heller, for permission to use a quotation by Lammot Du Pont Copeland, for permission to use a quotation by A.J. Barran, for permission to use a quotation by Robert W. Sarnoff, for permission to use a quotation by Leland Hazard, for permission to use a quotation by William C. Mott, for permission to use a quotation by David Rockefeller, for permission to use a quotation by Neil J. McKinnon.

QUILL, for permission to use a quotation by Frank Stanton.

SALESMAN'S OPPORTUNITY, for permission to use a quotation by Elmer Wheeler, for permission to use a quotation by E. Cabell Brand, for permission to use a quotation by Edward Whitehead.

SALES/MARKETING TODAY, for permission to use a quotation by Elmer G. Leterman.

SCHNEIDER, LOU, Business Columnist, Bell-McClure Syndicate, for permission to use a quotation by Ernest Jones.

SOCIETY OF AUTOMOTIVE ENGINEERS JOURNAL, for permission to use quotations by Norman G. Shidle.

SPECIALTY SALESMAN, for permission to use a quotation by Paul J. Meyer.

SUNSHINE MAGAZINE, for permission to use a quotation by Herbert Agar, for permission to use a quotation by W.R. Kelly, for permission to use a quotation by Joel H. Hildebrand.

SUPERVISORY MANAGEMENT, American Management Association, Inc., for permission to use quotations by Harold Mayfield.

TRIAL, for permission to use a quotation by Henry Ford, II.

U S STEEL QUARTERLY, for permission to use a quotation by Leslie B. Worthington.

WILLIAM FEATHER MAGAZINE, for permission to use quotations by William Feather.